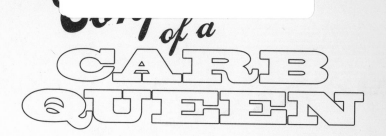

of a

CARB
QUEEN

WITHDRAWN

Confessions of a CARB QUEEN

of a

the lies you tell others & the lies you tell yourself
a memoir

SUSAN BLECH
with CAROLINE BOCK

Rodale books may be purchased for business or promotional use or for special sales. For information, please write to: Special Markets Department, Rodale Inc., 733 Third Avenue, New York, NY 10017.

Printed in the United States of America

Rodale Inc. makes every effort to use acid-free ∞, recycled paper ♻

Book design by Tara Long

Library of Congress Cataloging-in-Publication Data

Blech, Susan.
    Confessions of a carb queen / Susan Blech with Caroline Bock.
       p.   cm.
    ISBN-13 978–1–59486–776–7 paperback
    ISBN-10 1–59486–776–3 paperback
    1. Blech, Susan—Health.   2. Overweight women—United States—Biography.   I. Bock, Caroline. II. Title.
    RC628.B528   2007
    362.196'3980092—dc22
    [B]
                                                    2007030655

Distributed to the trade by Macmillan

2   4   6   8   10   9   7   5   3   1   paperback

RODALE
LIVE YOUR WHOLE LIFE™

We inspire and enable people to improve their lives and the world around them

For more of our products visit **rodalestore.com** or call 800-848-4735

To our father and mother,
Morris and Louise Blech,
with love

Author's Note

I'm not a weight loss expert, meaning I'm not a doctor or a nutritionist or psychologist or fitness guru. I'm the "anti-expert" expert. I'm the expert about what worked for me in losing weight and about why I sometimes failed and binged, and still do, though less and less now. No one is perfect, least of all me. I'm on a journey. I've written this book with my sister because for a long time I felt very alone, and no one should feel that alone and scared and ashamed.

Some names and identifying features of certain individuals have been changed in order to protect their privacy. Remembered scenes and dialogues are, well, *remembered,* and recalled as memory serves.

This is my story. It's sometimes shocking, sometimes funny and sad. I'm sharing my life with you, and that's how my life is sometimes.

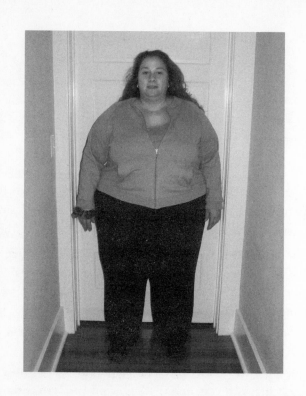

Prologue

My very first food memory involves the most basic of ingredients: bread, butter, and sugar. It's the summer of 1973. Richard Nixon is president. A hotel, the Watergate, is in the news. American prisoners of war come home from Vietnam. And I'm 8 years old. I make a white bread, yellow butter, and white sugar sandwich with my next-door neighbor, Cassie. She's a year older and shows me how.

I climb on the high kitchen chair. I take out a whole loaf of bread from the bread box and press the butter into the center of one slice. The bread tears apart.

There aren't any adults around to come to my aid. Nana didn't show up today, too hot for her. My sister is supposed to be watching us. She's 10, and she's probably in our bedroom, reading a book. My brothers are glued to the TV in the living room; the 4 o'clock movie is on. It's Godzilla Week.

We live at the end of the block, in a small white cape with the hop-scotch painted on the driveway. If you ask any of our neighbors, they'll say we're the house without a mother.

The kitchen, with its orange-flowered wallpaper and cracked gray and white linoleum, is just big enough for Cassie and me. The counter, where we eat breakfast and lunch, separates the kitchen from the dining room. A radio, covered in fingerprints, and a toaster, powdery with crumbs, clutter the counter. We're not supposed to stick knives into this old toaster, but we do; how else would the toast ever get out?

Containers marked *Flour, Sugar,* and *Tea* crowd next to half-eaten cereal boxes. The refrigerator groans and creaks in the center of the kitchen. At night, it sounds like a monster is eating our food. The stove is stuffed with pots and pans that clatter out every time the oven door is opened. Dishes multiply in the sink; laundry does the same thing in the basement; it's amazing, says my father.

Around the other side of the kitchen, I share a pink bedroom with my sister. My brothers share a blue bedroom. My father has his own bed-room. At the end of the hallway is the bathroom. In the mornings, we all battle for first in. Later, when we're teenagers, my sister and older brother will move upstairs, and we'll each have our own bedroom. I'll stay in the downstairs bedroom, closer to my father. He'll ruminate for years about adding another bathroom, but he never will.

Right now, it's 1973, and all I want is another white bread, butter, and sugar sandwich before my father gets home. I pull out the large container marked *Sugar* and shake it over the bread and butter. The sugar scatters across the Formica counter and onto the floor, alive like ants. Cassie and I scrunch the sugar under our sneakers, pouring out more. The counter-top and floor and my hands are sticky. With another attempt, I spread a layer of sugar on the bread like a fine white snow. I press one slice of bread on top of the other. Cassie laughs. My sandwich is lopsided.

Cassie has very long, straight brown hair that her mother braids every day. All this summer she's wearing a floppy white beach hat like Gilligan. She has buckteeth and is the youngest of 10. Her older brothers and sisters are "hippies," says our father. Even though Cassie's a year older, I'm taller. My hair is long, too, but thick, wavy, knotted in places I can't get to, a chestnut brown streaked with reds and never in nice braids like hers.

In my kitchen, I pull out the bread knife with its jagged blade. Cassie says to be careful. In her house, she's not even allowed to use a knife so big and sharp. I cut the sandwich in half, but one side is twice as big as the other.

"I always do things the hard way," I say, repeating what my father always says about me, not wanting Cassie to see that I'm upset. We each stuff a deformed half in our mouths.

When we were little, housekeepers lived with us. But now, David is 7, and I'm 8, Mark, 9, and Caroline, 10, and she's in charge. If she sees what a mess we're making, she's going to get mad. She'll make me clean it up immediately. Cassie and I have to work fast.

When my mother comes home, Caroline won't be able to boss me around. But Mommy has to get better first. She had a stroke when I was 1½. She lives in the Hudson River State Psychiatric Hospital. Ross Pavilion. Poughkeepsie, New York. We send birthday, Christmas, Easter, Mother's Day, and Halloween cards to her there.

Every few weeks, we visit. I can't wait to see my mother. Caroline and I always prepare spaghetti with tomato sauce, her favorite dish. We pack it in a bowl, cover the bowl with plastic, and bring a plate, a fork, and a dishcloth to tuck under her chin, like we're going on a picnic.

The last part of the 90-minute trip upstate is a long, curving driveway lined with trees. The hospital is built on a hill. The four of us bound up the marble stairs. My father has to catch up. He says we're too fast. At the top of the stairs, if I turn around, are mountains, the tops of apple trees holding up billowy clouds. The doors swing open and the smell of pee and bleach and cigarettes hits me. I take a step back. Every time, I hope that today my mother will walk out those doors and that we don't have to walk in.

Inside the lobby, the sunlight sifts in through windows covered in wire mesh. The lobby is crowded. Everyone smokes. The waxed marble floor is dirty, smudged with cigarette butts. Other patients shuffle along in slippers or in sneakers without laces, wearing layers of sweaters, even though it's so hot I feel dizzy and light-headed. They look blank and scared like the people in the Godzilla movies my brothers like to watch. A few hound us for cigarettes. I hide behind my father. He has to yell at them to go away.

My father finds us an empty corner of vinyl chairs. The chairs are orange and sticky. Candy wrappers and rolled-up newspapers and torn cigarette cartons are wedged into the seats. My father tells us to sit there and not to move. He strides to the elevator and it swallows him up.

I am glued to the seat until the elevator doors open and my father pushes my mother out in her wheelchair. Her chair looks like a bed on wheels. She's bent across it; her shoulders wedged one way, her feet, in unmatched socks, the other. Her head lolls back and forth. She's more lying than sitting, staring at the lights and flies flickering on the ceiling.

All four of us run over to her, calling out, "Mommy!"

I gag. She smells like pee and old vegetables. Her hospital gown is stained. A musty blanket covers her unmoving legs. Her hair is tangled and matted, needing to be washed. Her skin is rough and scaly and gray. I hold my breath, close my eyes, and kiss her hello.

My father attempts to hoist her upright. He props her up on a 45-degree angle, enough so she can see us. He yanks out the Sunday *New York Times* crossword puzzle from his back pocket, drops into a vinyl seat, and begins working on it. Caroline and I unpack the lunch.

Mommy can use only one arm. The other doesn't work anymore and looks more like a claw than a hand. Yet, even on her good hand, the nails are thick and yellowed, the knuckles chewed and raw. I don't want her to touch me, and yet I do. I want her to lift me into her arms. I want her arms to be able to lift.

I feed her the spaghetti. Caroline and I vie for turns. My mother doesn't have all her teeth, so we have to make sure the pieces are mashed up small. I dance around her, trying to get her attention. Her eyes stare back glassy and unreal, sunk deep into her skull.

She mumbles words. I can't understand her. I ask my father why Mommy can't speak like a normal person. I want to know what she's saying to me. I want her to say my name. He shrugs.

I see the problem. Her tongue is too big in her mouth. "Why can't the doctors give her a smaller tongue so she can talk better?"

My father lowers the crossword puzzle and says, "They dope her up."

I want a normal family with a father and a mother. I want her to get out of this wheelchair and come home with us. "When is Mommy coming home?"

My father ignores this question and chews his pen. When he's done with the puzzle, we'll leave. He'll jump up and say, "Time to go, Louise, we have a long ride back." My middle name is Louise. Everyone says I look like her.

I'll stand on tiptoes to kiss her good-bye and to encourage her. "Mommy, you have to get better soon, really soon, and come home. We need you. This is Susan talking. Do you hear me?" She looks at me, and if it's a good day, she'll smile at me. I don't want to leave her here.

After a minute or so, my father will say to me, "That's enough, toots." If my mother can't hug me, I want him to hug me. He doesn't. He's in a hurry. He wants to go—*now,* he says. *Right now.* He'll stick the magazine into the vinyl seat. We'll follow him out, down the slick marble steps and into our yellow station wagon. He won't ever answer my question, *When is Mommy coming home?* And soon I know not to ask him at all.

What happened to my mother is this: When I was 1½, my mother had an aneurysm that left her brain-damaged and paralyzed.

One day, when I'm 12, Nana answers the question. Nana sits straight-backed in a foldout chair in her usual summer place under the cherry blossom tree. Nana has short, steel gray hair. A huge hooked nose commands her face. A Roman nose, she tells us. White flowers blow onto the shoulders of her blue polyester pantsuit.

"When is Mommy coming home?" I say idly, swinging a branch, more flowers scattering to the ground until it looks winter, not spring, under the tree. Her watery eyes inspect me.

"You know, you look the most like Louise," Nana announces. "Same brown hair, same brown eyes. Too bad. She should never have married your father. But she wouldn't listen to me. You should take a brush to that nest of yours. Birds could lay eggs in that hair."

"When is Mommy coming home?" I say in a small voice, patting down my hair with hard, fast strokes, more flowers scattering.

"Never," she says, baring her full mouth of false teeth. "Your mother is never coming home. My heart breaks every day that my daughter is not here for me. Go get a brush. I'll get out those knots."

She glares at me until I run away, my stomach churning. I bang through the screen door and hurtle straight to the center of the house, the refrigerator. I open the monster up. My hair is wild across my face. I'm shaking, angry, wanting something to eat, anything.

That was the end of my childhood.

ut on this day, in the summer of 1973, with Godzilla trampling Tokyo, with all the windows open in the house and no breeze, and the afternoon lasting forever, Cassie and I use up an entire loaf of bread, two sticks of butter, and most of the white sugar. We're having a great time experimenting with how much butter and sugar to add, with cutting the bread in half or in triangles. We've eaten three or four sandwiches each.

And my father is home. He pulls into the driveway in the station wagon. He has his tie off and short-sleeve shirt open at the neck. His left arm is tan and freckled and his right arm is, by comparison, very white. He has tight, black, curly hair that none of us inherited. When he's in a good mood, he's strong enough to give all four children piggyback rides at the same time. Tonight, he looks surprised to see us run toward him, or exhausted, as if he's forgotten he had the four of us waiting at home for him.

An overflowing brown bag of peaches lies sideways in the front seat. "Right from the farm," he says, sucking a peach pit and carrying in an armful of groceries. The smell of peaches brushes off his hands, ripe and warm like what I think the color orange should smell like if colors had smells. The back of the car is filled with more food. Our refrigerator is never empty.

I throw my arms around his waist. I'm so glad he's home. He pushes me away. "Go. Go help your sister put away the food, and you can have a peach."

I love peaches and cherries and apples and all the fruits and bakery cookies and cakes and loaves of fresh, still-warm Italian or Portuguese or Jewish rye or Russian black with raisins that he brings home with him, almost every night. But tonight I grab some Italian cookies in my fist. I'm not helping.

After dinner, we all race back outside—me, David, Mark, Caroline, and Cassie. Cassie's stayed over for dinner again, though she didn't like the spaghetti and meatballs Caroline had cooked. Her mother doesn't make it with so much sauce or the meatballs so big. We play freeze tag or kickball or Red Rover, and when we can't run anymore, we set up charades. The person acting out the title stands in the street. The rest of us

sit on the curb, guessing our favorite TV shows: *The Partridge Family*!
The Brady Bunch! *The Courtship of Eddie's Father*! None of the TV fami-
lies have their parents intact, and I love them for that.

A full moon rises. Fireflies dance around. Mosquitoes bite us up. Two
doors down, Cassie's brothers work on their Corvettes under special
lamps, like doctors. Their eight-tracks drift out rock 'n' roll. "The Doors,"
informs Cassie.

The streetlights blink on, throwing pools of shadows into the street
corners and us into darkness. When Cassie's mother calls her in, she runs
home right away. The four of us are sitting out there on the curb, waiting
for a mother's voice, or at least our father's, to find us.

But our father is inside working. His cursing and clattering, typing up
his sales orders on the IBM Selectric, competes with the crickets. He's
always working.

Tonight, we stay outside until the grass is wet with night-dew, until
we've all made wishes on a first star and fought about who had seen their
first star first. David, my little brother, asks if the moon is made of cheese,
and Caroline sets him straight. Men had actually walked on the moon.
They're called astronauts, she says in her know-it-all way. He rolls on the
grass like a puppy. We're outside waiting, listening for our father to call
us in, until Caroline says we could all use some ice cream before we go
to bed.

And we race inside, my legs light and fast. I beat David into the house. I don't want to be the last one left outside alone in the dark.

On the kitchen countertop, my sister lines up four bowls and four spoons. She scoops out the vanilla, chocolate, and strawberry ice cream, doling out equal shares, more or less. Mark gets more chocolate because that's his favorite. We're laughing, talking, jostling, and safe inside our house with the comfort of ice cream. I promise to make everyone my famous new white bread, butter, and sugar sandwich the next day. I ask for seconds, not wanting the night to end, but it's time for sleep, and we put ourselves to bed.

Later, I'll wake up in the middle of the night, with such vivid dreams of my mother that I have to go find her—but, of course, she's not home, not yet. I go to the kitchen and I'm alone. I eat spoonful after spoonful of ice cream.

It's like a dream, a bad dream, the worst dream in the whole world, to wake up years later, age 35, alone in my apartment in Long Beach, my hair matted to my head, my head hanging to the side, strangled by my own breasts, heavy like weights up toward my neck. I heave my body up on my elbows. My stomach drags on my thighs. My ankles are the size of a big man's forearms, but soft like sponges. Varicose veins crisscross my legs, collapsed blue and red blood vessels pulsating to the surface. Even the ends of my fingers are swollen and tender.

I weigh at least 400 pounds, maybe more. I don't know how I got this way. I don't even own a scale so I don't know exactly how much I weigh. *Buy a scale. Add that to the list.* But I'm going to be really good today. I'm on a diet. Everyone knows that I'm on a diet. I haven't eaten anything all day.

I don't want to think of anything except getting up. I must get up and dressed; it's almost 5 o'clock in the afternoon. I'm meeting Marcy, thin Marcy, my best friend, for dinner out.

Sweat pours down my temples and armpits and sides of my thighs. Bile rises in my throat. I force it back down. I can't lift myself. I fall back flat on the bed. I don't know how I woke up like this, like a giant bug flaying on its back.

A familiar sadness overcomes me. While I napped, I had a beautiful dream. An endless summer day, I was 8, and eating white bread, butter, and sugar sandwiches with my old friend Cassie. I haven't seen or heard from Cassie in years. I remember how creamy and sweet and how many of those sandwiches I made. Even Caroline liked them. But in that dream, I had a mother, a real, normal mother, to help me make those sandwiches, cut them in equal halves. We shared one sandwich—that was enough.

After, she hugged me and told me how proud she was of me. I'd love a sandwich now. I push the thought away. My refrigerator is always empty. Maybe there's some old chicken breast or yogurt on a shelf, but certainly not white bread, butter, and sugar; not when the all-night deli or Chinese take-out are only a phone call away. But not today; today I'm going to be really good.

I fling myself to the side. My legs flip to the floor. With the nightstand for leverage, and gathering all my strength, as if I'm still bodybuilding and deadlifting weights, like I did in my twenties—except I'm the dead weight now—I hoist myself upright.

My clothes-strewn bedroom—the scattered invoices needing to be sorted and entered into the computer—the eaten-out ice cream cartons flung half under the bed—fill me with rage. *How can I live like this? How did I get this way? Four hundred pounds, or maybe even more.* The thought is too frightening. Because of the condition of the room, I have to leap, not walk. And I can barely walk.

I'm also furious at myself for oversleeping. I had planned only on an hour nap. I slept all afternoon. Yet, I'm exhausted. I need to eat.

I should have gone to visit my mother today. I'll go tomorrow.

My back and shoulders ache. My eyes are ringed with black from sleep or mascara; I can't tell which in my half-hidden mirror. I need to eat so bad. But when I see Marcy, I want to feel thin.

My answering machine flashes urgently. My sister, my brothers, and my father have all called. Everyone is concerned about me. I'm tired of them worrying about me as if I'm the family's charity project.

I'll call them back later—I'll tell them about my new diet. I'm always on a diet—I'll tell them how much I'm exercising instead.

I get out of bed.

Marcy's message reminds me that we have dinner tonight, and to please, please, please call her immediately if I'm canceling again. Bobby is the last call. He's concerned, too. I definitely don't want to talk with him. It's over between us.

I erase the messages. I don't want to go to dinner. Going to a restaurant with Marcy, or with anyone, automatically means I have to be good because everyone knows I'm on a diet. I'd rather stay home, order in from the pizzeria or the Chinese take-out, or both, and be by myself.

But if I cancel again, Marcy will be furious with me. So I'm going. I'm going to be good. I'm not eating anything before I leave. I'm not even drinking a glass of water.

I can convince myself of anything, and tonight I want to convince myself that I feel thin. I try to hold in my stomach and lift up my arms. I can't. *How did I get this way? How can I be over 400 pounds?* I have to move. *Move.*

Chapter 1

The bridge comes into view, the traffic slows, but I don't. I'm late. I'm hungry and tired and angry and frustrated. I'm angry that I want to eat. I just want to eat. But I'm going to be good. I drive faster.

I don't want to think of Bobby.

We're over.

I broke up with him.

I'm 35 years old. I had to get on with my life. I don't know where I'm going, but it can't be with him.

I don't want to think of this, but I do: Bobby and I wanting to make love in my shower. We can't. I can barely stand up. My legs hurt. My calves and ankles are blown into one mass. I call them "cankles." I can't see my toes. The oversize square pink 1970s bathtub has a wide ledge, so I sit. I tell him it's easier and more fun this way. My stomach folds onto my lap, almost to my knees. I don't translate *sexy*. It's another language. *Feminine* is far away. *Human* comes across only because I'm breathing.

I try to remember myself thin, to forget who I am now. The water cascades off his broad, strong back. The shower smells like vanilla, the scent of my liquid soap. He says he wants to make me happy. I laugh and tell him I'm hungry. I end up doing what's easier, sitting on the porcelain ledge—and giving him a blow job—even though it hurts inside, to the core of me, and I'm even hungrier afterward.

I don't want to think of sex. I can't believe I broke up with him. I can't believe I'm going to be alone. I want to think of what I'll eat tonight. I don't want to think of how I'll ever meet another guy. I don't want to think of me: how my stomach presses again the wheel even though the seat is pushed all the way back; how my thighs spread across the seat; and how my hips roll against the door on one side and the gearshift on the other. I can't even sit up. I have to drive as if I'm lounging, as if I'm comfortable. I don't want to think that my seat belt doesn't fit, hasn't fit, for months. I want to eat, now.

I drive even faster.

The Cross Island Expressway curves around the bay in two tight, narrow lanes. On one side is Queens and on the other side of the water is the north shore of Long Island, with its rich towns like Sands Point, Great Neck, and Kings Point. In front of me, the sun sets hot pepper red, holding the haze and heat. The day doesn't want to end.

I haven't seen Marcy in weeks, or has it been months? She wanted to go to the city together. I love to see her. But no way; I'm not traipsing around Manhattan.

I squint into the sun. I put on my new dark blue aviator shades and think I look hot. I pound the steering wheel, blare Mariah Carey, and pass 70, 80 miles per hour when I should be doing 50 at most.

Van lights swerve in front of me. I won't let him cut me off. He's going to get us both killed. I rev the car.

Where are the chips? I have a bag of chips in this car, don't I? I have to eat something. That's not really eating, not when I'm in the car. I blast Mariah Carey louder. I swing around another car, no fear, one-handed.

I'm definitely, totally, back on my diet on Monday. Even though I woke up feeling fat, I'm not that fat. I need to lose a few pounds. I know I'm a little chubby. The last time that I was on a scale was when I tried Caroline's scale, but it was off. But that's just like my sister, owning a cheap scale that only went up to 300 pounds. Of course, I may be a few pounds heavier than that. But who cares?

If I can reach, the chips should be crumbled under the passenger front seat, where I hide all the evidence. They should be there, crunchy, salty— a half-bag of pure saving grace.

My turtleneck pulls over the stomach as I reach for them. I bought a new ribbed turtleneck for tonight. I love these turtlenecks. I have them in every color and wear them all year round. This new one was a size bigger than the last one I bought. But I know I look good. My hair will look great once I fix it and curl it down around my shoulders, though right now it's piled on my head, knotted back, a mess.

Where are the damn chips?

I straighten up. Take a breath. I'm sweating. I need to distract myself. A truck, a semitrailer, honks. This truck probably shouldn't even be on this two-lane highway. But I can't help it: I pump my arm up and down for him to honk his horn again. My arm hurts to reach up and down, heavy like someone else's arm; it's too big and bulky to be mine.

The trucker pulls his horn, a long satisfying pull, and I smile. I can't help it. I love playing with truck drivers, but the horn is loud and angry instead of what I expect from him, something short and playful, more like a wink, more like a *Hey, babe.* What the hell is his problem? I speed past him.

Screw him.

I know I need to work out more. *Add that to the list.* I have my lifetime gym membership. I just have to get there a few more times a week. I could be back in shape in no time. Maybe I should even get back into bodybuilding? Maybe even hook back up with Gary, now that I've broken up with Bobby.

But Bobby was different. He accepted me the way I am. He didn't care if I was a little chubby. He loved making love to me. I'd ask him why all the time. I was twice his size. He'd shrug his big guy shoulders and grin.

What am I doing? I know I'm driving too fast. I'm doing 70. *Ease up.* New York City, one of the biggest, most powerful cities in the world, shouldn't have skinny, narrow highways. I can't drive this slowly. I'm pushing the car. I speed up, cut in between another car. I forget to put on my turn signal. Brakes screech from somewhere.

How long did I go out with Bobby? Two years, on and off. I know I should have broken up with him sooner. I should have broken up with him when—

I can't even think of it. Not now.

We made love for the last time last week. I put my head on his chest. He ran his fingers through my hair. He asked me to marry him again. I reminded him: I was breaking up with him.

He was naked first. I tickled his recently slimmed-down-to-190-pounds torso. I was losing him as he lost weight. He insisted that I wasn't—that it didn't matter to him "if you're a few pounds heavier, Sue."

He was right. It didn't matter; I had to break up with him anyway.

He helped me off with my turtleneck and black stretch pants. I couldn't move. I was lead. But this devolved into breakup sex and since I hadn't broken up with too many guys, I didn't know the rules for it. All I wanted was for him to leave and for me to order from the deli.

"I'm scared," I said. How did I get to the point where I was scared to make love?

My Altima's air conditioner bursts out full blast as if it's a signal for me to pay attention to the road. Samples, boxes of pens and pads, heavy catalogues, toners from the business rattle in the backseat. I don't even want to think of what I've jammed under the front seat. I need to clean the car out. *Add that to the list.* I open the window. These days, I'm always hot and the air conditioner is not enough. Bobby said he liked me hot-blooded.

I hang my face out the window. I'm singing out loud to Mariah Carey. I'm blocking out any thoughts about his body, my body, sex.

I should turn around. Head home. Just go get a few things to eat by myself. But there are no exits. I gulp in the city's steamy air, exhaust fumes, and the heavy, low tide, the stench of the bay. I swallow as hard as I can.

I can't clear the wedge in the back of my throat. It never seems to go away unless I'm eating. My mouth is dry, my throat scratchy, almost like it's blocked. I need to eat.

But I can't eat before I see Marcy. *Thin, thin, I have to feel thin.*

Why didn't I leave earlier than this? Why did I have to stop at the deli? And where else was I today?

I push it out of mind. The last time I ate was Friday night, more than 24 hours ago. The drive-thru Dairy Mart. The Italian deli. The Chinese food delivery.

Friday was a horrible day. I was on the phone all day, taking orders, trying to drum up business from the office in the dining room. I did make a couple of sales on printer toner today. I hate printer toner. I hate thinking of it.

I step on the gas. Pain shoots through my foot. I need to go see the doctor about this and get another cortisone shot. But I hate this doctor. What the hell is his problem? Head of Podiatry, my ass! He can't seem to make my foot less swollen, less of a battering ram with open nerves. *Get a different podiatrist. Add that to the list.*

My neck hurts. Somehow, a knob of fat has formed at the base of my neck. I think the turtleneck covers it up nicely. I need a massage. But last time I saw the masseuse, I broke her table; it must have had a crack in it. I paid her for the table. Yet, how can I go back? She was so irrational about it. *Find a new massage therapist. Add that to the list.*

I'm an idiot.

I really need to eat something.

I can't find the damn chips! I need them—I can't do this—I can't be in the car without eating.

I see the bag of Doritos.

This is the worst, seeing the chips wedged between the seat and the passenger door and not being able to reach them. I see what else is stuck over there, under the seat: an empty pint of mocha chocolate chip, Butterfinger and Heath bar wrappers, and smashed-up boxes of fast-food containers, the hidden evidence. *Add that to the list; clean out the car.*

Dammit. I should pull over. But there's nowhere to pull over. There's no shoulder on the road. I'm hemmed in as if there's not enough road for me.

I lean as far as I can and try to grab the bag. I nearly drive into the concrete divider, and I straighten up as fast as I can.

A big fat gas-guzzling SUV careens in front of me. I swerve around it. Idiot! I slam my fist into the horn. I'm careful with my nails. I just had them done, and they look great, long, hot red. Unfortunately, my fingers are still a little swollen. I couldn't wear any rings out tonight. I'm retaining water these days.

Bastard! I laugh. The SUV cuts me off, again.

I don't care.

I've snatched up the bag of chips.

The smell of the still-fresh, salty chips wafts over me. I'll only eat a few, just a handful, just enough to tide me over until dinner. There's half a bag left.

I've been in the car 45 minutes. I deserve them.

I take one, and another, and another. My heart races. These are so good. The phlegm in the back of my throat softens. I calm down.

I don't want to think of this. But I remember teasing Bobby, saying that instead of breakup sex we could have a breakup dinner. "We could go back to our Italian restaurant in Queens," I said, stroking his chest and stomach. "Family-size portions?"

I munch through the chips. That helps. Keeps my mind off the traffic, even though there's not that much traffic for a Saturday night.

Dinner will be fine. I'll be good at dinner. But I know how I'll get through dinner with Marcy. I'll focus on what I'll eat after I'm done with my night out with her. Now that I've broken my diet with the chips, it shouldn't matter. I'll start again on Monday. But tonight, once I'm by myself, I can really eat. I need to be alone to really eat these days.

That's what I told Bobby, something like that, something that made being alone seem like the right thing.

He said he loved seeing me naked. I didn't believe him. I don't believe him. I had long ago hidden my full-length mirror behind the dresser so I wouldn't have to see The Body. Lingerie no longer fit.

Once, Bobby and I shopped at Victoria's Secret together. What was I thinking? The tight-lipped salesgirl suggested we try Lane Bryant. Nothing fit at Lane Bryant either.

The sight of my naked body made me queasy. Naked, it felt like somebody else's arms, thighs, hips, stomach. In my head, my body was still the one I used to have. That body was into bodybuilding for more than 10 years; that one wore a size 10. *That* was my body. I didn't want him to touch this body, The Body, with its stretch marks, with its loose, rubbery, spreading rolls—at the same time, I only wanted him to hold me. His arms couldn't wrap around me.

I don't want to think about it!

I love these chips. But I don't want to eat the rest of the bag. What kind of person eats a whole half-bag of chips? There are definitely some chips left in the bag. I could eat them, but I don't.

I lick the salty ranch flavor off my fingers. My lips stretch sore, a nice sore, raw from the salt. I'll put on more lipstick once I get over the bridge. I have my Chanel lip liner, my MAC lipstick. I have plump, perfect lips. I have lips other women pay a hell of a lot of money to have.

I crumble the bag up and stuff it back under the seat. I can't bear to see Marcy's "pity" face if she sees a bag of chips in my car.

It makes me think how Bobby's skin always tasted salty. He liked to use a lot of lotions, and he always smelled good. The last time we had sex, I wouldn't kiss him. I climbed up on the bed, and said, "This is the way we have to do it." I got on my knees; bending them hurt. Everything hung: my breasts, my stomach, even my thighs.

I didn't want to have sex. I wanted to eat. But it was too late.

He moved in from behind. I cringed when he put his hands on my hips. He squeezed the cliffs of my hips playfully, and I wanted to cry.

We had sex, for the last time, for the absolutely last time, doggie-style.

We had to do it doggie-style. This was the only way for us to have sex. I knelt, more like in prayer than in sex. I dropped my head. My arms, knees, and the backs of my legs pulsated. I felt dizzy from the effort. I shut my eyes. Bobby clutched my ass as if it were a life preserver, though I was the one who was drowning.

I made him leave after it was over. I called the deli and had delivered what we always had together after sex, what made it better—the sex—the breakup—my life: two tuna subs on grilled Italian bread with extra mayonnaise and oil, along with a side of eggplant parmigiana, Doritos, a pound of macaroni salad, and a bag of Milano cookies. I was disappointed that the deli didn't have the chocolate-covered ones. They always made the night.

Stop it, Sue! Just stop it! I have to think of anything else. But I'm hungry and tired.

I squeeze my eyes tight. I will not cry.

I keep my eyes shut one second more. A thrill rides up in me. I'm driving on the Cross Island Expressway with my eyes closed. I could be killed.

I open my eyes, tentatively.

I'm still here, I laugh. I can eat another today. I mean—live another day.

I glance at the rearview mirror and stretch out my neck. I hate when I look like I have a double chin. The turtleneck must hide it, though.

I double-check my eyes. I focus on what matters: My makeup looks perfect. The sparkling eye shadow lights up my eyes. I practice a smile. I want tonight to be normal.

And nothing is wrong. Nothing, except that I finally broke up with Bobby. I should have done this 2 years ago. Nothing else is really wrong.

Normal, think normal, Sue.

If only I could meet a guy tonight, or soon, who would look into my eyes and understand what I'm feeling. But someone with a real job, a real future, whom I can introduce to my father and sister and brothers without excuses. I'm 35 years old; it had better be soon.

How am I doing?

That's what my therapist used to ask me twice a week. I loved her as my therapist, but I don't need her anymore to ask how I'm feeling. I don't want to feel anything.

I just want to eat and go to sleep.

I should call Marcy and tell her I'm late. She knows I'm always late. I can't help it. I had to stop at the deli.

I should call my sister, too. She wants to see me. But I don't need another lecture. I don't want to see her. I'm tired of her telling me what to do, my whole life; she thinks she knows it all. She's the one with the problems, working 70, 80 hours a week with a little baby.

I'm not going to call her. I'm not calling anyone. I'll show up when I show up. I'm so tired of everyone. But I don't want to eat before I see Marcy. *Thin, I have to feel thin.* And I do. I feel empty and dead, and that almost equals thin.

Pay attention to the road.

Slow down.

All I need to do is get over the bridge. At this restaurant, they have the best bread with different dips like creamy, fresh hummus. I won't have the bread. Okay, maybe I'll have one piece, one luscious piece. One piece can't hurt me.

The moon rises, too early for the moon. It looks dropped in, faded and fake in the still-blue sky. What if the moon really was made of green cheese? Can you eat green cheese? Isn't cheese just mold?

At full speed, I veer onto the bridge. I'm too hot. I'm too hungry. I'm thirsty. I'm not eating and that wedge is back in my throat. I'm so thirsty.

What I need right now is a large Dunkin' Donuts decaf with skim milk. My Dunkin' Donuts ritual is this: two French crullers along with an everything bagel with egg, American cheese, and vegetable cream cheese. But I have to get this all at the Dunkin' Donuts drive-thru on Long Beach Road; they know exactly how to make it for me—and yes, of course, three big chocolate chip cookies.

I'm so hungry. Taillights flash red in front of me, and I'm angry and frustrated. I can't believe there's nothing else in the car for me to eat, nothing in any of the wrappers. There are signs to slow down for the tolls. But I'm late and hungry and tired, so I don't. Those signs are for other people who don't know how to drive. I speed up instead of slowing down. *Dammit! I have to eat—*

I slam on the brakes. My hand hits the windshield. My sunglasses go flying.

My Altima squeals. The back swings out. Paper flies through the car. Catalogues crash into the back of my seat. My foot jams down, pressing the brake pedal to the ground. My foot pulses, the tendons stretched. Bored policemen in bright orange traffic vests watch the line of cars and trucks inch forward; not one comes over to me.

I just missed slamming into the car in front of me. I'm sweating, panting, trembling, in absolute disbelief that this is happening. Did I almost just kill myself?

I grip the wheel, for the first time tonight, with two hands. I lean forward, mashing my stomach into the steering wheel. I put the car in park. My Altima shudders. I can't lift my foot from the brake. Everything about me feels heavy, dead.

The old man and woman in the car in front of me turn around, frightened or angry or both. They are a wisp of a couple, pale and fragile. The man curses at me before driving slowly away through the toll booth.

"I was nearly killed!" I want to scream.

Oh my God. I was nearly killed. This is crazy. Oh my God. I need to calm down—I need to eat something. I paw through garbage under the passenger seat, the wrappers, and fast-food boxes. Isn't there anything in this car to eat? I'm red-faced and my body is shaking. I can smell leftover french fries from inside one of the bags. I shove my hand inside. Burnt ends of stale french fries are hidden there, covered in old ketchup. I eat them and lick the ketchup like thick blood off my fingers and wrists. But it's not enough. I'm ready to cry in frustration.

A taxi driver gets out of his car and taps on my window. He wears a turban. He has kind eyes but smells of incense, too sweet, like rotting peaches. I catch my breath. He's offering me an unopened can of 7-Up, and asks me if I am okay.

All I think to say is: "I don't drink regular soda, only diet."

Chapter 2

I'm late for dinner with Marcy. But in the restaurant's parking lot, I clean my car out first—well, actually just jam all the evidence of food under the driver and passenger seat—and think: *I can do this. I can have a normal meal.*

Marcy kisses me a big hello. Marcy's always been thin; she was born that way. Her jet-black curly hair falls beautifully to her shoulders. We've been friends forever, since Mrs. G.'s first-grade class. I follow her.

The waiter seats us to the side of the restaurant, my back to the other patrons. A basket of fresh rolls is immediately brought to the table. I take one roll and break it in two. Seeds drop around the white tablecloth. I brush them into a pile and pat them up daintily with my forefinger. A piece of crust sops up the flavored olive oil. I work on eating the roll slowly, though what I want is to eat it as fast as I can and have another.

The waiter stares at me with a frozen smile that he's trying not to turn into a grimace. He doesn't think I see it, but I do.

"Excuse me," I say. I want his attention, not on my stomach, or hips or thighs, but on me. "Excuse me, I'd like to order." I want to scream, *"Look at my face!"* I have a great face: Look at my great skin, cute nose, kissable full lips, or high cheekbones. Look at my face, not my thighs.

I calmly order the Chilean sea bass, grilled in olive oil with capers and olives, even though I'm not calm. I could eat all the bread in a minute and want seconds or thirds. Instead, I ask for extra vegetables instead of the potatoes. I want to show Marcy, and this waiter, that I'm being good. I'm in control.

I order wine because Marcy orders a glass, even though I'm not a big drinker. I like white wine. Red stains the teeth. After a couple of sips, I'm doing pretty well. Our dinners arrives, mine with vegetables—and with the potatoes I didn't order. I don't say anything. We're talking about guys, her ex-husband and my ex-boyfriend, and I'm relieved. I'm wonderfully normal. I'll eat fish now. I like fish. Right now, that's all I want to feel: normal.

I ask Marcy about what it's like to be dating again. But what I'm actually doing is trying to distract her. I want more bread. She's laughing; maybe she made a joke, so I smile. I pluck a roll out of the basket. I quickly break it into pieces so that she doesn't realize I have another. She keeps talking. I dip the bread happily into the hummus, nod my head toward her, and think how I'll go out for a little something after I leave her: a little ice cream, or a burger, or a slice of pizza, or maybe a slice and a burger, or tuna fish on a bagel from the all-night deli—or—I cut my fantasies off. She's thrown me a question.

"Do you want dessert, Susan?" Marcy asks, almost too innocently. But I've known her too long. She's testing me. "Chocolate cake. We could split it?"

"If you want to," I say tentatively.

I want a whole piece of chocolate cake.

"But I shouldn't have it," she negotiates. "I've been pigging out a lot lately. What do you think? Do you really want it?"

"Only if you do."

I actually don't want it, because I'm on a diet, and people on diets don't eat dessert.

"You know how I love chocolate. I could even eat a whole piece by myself, but I'd feel so *fat*. What should we do?"

"I don't know."

"One bite each?" she says. "Could we eat just one bite of anything?"

I stop playing along.

Marcy doesn't order the chocolate cake. Neither do I. I'm ready to go.

"It's early," she says.

"I'm tired and—" I don't say "hungry." It wouldn't be normal to be hungry after dinner. But I am. All I can think of is, how quickly will this night end so I can go and really eat?

We drive around Larchmont and Mamaroneck, towns on the Long Island Sound not far from where we grew up together, in New Rochelle. Marcy leaves her car at the restaurant. It would be a tight fit in her two-seater, but I'm never comfortable in someone else's car anyway. We drive past the country club, where Marcy had been married the year before and where I was a bridesmaid.

We don't talk about the bridesmaid dresses. I had to pay for two green dresses, each with their tiny white flowers around the square neck and each with their big satin bow in the back. The store sewed them into one giant, size-32, green monster of a dress that I was almost too embarrassed to wear.

We park at Mamaroneck Harbor. Boats bob in the water, sailboats and yachts. Lights from across the Sound flicker and sparkle. Marcy wants to hike through the park.

My legs ache as if stones are tied to them. My feet swell, pulsate, swell. I'm dizzy, probably from the wine.

"Let's just sit here?" I say, torn between wanting to please Marcy and my inability to walk.

"Okay," she says agreeably. "We'll do what you want, Sue."

What I want to do is run.

We stay out until two or three in the morning, until a cool wind whiffs across the water, until Marcy and I can't bear to talk anymore about our exes, until we stare at the boats and lights and the peaceful expanse of Long Island Sound, and I am so hungry I am going to faint, but I only say, "I have a long way home" and drop her off at her car and go.

I race back over the Throgs Neck Bridge, toward home. There are no cars on the road. I can drive as fast as I like, and I do. I drive furiously. I bite down on my lip until it bleeds. A landslide of rage fills me—I slam my hand on the wheel and drive faster.

I don't want to think, or feel.

Soon I'm near home, like I've been zapped here. Now I can eat. Now it's time for Sue, not Bobby, not Marcy, not my sister or mother. Now I don't have to think of anything but food.

I pull into the 24-hour McDonald's. This McDonald's is 15 minutes from my house, a desolate area of cheap strip malls and small industries, on the border of Nassau and Queens. The McDonald's is deserted, and I'm desperate.

I order a fish sandwich with extra *extra* tartar sauce and extra *extra* cheese. And, what the hell, I order a burger too, with extra cheese, and french fries.

"And yes, supersize both orders for us," I cheerfully say to the Hispanic voice taking my order. "Supersize us. It's only 10 cents more." I can never turn down a supersize offer even if I have to pretend it's for me and some-one else.

I almost order 18 cookies, but it's so late. So I order nine. I think to myself, *See, I can cut back.* Of course, I order diet soda; the extra-large cup is handed to me separately from the two bags of food.

The first fry is full of salt, grease, and melt-in-my-mouth heaven. I'm home free. Happy, almost giddy, and relieved—I'm eating—and the rage is easing.

I pummel through one bag of fries before I leave the parking lot. I dive through the second bag heading back home. I keep my hand near my face so I can lick the grease and salt off, finger by finger.

I could make another stop. I know where there's a 24-hour Wendy's. I could go to an all-night deli and buy a box or two of Yodels, my favorites. Some nights I do. But tonight, I feel okay. I just need the McDonald's to tide me over.

All the late-night places are on my inner GPS. Every 24-hour fast-food place, every all-night deli, bodega and doughnut shop, I know them all from Long Island to Brooklyn to Queens and Manhattan. They're all my wonderful secrets.

Parked on the street outside my house, I unwrap the burger. My car is dense with the smell of grilled beef, actually, two all-beef patties, special sauce, lettuce, cheese, pickles, onions, on a sesame seed bun. I can almost sing the old jingle to myself, I am so thrilled to be there.

The two-family house I live in is almost equal distance between the Atlantic Ocean and the bay. This neighborhood, on Long Beach's West End, used to be a summer vacation area, and many of the houses look like bungalows. Even now, several of the houses rent out during the summer.

But most of the places are owned year-round, many by New York City policemen or firemen. I always feel like an outsider.

The houses crowd in together. Several have front porches, and American flags lie limp in the summer heat. On Friday nights, groups of beefy guys and girls in bikini tops, or couples with two or three children at their feet, gather on these porches drinking beer and kicking back to celebrate the end of the week. I see them from my car. I rarely have anybody over. None of my friends wants to visit me in this old beach town.

I finish the Big Mac and start on the Filet-O-Fish sandwich. I eat the sandwich as fast as I can. The faster I eat, the better. I will *feel better* is the point. The fish sandwich takes three bites. The nine cookies are gone too fast. I should have ordered 18.

But I'm okay. I feel good—comforted, satisfied. My head is clear. I close my eyes, a sense of calm spreads down my throat, over my chest, stomach, legs, and even into my heart, which, for the first time all night, slows.

I rest. I could sleep in my car if I let myself. Once, after a huge meal at our Italian restaurant in Queens, Bobby and I did fall asleep in the car in the parking lot. We were drugged on chicken and eggplant parmigiana, pasta, and bread. A kitchen worker rapped our car window, thinking something had happened to us, and scared us awake. We were slugs. We couldn't wake up. We laughed when we did, held each other, and kidded each other about getting another meal. The memory makes me smile, slowly, lazily, licking salt from my lips, Bobby far away, mind numbed, the glory of fast food taking over.

It's four in the morning. The stars are so close. The smell of ocean wafts up the block. The car windows fog up. My breath slows.

I psych myself to go up the stairs. There are 16 stairs, which seem more like 24 or 36; the number seems to grow. The stairs are steeper every day.

I crumble up the McDonald's evidence. I'm moving. I'm opening the car door. The street is dark and silent. I heave myself out of the car. My legs and ankles pulse at the effort like drums. Each step is an effort.

I throw out the fast-food trash in the neighbor's garbage can. Tomorrow I'm going back on my diet. But tomorrow is hours away, after I go to bed, after I sleep.

I lock the front door behind me, even though this is a safe area with all the firemen and policemen living by, and climb up the dark stairs, one by one. I rest halfway up. I'm breathing hard. Sweat thickens under my arms and rings around my throat. It's airless on the stairs. I have to get to my bed. But tonight there must be at least a hundred stairs.

The first-floor apartment is waiting to be rented out. I don't have to worry about waking anybody up. If anything happened to me, climbing up the stairs, I don't know when someone would find me. I push that thought away. I have to get to bed.

I grip the wrought-iron railing and pull myself up another stair. *Dammit! When did this get so hard?*

My heart palpitates as I reach my apartment. I stare into the shadows at my living room and dining room, which isn't used for dining at all; it doubles as an office. I can do my sales, live all my life, without ever going out—and some days, I do. Tonight, I feel like a prisoner who's come back to her cell.

I whimper: *I have to get to bed.*

Off the dining room is an eat-in kitchen that I hardly ever use because I like to eat in my car. Eating in the car or having food delivered makes life so much easier. Off the kitchen is a door and back stairs leading to a narrow strip of grass that separates my house from the neighbor's. I never go up or down those stairs.

I see well enough through the shadows to go the bathroom. I don't want to turn on the light. I don't want to see myself. On the toilet, I'm too exhausted to bend around and wipe myself. I can barely reach on good days; it's too much work. I let myself drip dry. I pull off my black stretch pants and underwear and leave them on the floor.

In my bedroom, I strip off the rest of my clothes without looking at The Body, at the folds upon folds of my stomach, at the rolls around my hips, at the thighs pockmarked with cellulite upon cellulite, without looking at my ankles swollen to the size of a man's forearm, without looking at my feet, which I can't see anymore standing up. I look at nothing but my bed and its 600-count, forest green cotton cover, cool and silky and welcoming.

Usually, I sleep in a T-shirt. Tonight, I want to feel light. I don't want anything to touch my skin but my comforter. I want to float away.

I don't turn the air conditioner on because it blows lukewarm air instead of cold. I have high, narrow windows in the bedroom, and they're open. I hope for a night wind, something almost magical, so I'll wake up thin.

I punch my pillows up. I sleep sitting half-up so I can breathe a bit better. If I can get my pillows just so, two behind my head and one behind my back, I imagine myself in a really comfortable recliner. Some mornings, though, I wake up on my side, in a fetal position, my boobs around my neck like chains, and I can't breathe. I've started to be afraid that I'll suffocate myself, so I arrange two pillows to the side I usually sleep on as well, as if to catch me.

Tonight, I'll be fine.

My bed takes up most of the room. I have a new box spring. For some reason, my old one broke and the mattress company wouldn't honor the warranty. They sent me some letter about "excessive use." I had only owned it for 2 years. I had to pay for a new one.

A long, black dresser my sister gave me is pushed against one wall, a makeup table is piled high under the window, and a double closet with clothes ranging from size 10 to size 32 takes up the other wall. Even the 32s are getting a little bit tight these days.

I turn the television on to one of the 24-hour news channels so that I'm not alone.

And finally, with a deep breath, I climb into bed, my wonderful refuge. I wrap the forest green of my comforter around myself and create a safe cocoon.

For a second, the taste of meat retches up in my throat. *I'm not going to throw up tonight,* I think. I won't. Anyway, tomato sauce usually makes me throw up, not ketchup.

I swallow hard and taste the meat and grease fighting their way back down. I do the only thing that will help me sleep: I make plans.

At one time, I used to think of guys, guys built strong and muscular, guys who wrapped firm arms around me, guys with dark curly hair and confident laughs and sweet kisses—and touch myself. But I can no longer reach. My arms seem to have shortened over time. I know the truth, but I don't think of it except for a second: I can't stretch over my stomach. I can't raise my legs. My hand, by itself or with help, is useless. I don't even try anymore to do what I what once did so easily, so lightly, so intensely, so normally.

I don't want to think of guys anyway. I don't want to think of Gary, the bodybuilder/stockbroker/perfect nice-Jewish-guy-to-marry who told me when I was 170 pounds that I would never have a perfect body. Schmuck.

27

I don't want to think of all the guys I've met—online and in newspaper personals—after describing myself as "just a little chubby." Not one so far has asked me out on a second date. Schmucks.

I don't want to think of Bobby, poor Bobby, who was so wrong for me, who worked in data processing, and who cheated on me. He did worse, but I won't think of that now. Schmuck.

I don't want to remember the disgusted face of the waiter tonight who couldn't look at me, but I do. He gets a "Schmuck" out loud, and I laugh, counting at least eight schmucks in the last 5 years since I became a little overweight.

As the sun rises over the beach, I sink back into my pillows and plan . . . a trip to the grocery store. I'm passing the on-sale bakery items right in the front. Tonight, I'm here for the chicken wings, hot sauce, and ketchup. Damn. I should get celery. What are chicken wings without celery? I'll get a stalk. Oh, the Marie's Blue Cheese dressing. What was I thinking! I can't have chicken wings without Marie's Blue Cheese Dressing. I debate, as if I'm really buying them: Should I get a single-serving pack with 12 wings or a family package with 24 wings? I go with the family package and throw in a family-size bag of ranch Doritos. And Yodels. I'll put them in the freezer when I get home, and they'll be cold, crunchy chocolate on the outside and layers of creamy sugar on the inside. I run my tongue over my teeth. I take a deep breath, hold, and exhale, almost tasting a Yodel. My mouth is very wet; the part I can't reach is wet too.

Sleep engulfs me; it's a mindless, numbing, satiated sleep. I don't dream. I'm in a food coma.

Chapter 3

I don't hear the knocking. I don't hear the screen door being torn off. I don't hear the kitchen door crack open. I'd see, later, that the white wood door was broken off its hinges. The doorknob ripped off.

I don't hear him pound the walls. Later, I'd see his dirty handprints in the hall and the cracks in the plasterboard.

I don't hear him stumble into my bedroom.

I don't hear him fall.

I don't wake up, not immediately. I had only gone to sleep an hour or so before. I open my eyes, slowly. They're puffy and swollen from lack of sleep.

For a second, I think it's David, but of course it isn't. Hadn't I talked to my younger brother earlier today? Wasn't he thinking of moving from Chicago to Atlanta? Or was he already in Atlanta? Why would he be here? Maybe he's surprising me? Maybe it's a dream?

He sees me looking at him. He's kneeling at the side of my bed. His face is in my face. His eyes are red, dilated, drugged. He smells of beer and cigarette smoke and pee. He has brown hair and big hands, and he's spitting out words, not making any sense. I try to pull away from him. But he reaches for my forearm. I pull it away.

I'm naked under my green comforter.

Oh my God! Oh my God! Oh my God!

He's taller than me, his stomach hangs out from his T-shirt, hairy and protruding, over his jeans. He's around the same age as David: late twenties or early thirties. He's grunting, trying to tell me something, arguing with himself, his hand on top of my comforter—

I can't breathe. I'm afraid to move.

I can run out of the bedroom. I can run downstairs. I can get to my car.

But I can't run.

I can't move that fast anymore. I can't even sit up. He towers over me.

He circles the end of my bed and sees the television. He mumbles as if he wants to tell the newswoman something. *Oh my God. Oh my God!*

He's here either to kill me or to rape me. He isn't going to rape me.

He's going to have to kill me before he rapes me.

The phone. Where's the phone? I have to get out of bed. I'm naked. Why of all nights did I go to bed naked tonight? How am I going to get out? Out of this bedroom? Out of this house? What if I try to run? I can't. I can't run.

He whirls on me.

"Why don't you relax?" I try, using my most level, most reasonable sales voice as I frantically search for the phone. "Watch a little TV? There's a good show on."

He drops on the bed, grunting and drooling.

"Relax, calm down," I say, soothingly. "Watch some TV—" I find the phone next to my bed. I hide it under the covers with me. I dial 9-1-1.

Whispering into the phone, I say to the 9-1-1 operator, *"Oh my God. I have someone in my apartment. I don't know who he is. He's in my bedroom."*

He focuses on me, bleary and red-eyed.

"Don't worry, you. Watch the television . . . " I say to him, my throat closing, my voice hard to release.

"Yes, yes, he's right here. Yes. I won't get off the phone. I'm here. Please. I'm not getting off the phone."

I smile at him again. I grip the phone. My heart is jacking up in my throat. The operator says that she's calling the police.

Something has caught his attention on the television. He jumps off my bed, paces, dribbles words out of his puffed-out mouth. He's incoherent. Muscles in his neck pop. He falls onto my bed.

"Help," I whisper into the phone. "Help me. Please hurry. Please."

Boom. Boom. Boom. Boom!

I'm still on the phone with the 9-1-1 operator when I hear the crash of boots. The intruder stumbles toward my bedroom door.

I'm paralyzed. I can't feel my arms or legs. I can't scream.

Four Long Beach cops race into my bedroom with guns cocked. They line up shortest to tallest.

The shortest, blondest one screams at the intruder, "What are you doing here?!"

This is the first time I have seen a gun up close, and I stare at four of them pointed at me and shiver in fear.

"What the hell are you doing here?!" the cops bark.

No answer. He backs up as if he's shocked to see cops. He flings his arms out and yells. "What the hell?!"

The cops throw him into my closet. Everything is happening in slow motion.

I scream. I start to shake and cry. I'm hysterical. I'm clutching my comforter and screaming. I'm outside myself. I sense as much as see this happen: banging, the smell of too many men in too small a space, grunting and yelling, the taste of meat thick in my throat, my skin cold, my tears hot. I want to run and can't.

The cops fight him to the floor of my closet. My clothes, all sizes, tumble down on him.

33

I scream louder.

They yank him up and put him in handcuffs. Guns point everywhere. They push him out of my bedroom. I hear the cops drag him into the kitchen. Two cops immediately return.

"Is there anyone you can call?" says the blond cop, holding up the phone for me.

"She's hysterical. Look at that," says the other.

"She's going to have a heart attack—look at the size of her," says a third.

I can't recall my sister's new phone number. I'm heaving and groaning and choking. I'm clutching my comforter around my neck. I can't believe that someone broke into my apartment, that I could have been raped, that I could have been killed.

I can barely hold the phone. I call Marcy, and for some reason, thinking that I'm thinking rationally, I hang up. It's too early to call Marcy. "I don't have anyone else to call," I scream at the cop.

Marcy calls back. I can't talk. I'm holding myself, crying, rocking. I hear the blond cop tell her what happened. One of the cops throws me a long T-shirt. I put it on under the covers as best I can. My hands fumble. I can't find the sleeves. I can't do it. The cops don't look away—they leer at me, these big Irish cops.

Where are my pants? My clothes are flung over the floor. The cops are stomping over a business suit. If I get up, they'll have to see my legs. I want to hide. I want to die.

A fireman appears, looking as if he had just awakened. Unshaven, in his pants and suspenders and without a jacket, he clearly isn't happy to be here at dawn. Quickly, he checks my heart rate. I haven't stopped crying. My nose runs. I'm covered in sweat. My stomach heaves. I need to eat something.

He attempts to take my blood pressure, but the first cuff doesn't fit, and he looks annoyed and disgusted, and I can't stop crying even though he says flatly, "You have to calm down." He digs around in his bag for the larger cuff, finds it, and makes a face as he wraps it tight around my arm. I'm sure it's going to explode.

"High," he pronounces.

I cry and shake even though I try not to do either.

"But you're going to live," he says in a half-assed way, ripping the cuff off my arm.

I hate him. I pull my arm back. I sniffle, alone and hopeless.

I stumble out of bed. Makeup smears down my eyes. My cheeks and eyes are black with mascara. I taste bile in my throat. I'm going to throw up. I can't stop crying.

I push past the firemen and cops, who idly stare at me, at my thighs, which are red, raw, and hugely naked under the T-shirt. I shuffle the few steps into the kitchen. For a second, all I can think is, *Thank God there aren't any pizza boxes or ice cream pints or fast-food bags around for these cops or that fireman to judge me by.*

I see handcuffs. He's facedown on the kitchen linoleum with his arms tight behind his back in bright steel cuffs. I scream at him. I kick his legs with my bare feet.

The cops smirk.

I kick him again in his stomach. I kick his thighs. I kick his forearms. I want to kick his balls but he's lying on them. I see the kitchen door smashed off the wall. The wood frame where there should be a door is wrecked and splintered. I see the outside and the neighbor's vinyl siding. *How did I sleep through this? How did I live through this?*

I cry and scream. I'm out of breath, and scared to death with four cops and a criminal in my kitchen, and I want everyone out. But the cops let me continue, so I do. I bend down and smack his head and grab a fistful of his hair. I yank his hair. His head smashes into my kitchen floor.

I think of every guy who ever hurt me, and I snap his head back and down as hard as I can.

He screams, but I scream louder.

I gulp for air. Through my tears, I can't see anything but his head flying up and down. Blood smears on the linoleum. His wispy hair comes out in my hands, and I fling it off my fingers, hysterical. I don't want his strands of light brown hair on me.

I grab his forehead. "You fuckin' asshole. You asshole. You fuck. You fuckin' asshole!"

I'm so exhausted.

I'm also in the kitchen surrounded by cops in a long gray T-shirt and nothing else. They stare at my legs, at the bulging rolls of rubbery fat and cellulite, each one thicker than their waist, each one with large, lopsided, black and blue bruises from squeezing through small spaces. *A man could suffocate between those legs,* they're probably thinking.

I stumble back into my bedroom to put on a pair of black stretch pants, lurching forward, rubbing the boils on the deep insides of my thighs together, feeling like my legs are on fire.

In my bedroom, another group of policemen write up their reports. I ignore them, and they seem to purposely look away from me. That's okay. I want to be invisible. I bend into my closet for the pants and scream. White powder is sprayed over my shoes. In one of my shoes, I see a bag of white powder.

"Don't touch it," yells a cop.

"What is it?"

"What do you think? Cocaine, probably."

I stumble back on raw, naked, fat legs.

At about seven in the morning, they leave. I remember my sister's new number and call her. She says she's coming right over.

Marcy calls back again. She lets me rant on the idiots, morons, and assholes of the world. "When is this going to be over? When am I going to have my life together?"

She asks me if I'll be okay.

"I'll be okay. My sister is coming."

My sister arrives. I find a pair of my black stretch pants. I barely have the strength to pull them on. I'm so glad she's here. But right away, Caroline says that she can't stay long—the baby, of course. She's efficient and full of good intentions and distracted as ever about her job or her baby or her husband or her house when I want her to understand that I'm scared and desperate and I don't know what to do next.

"You'll be okay," she says.

"I know! I'll be okay!" I scream at her.

We go out for breakfast at the diner, and it's okay for me to eat in front of her because I'm in such distress. I have an omelette and hash browns and buttered toast and ask for more toast and more coffee, and more toast. At some point, I stop crying.

Later in the day, two detectives arrive and ask questions. I learn that the guy's brother lives down the block. Months later, a plea bargain will include jail time for the cocaine, along with a new door and a burglar system for my apartment, paid for by his family. I never see him or hear from him again.

Late that afternoon, I am alone and on my way out to get a little bite to eat—*that's all, a snack*—when a neighbor who has always stared at me and pretended not to calls out to me from across his porch. He asks me what happened. "I thought I heard something like a door breaking down this morning," the jerk admits.

I climb into my car. I'm shaking at the idea that he could hear some-one breaking into my house and do nothing to help me. *Was it because I'm fat? I'm not a person? Maybe he thinks I'd like to be raped . . .*

I drive off. Away. Out.

First, I have Chinese take-out delivered to me right outside the restau-rant in my car: steamed vegetable dumplings, Chinese chicken wings, General Tso's chicken, fried rice, and two egg rolls. Next, even though I don't want to go into any place and order food, I make an exception for Baskin-Robbins. I go for it and order a chocolate-dipped waffle cone with one scoop of chocolate peanut butter and one scoop of mint chocolate chip, and extra *extra* rainbow sprinkles on top. I carry it back to my car like a prize.

I'm not finished.

I'm filled up, but only with anger. I hate the guy who broke into my apartment. I hate the stupid cops. I hate the stupid fireman. I hate Marcy's chocolate cake tease. I hate that my mother is sick, my father is in Florida, and my sister is a know-it-all.

I know! My life is in chaos. *I know!* I should move out of the apartment. But I have nowhere to go. I don't have the energy or money to move. I'm trapped. *I know!* I hate myself most of all.

I drive from one fast-food drive-thru to another, unable to stop.

I don't want to think. I don't want to feel. I want the food in my veins. I want to forget the day—to be numb—to be nothing.

Chapter 4

      I was born on Mother's Day, May 11, on Morris Park Avenue in the Bronx, to Louise and Morris Blech. My parents had been married 3 years. They had three children. I was the third.

Yet my very first memory is of Tillie—huge, slow-moving, good-hearted Tillie, our last housekeeper. She fed us fried plantains and fried fish and hard, delicious biscuits she called pancakes. I'm 7 years old and I wake up. I'm alone. I cry. My back tooth burns. Tillie carries me into my father's bedroom, and swabs my teeth with bitter brown water, "a little whisky," she whispers. She lays me down in her arms. I suck my thumb and sleep. My father had to let Tillie go when I was 8.

I attended George M. Davis Elementary School, Albert Leonard Junior High, and New Rochelle High School. I spent a year at Syracuse University before ending up at Florida State in Tallahassee. I graduated with a degree from the School of Education and a 23-inch waist. I had unlimited interest in bodybuilding and in one particular steroid-shooting bodybuilder. Back then, I was all about looking hot in spandex workout pants and skintight tank tops. I was a size 8.

This night, I'm not a size 8.

I don't know what size I am. I can't look at myself in the mirror. Luckily, I have hidden the mirror. It's holiday time, December 2002.

And I've been good, I remind myself. This fall, I started working with a nutritionist and I have basically been following a low-carb diet, which to me means all the chicken wings I can eat. When I checked with the nutritionist, "I can eat an unlimited number of chicken wings?" and she said yes, as along as I didn't eat blue cheese, I knew I'd found the diet for me.

The nutritionist's office is downtown, in Tribeca, about 45 minutes from my house in Long Beach if I don't hit any traffic. But I always hit traffic. I'm always running late, and I'm erratic about visiting her. I'm supposed to go once a week. She's a painfully thin nutritionist with a round bump that screams: I'm fit and pregnant. She sits behind a very small desk. I hunch forward on a chair for petites that's on the other side of her.

But my unlimited chicken wings diet has translated into at least a 24-piece family pack of chicken wings. I debate buying an even larger family pack in the grocery store, but I usually stick with the 24. Slather all 24 pieces with ketchup and Tabasco sauce, 20 minutes in the oven at 350°F, and I'm ready to go at least once a day, sometimes more. The chicken wings just pull apart and slide down, hot and tender. Chicken wings and two fruits a day, and I've lost about 60 pounds.

I may not be in spandex, but I do have a new maroon turtleneck over my black stretchy pants, and I'm going out. I haven't ventured out in weeks. I've been connected to the outside world only via phone, the Internet, and take-out.

But tonight, months after the break-in at my apartment, I'm off to the Manhattan Jewish Experience holiday party on the Upper West Side with one very close girlfriend, Laurie, and Donna—skinny, scornful Donna, who is really Laurie's friend.

There's no parking anywhere on the Upper West Side. I circle and circle in my Altima looking for a spot close to the temple. But there's none. I'm forced to park two blocks away, which is not really far, except for me.

It's a cold, clear night, but I don't wear a coat. I'm huffing and sweating down the sides of my face and under my arms. My sweat tastes salty and hot, more like tears than sweat. Laurie slows down to pace next to me; she's chunky, bubbling, laid-back. In another life, she would have been a Deadhead or a '60s hippie. Laurie has only known me heavy, unlike Marcy, or any of my other old friends. I'm her fat buddy. I'm fatter than her. *I know I make her look good,* I think bitterly, and then take it back. Laurie's a good friend.

Wrapped in a long wool coat and matching hat, Donna charges ahead.

I'm having trouble breathing. Maybe I have a cold coming on. My feet are sore, swollen, aching, and squishing in my black rubber-soled shoes. My head pounds. I have to rest. There is nowhere to sit, nowhere but the sidewalk, and if I go down I'm not getting up without a lot of help.

Why am I doing this? I'm never going to meet anyone. They'll look at me and know my secret. They'll know I'm a fake. This doesn't have anything to do with my weight. I can convince myself that I'm only a little chubby. I've spent a lot of time on my hair; it's soft and wavy and streaked with reds and blonde, blown down past my shoulders.

It's my last name that hides my secret. *Blech* in New York says loud and clear: "Jewish"—it actually means "tin" in German—but according to 99 percent of the Jews in the world, I'm not Jewish. My mother, Louise, is Italian and Catholic. I'm an impostor, a thin person trapped inside a fat person, a Jewish soul with a baptismal certificate. *I should just get back in the car. I'm safe in the car.*

Donna looks back at Laurie and me. She's impatient. She's thin. She's more than thin; she's a mousy wisp of a person. But now, a few steps in front of us, she stops and looks around as if waiting for someone, anybody else but me.

Laurie says, "We're not in a hurry, Sue."

But I'm in a hurry. I want to run. I want to throw off this fat suit and run. I want to turn around. And I don't want to be part of the Manhattan Jewish Experience or any experience that doesn't involve someone asking me "fries with that?"

After a moment, I'm okay. I want to go, I assure Laurie. I take a breath and a tentative step and another.

The synagogue lobby is packed with singles in their twenties and thirties. I'm the only girl in black stretchy pants, or in pants at all, since this is an Orthodox shul and the women know to wear skirts.

But I can't wear skirts because I can't fit into pantyhose. My thighs rub together and tear through pantyhose, boring the skin open, blistering, raw and bleeding.

I wonder what they'll have to eat, though I don't plan to eat anything here, of course. Like everyone else, I'm eager to get upstairs to the party, but it's an old building with slow, creaky elevators.

There's a festive air of people coming in from the cold, stomping their feet, blowing into their hands, taking coats off. I try not to sweat. I want to make myself invisible as I inch toward the elevators. But I don't have to try too hard. Donna ignores me, even Laurie is suddenly busy with her coat, and I'm standing by myself, in the lobby. A whir of greetings and shouts surrounds me. People glance at me with that blink of disgust and shift their gaze elsewhere. I have nowhere to look but straight ahead.

The elevator creaks open, and eight to 10 of us rush in. I automatically check the weight capacity on the elevator. I always do this. The old faded sign says I'm fine. I'm under the weight limit. I've always hated small, enclosed spaces.

The elevator jerks upward.

I'll stay only a little while. I'll make an excuse to leave alone. Laurie can get home with Donna. I need to go. I'll need to eat. I hadn't eaten anything for dinner. My stomach churns.

The elevator stops. We wait. Someone makes a joke about too many girls at the event. They want all the guys to themselves. That person is me. I'm laughing and making jokes when all I want to do is get out of the elevator. The guys laugh nervously and look at their feet. They are prey at these events for most girls. But I know, *It's me, they don't want to look at me, they don't want to acknowledge me.* I'm the girl they are not going home with tonight.

After a minute or so of not moving, cell phones fly out. An emergency button is pushed. Someone bangs on the door. I can't breathe. I'm laughing and smiling, and assuring everyone that the elevator will start up in a few minutes or that we could have our own little party right here, but I can't breathe. My first thought: *It's my fault. The elevator stopped because of me.*

Before I can sink too far, there's a banging on the elevator. The elevator doors are pulled open. We're caught between floors. We're about 5 to 6 feet below the floor where the event is taking place. We can hear the music. The band is a clash of modern rock meets klezmer, Jewish folk music. I expect that we'll be told that the elevator will start up in a few minutes. Instead, we're told that the elevator is out of commission. The fire department arrives.

A crowd has gathered by the elevator and watches as if this is live theater. I wave to them and shout, "How's the band?"

Soon, the firemen peer down at us. They're going to lift us out of the elevator one by one.

"No one's lifting me," I joke to Laurie. "I'll stay right here."

The firemen are afraid the elevator could give way and drop to the basement. The elevator shudders. If this drops, could I be paralyzed? What do you do? Do you stand or crouch? I can't crouch. I can't bend my knees.

But the firemen are calm. They'll get us all out. Two big firemen start lifting out the women. Donna and Laurie are among the first. The firemen pull on their arms and shoulders and hoist them up 5 or 6 feet and onto the floor, where they scramble up. Everyone cheers. I'm the last girl left with three or four worried-looking skinny guys. I want to sink down into the corner of the elevator and disappear. I look up and see Laurie waiting for me. Donna has sauntered into the party.

The first two firemen glance at each other, and two more appear. Four firemen stare down at me. They are handsome, strong men with heavy equipment belts around their waists, looking at me with brutally honest faces.

"You're next," calls one.

"I can wait," I laugh lightly.

"Let's go," he says, stone-faced.

"I'm okay here," I say, giggling at the skinny guys. They don't join in.

Two firemen lean into the elevator. "Raise those arms up. Let's secure her, boys," says one, harshly, like I'm a box or container.

The two pull on my arms and call for two others, who grab the rolls around my hips.

"Look at me," I laugh to no one. "Can you believe this?"

Four pairs of large hands snatch and grab my fat. Their hot breath pants on my neck. They are grunting and cursing, and I'm laughing uncontrollably.

"You have to stop laughing," says the strongest fireman, his sleeves rolled up, his biceps bulging with the effort to help me.

My body convulses in laughter. I heave up the laughs. I can't bear to stop.

"You're only making it harder," he grunts, his arm tightening around me. Does New York City only recruit gorgeous firemen? "This laughing is making you heavier. This isn't funny. Come on, now."

But it is funny. It's the most hysterically terrible and embarrassing thing that has ever happened to me. And I can't stop laughing. Two of the skinny guys push from behind. Their hands dig into my ass. I'm so ashamed.

Tears and laughs curl together.

I try to help, try to lift my legs up, but they're like dead weight. I'm floundering, grasping for a wall, and flapping my legs in the air. My face hurts so much from laughing. One of the firemen almost loses his grip. "I can't believe this is happening," I say over and over, as they pull and yank and push and finally hoist me out of the elevator.

My cheek streaks against the wood floor. They leave me there, beached. I'm red in the face, lying on the floor, unable to move, not wanting to move, and I'm hysterical, laughing, more embarrassed than I have ever been in my life. People avoid looking at me. There are no cheers. Someone clomps over my leg. I can't raise it. All I can think of is: *Get me out of here.* I can't stand up. I'm on my knees. My black pants are covered in dust and dirt. The skinny guys scramble out and give me wide berth. The four firemen glance at me, disgusted, and pick up their gear and go.

I'm not laughing anymore. Finally, Laurie helps me up. She doesn't make it a big thing, and I'm so grateful. Donna rolls her eyes at me. She looks purposely away as if she has forgotten something important.

I straighten up and fling back my hair. I can't manage to bend over and brush off my pants. No one will notice them once we're in the party. I'm not going to forget this for a long time. I hope nobody will recognize me as the girl who had to be pulled by four firemen from the elevator. I smile at Laurie and say, "Ready?" I switch off the image of myself as the girl pulled from the elevator by four firemen.

"Are you really okay?" asks Laurie.

"I'm great."

We plunge into the party room. Music drowns out everything. I'm someone else.

I scan the party. I have to know if I'm the heaviest person there. I hope I'm not. I hope to make eye contact with another chubby person. I don't actually want to hook up with a fat guy, or make friends with a fat chick. But I don't even *see* another fat person. I'm all alone. I squeeze into the crowd, miscalculate, bump one guy's elbow from behind and send his drink flying. Apologizing 10 times doesn't help; he just shakes his head and dashes away from me.

My face freezes. I'm smiling at no one and at everyone. I want to lop off my ass. If I had a knife, I'd cut off its round flopping cheeks. I want to find a place to sit, to hide my ass. From somewhere, I smell potatoes frying. Plates of latkes, flat, crispy, oil-drenched potato pancakes, appear from nowhere and settle across the party alongside bowls of sweet applesauce and white mounds of sour cream.

This time, I turn around carefully, maneuvering my backside through the partygoers as they surge toward the latkes. I can't eat here in front of all these people, though that's all I want to do. I hurry from the encircling smell of food that is supposed to celebrate freedom.

I find Laurie and Donna at a round cocktail table, talking with a guy. I get a diet soda and join them. The room is crowded and hot and this guy is cute. Sanders jockeys up to the table like a man who knows what he wants. I force myself into the conversation. I will not be ignored.

"Fun party—" I venture, never shy.

Laurie doesn't seem interested in him. Donna is already checking out other guys. "Do you work out?" I asked without any awareness that this may be an odd question from someone nearly 400 pounds. "I used to be a bodybuilder," I say with confidence. "I'm getting back into it," and at that moment, I mean it. Monday morning, I'm starting a new program of weights. Maybe I'll get a personal trainer. *Add that to the list.*

He looks me right in the eyes—this is incredibly important to me, he sees me, I'm not invisible—and smiles, slow, cool. Soon I have him laughing, telling him of what happened with the firemen as if it were the funniest thing that had ever happened to me instead of the most embarrassing. But he laughs too. By the end of the night, he's asking me for my phone number, which I eagerly write out for him.

Later, I learn that he has collected at least a dozen girls' numbers. But at that moment, I'm sexy and hot. Someone has asked me for my number. After an hour or so, I leave with Laurie. I want to play a little hard to get with Sanders. I don't want to be the last one at the party. Neither Laurie nor Donna have met anyone. I have.

I drive home with Laurie. I'm buzzing the whole way, and starving, but we don't talk about that. We talk about how meaningless and hopeless and useless these kinds of singles events are, except that I've met a guy, a nice Jewish guy. *He must think I'm Jewish. I passed! And I'm not so fat either.*

After I drop Laurie off, I figure I'm not going to go out with him for 2 weeks, so I can eat tonight and then restart my diet and look great when I do see him again. I drive to the 24-hour deli at the end of my block. It's two in the morning. A scrawny teenager works the counter. I'm invisible—the teenager doesn't say anything to me, and I say nothing beyond my order—an everything bagel with tuna, lettuce, and tomato, a pound of macaroni salad along with a large bag of Doritos and two Tollhouse cookie ice cream sandwiches. I always like salty and sweet things together.

Tonight, it's too cold and late to eat in my car. Anyway, I deserve this snack. I climb into my spacious bed with my treats, tear open the Doritos bag, dig into the sandwich and macaroni salad, alternating my way through the Doritos and ice cream sandwiches, the salty and the sweet dazzling me. I fall asleep in my clothes, dreaming of firemen.

The next day, Sanders calls and asks me to see me—that day!

He invites me to his house. He offers to make dinner.

This will become a pattern. We'll see each other, have dinner, kiss and make out like we're in high school, and that will be the night. It takes me a while to figure out that he doesn't want to be seen with me in public. He isn't the only one.

Chapter 5

We have blueberry bushes along the back fence. My father sends us out with empty pots to battle with the birds and pick the berries. Bowls of blueberries are stirred up with sour cream and sugar. We have cherry and apricot trees dotted all around the house. On our suburban street, we're the red cardinals' and blue jays' and even the ordinary sparrows' favorite house. One fall, my father plants pumpkins on the front lawn—leafy, wild-looking plants instead of lawn. The air buzzes with bees. The largest pumpkin, like the Great Pumpkin of *Peanuts* fame, gets carried up to the flat roof of our garage. Neighbors stare. They know we live in the house without a mother.

In my late teens and twenties, food became an obsession, but in a completely different way from what would happen later in my life. I was wild. I stayed out all night. My father didn't like my friends. We fought all the time. I discovered that I liked working out, aerobics, jogging, and in particular, bodybuilding. I could focus on nothing but the pull of the muscle.

After my freshman year, I left Syracuse University, took a year off, and moved back home with my father, except home wasn't my home. My father had relocated to Coral Springs, Florida, for the warmer weather. For the first time, he was living with his longtime girlfriend, a middle-aged home economics teacher, a Martha Stewart facsimile without the flair. I knew my mother was never going to get better, never going to come home, but this woman was taking her place. I moved in. Nobody wanted me there. I didn't want to be there. We fought all the time.

I worked as a waitress in a club down by the beach, a fading spring break dive. I met a bodybuilding, surfer-blond bouncer there. I took a few aimless community college classes, my father was all over me to go back to school, but what I threw myself into was bodybuilding.

A whole community practically lived at the gym. Everyone knew each other. Everyone looked great. I was part of an exclusive club, soon working out at least 2 hours a day. In the gym, I could be hyper-focused on deadlifting up to 225 pounds. I pushed myself into a zone where I didn't have to feel anything but the strain of my arms lifting high. I had found a home.

About 700 or 800 calories a day is all I consumed. I compulsively wrote down everything I ate. If I ate an extra FrozFruit pop, I'd go back to the gym. If I argued with my father, I'd run back to the gym. I was at the gym all the time.

I kept a diary of my body parts. I'd measure every part of me—my hips, my thighs, my ankles, my wrists. My waist was 23 inches. I'd measure my fingers to see if I could lose inches and weight off my fingers. My fingers are long and naturally slender, but then, the bones were stark against the skin, the tendons strung strong and tight. I had skinny fingers.

I jogged with the owner, about 6 miles every night. She urged me to get into bodybuilding formally. She wanted to sponsor me. If I took "a little bit" of steroids, she was sure I could win.

Everything revolved around the gym. I felt like I was in another world.

One night I came to my father's house and caught him rifling through my purse.

"You're doing cocaine," he accused.

"What, are you crazy?" I said. I didn't do cocaine. I didn't smoke pot. I didn't snort or smoke or shoot up anything. In high school, I once smoked pot laced with PCP, and it totally freaked me out. But most of all, I knew my father. He was no-nonsense about drugs. I didn't even smoke cigarettes because I knew what he thought about that as well. I wanted him to be proud of me.

"You're too skinny, Susan. Something's wrong."

"What do you mean I'm too skinny?" though I was secretly happy that he noticed. "Give me my purse back." And part of me thought, *At least he still cares enough to search and ask.*

"You got to have your head examined, Susan. You do. I want this to stop."

I grabbed my purse back. "Stop what?! This is my life!"

"I want you back in a 4-year college. You should be living on campus!"

"Let me live the way I want to!"

I fled to the gym, where I forced more and more weights on the leg presses, pushed my body to do more squats, more biceps curls, until I couldn't lift my arms up, until I was feeling nothing but the pain of exertion and exhaustion.

Soon I was staying all the time with my bodybuilder boyfriend in his apartment by the beach. But we really lived in the gym, a hard-charging, weight-lifting, muscle-man gym, where my bouncer-boyfriend epitomized the bodybuilder life. He was strong, powerful, and won a lot of bodybuilder competitions. He was cool.

My boyfriend also shot up steroids—and I helped him. I shot him in his butt with steroids widely available at the gym.

I was the luckiest girl. I had a boyfriend who looked like he was carved from marble. I had found something I was passionate about: fitness and bodybuilding. I pursued weight lifting and weight loss obsessively, and it showed.

One night after a year or so together, I was going out dancing with a girlfriend.

"You're not going dancing," my boyfriend screamed. "Tell me where you're going."

"Yes, I am," I said, backing off in my black miniskirt and white cut-off T-shirt and pointy high heels. My legs were long and toned. My hair was an awesome blonde and big, really big, topping off my whip-it-thin body, a totally '80s babe.

"No, you're not!" he shouted, blocking me.

I pushed past him. His torso was as hard as a stallion's. He even glistened like a horse (though that's as far as the horse metaphor goes; he had been impotent since his last steroid cycle).

His head flew back and he roared. His harsh sweat spit across the room. He heaved a kitchen table at me. As I backed out toward the door, the cheap wood smashed to the linoleum. I felt low and trashy and wondered if everyone heard.

"I'm out of here!" I screamed.

This was the first time—and last time—anyone ever threw a table at me. And that was the last day he saw me. I soon enrolled in a 4-year college, Florida State University in Tallahassee, and "majored" in an extreme fitness regimen.

After college, I moved to Manhattan. I had always wanted to work on Wall Street. I got a job in the World Trade Center at the Commodities

Exchange. I lived in the city. I became a corporate securities paralegal, dreaming that maybe I'd be a lawyer or a stockbroker.

But what I remember of my late twenties and early thirties is how I couldn't sleep. I had to have noise—television, radios, and music—anything that blocked out my thoughts. My life was lived at full volume.

I stayed out late, hounding bars and clubs with friends. I fought with my family. I knew what was best for Susan, not them. I was toxic.

Why didn't I get involved with drugs like alcohol? Somehow, I'm not programmed to drink. A very occasional glass of wine is enough for me. Why didn't I dive into sex? Now that's tempting. I had a lot of dates. And it's not that I don't like sex; obviously, you know from reading this book that I do. But I don't do one-nights. I'm deathly afraid of diseases.

By age 31, I had moved out to Long Beach, thinking that the city was the problem. I had quit my job as a paralegal, sure that the job was the problem. I began to sell computer products out of my new apartment. The radio or television or boom box blasted all the time. I didn't like myself. I was going to kill myself or kill someone else. I was exhausted. I found a therapist.

At this point, I weighed around 190 pounds. My weight had been yo-yoing up 10, down 20, up 30, down 10, etc., every few months since I had stopped hard-core bodybuilding. This happened even though I was always on a diet and had a lifetime gym membership.

I saw a therapist twice a week. I rarely missed a session. My first fast-food binge occurred when I was about 5 months into therapy. I was at a session. I was demanding to know why. Why me? Why my mother? *Why?* I wanted her back. I wanted her for ordinary things, to help me buy shoes, to go to lunch with me, and for what I needed most: the reassurance that I would be okay. Five months' worth of therapy exploded.

"Enough!" I shouted. "Enough!" I had talked enough about my mother, my father, my loss, my stupid choices. I was shaking. I wanted the session to end. More than that, I wanted my life to be over.

"How are you doing?" the therapist asked in her sympathetic way. She was an older woman, a handsome, petite woman, who spoke in careful, firm tones. "Are you okay?"

"Yes," I said, gulping for air, swallowing tears. I said yes, but I thought, *If I said no, what would you do? You'd do nothing. You can't do anything. I can't do anything.*

I tore out of her office. I was on a diet, but I was always on a diet. Screw the diet. I don't care about the diet. I'm sick of dieting. I'm sick of worrying all the time about my weight. I didn't want to be responsible all the time. I didn't want to think. I drove to the first open place: Dunkin' Donuts. I don't even like doughnuts. I bought three. I scooped out the red jelly insides and ate only that. It wasn't enough, but it helped. The sugar rushed into me. I felt a little better. If I ate more, I'd feel much better.

I hurried back in and bought six chocolate chip cookies. These really helped. These did it. These quieted the thoughts, like a shouting match, in my head. The first three calmed me down. The next three numbed me. I liked the feeling of not feeling. I liked it a lot.

So that became the routine: After each session, I ate. I soon got to the point where I had to eat. I couldn't sleep if I didn't eat. I needed to eat; it helped to ritualize the therapy, it gave me something to look forward to, my reward for revealing myself. I could always start my diet again on Monday.

My father flew up to join me at a session, which meant the world to me. He had broken up with his longtime girlfriend and rebounded into a short-lived marriage. We had never talked together about how I felt so motherless, so abandoned, with a mother in the hospital and a father who retreated into his work. He had kept the four of us together, he had fed us and clothed us, but it wasn't enough. He listened. He flirted with my therapist a bit. But mainly, he listened.

"I love you; what do you want me to say?" he said, trying.

"I want you to say you're proud of me."

He shook his head like I was crazy. He looked to my therapist for direction and flashed his dimples at her. He rushed out, "I'm proud of you. Okay?"

I wanted him to say it like he meant it.

I felt raw and exposed. Ten other emotions between rage and grief exploded in me.

I couldn't take talking about me anymore. My therapist begged me to stay. I needed a break. I was drained. I had gained about a hundred pounds. I was teetering at 300 pounds.

"If you leave now, you're going to gain more weight," she warned me gently.

"No way. No, I won't."

I was in control.

Chapter 6

So, now I'm over 400 pounds. It is spring 2003, and I've gained back the 60 pounds I lost while seeing the nutritionist. But she abandoned me. She went off to have her baby. I'm inhaling my second family pack of chicken wings doused in Tabasco sauce and ketchup. It's late. I check out various dating sites. I spend 3 to 4 hours online every day, waiting for The One to pop up. This night, one does, in a very odd way.

His name is Adam or that's how it starts.

Adam instant messages me out of the blue, based on my very tight face picture posted online, only slightly dated, and my profile. The text includes my occupation as "go-getter" and my hobbies/interest: questioning man's existence.

Adam thinks that his friend John would like me. Adam sounds normal and sweet, and I'm alone and we're instant messaging each other, and soon we're talking on the phone. He's going to bring John around the next day. I know it's crazy, but I think, *Why not? Why the hell not?* I have nothing else but chicken wings and toner to think about.

The next night, Adam and John arrive. I position myself behind my office desk, which I have situated on the left end of my living room, where a dining room table should be.

I've filled the dining area, since I never dine, with a large computer desk, file cabinets, and thick computer supply catalogues. I'm the accounts receivable, bookkeeper, receptionist, office manager, and salesperson for a chaotically run small computer-supply business that plans to be big one day, a day that never seems to come. The apartment has three bedrooms; two of the three are used for the business. I still have a living room area—a set of burnt orange buckskin couches surrounded by a huge square cocktail table crammed with photos, but I never relax on those couches. Except for my office chair, everything in the house has grown too narrow or small or constraining. The living room is like a set, to show that I have a normal life.

I've told Adam that I'll leave the front door open. That way, Adam and John cannot follow my ass up the stairs.

I'm so excited. It's like I'm expecting a delivery, but this time it's a man.

John bounds up the stairs—he's full and broad and substantial in the way I like guys. Blond, thick curls spring from his head in all directions and he has dreamy blue eyes, the most Aryan Israeli I've ever met. He claims he's 20 years old. I suspect he could even be 18. He lives at home with his mother. Even at 20, he's at least 18 years younger than me. Technically, he could be my son. But I don't think of him in that way at all. I have absolutely no maternal feelings toward him.

I want to kiss his full pouting lips. I want to make him smile, though it's hard. He's careful with his smiles. I'm doubly rewarded when I get him to ease one out of his brooding face.

For months, I didn't even know his last name, or his real first name. He's playing a game and so am I.

He's not John, he's Isaac. I know it's weird.

We start seeing each other and one day, I show up at his store after closing. We watch television. He likes game shows. I don't want to be there. I hate game shows. We go in the back. I give him a quick and dirty blow job amid the file cabinets. It's dangerous and fun and flirty. I'm someone else, someone thin and sexy, even though I can barely bend over and he has to help me get up.

I ask him to whisper something dirty in Hebrew. I don't understand, but it sounds like prayers. I laugh and say, "You could be telling me to do your laundry." But what I think is: *He could be calling me a fat pig in Hebrew.*

He wouldn't.

He wants to reciprocate, but I won't let him see The Body. He undresses. I fold his clothes. I nuzzle into his broad naked chest. He can't hold me. He can't fit his hands all the way around my folds and bumps and lumps of fat. But he's so nice, he kisses me lightly all over my face.

I ask him his last name.

"What's the difference?" he says, shrugging, turning away, liking his mystery or not wanting me to know more about him, I'm not sure.

I make like it's a joke, teasing him, making up improbable last names like McCormick or Sinatra. But I feel so dirty that I don't know his last name. He doesn't answer, and I don't push him. I want to see him again. I don't trust him, but I want to be held and kissed.

Another night, he's at my apartment. I say: "I have to go the city the next day and get my hair colored." He lies back on my bed and tells me that his brother's a colorist. I carefully balance myself on the edge of the bed, huge and awkward and wishing I could hide my swollen, pulsating, vein-scarred feet. I ask his name.

"That's my colorist!" I shout, bouncing slightly up and down on the bed, careful not to jump near him. I wish I could curl up next to him.

"That's my brother," he concedes.

How small this world is.

His brother is a colorist, my colorist, and he's famous, having dyed, streaked, and highlighted the hair of many celebrities. I kid him, "Now I know your last name."

I lay my head on his pelvis and stroke him up and down and get him hard again. I'm too big for my body. I can't bend over. I hate myself. Shame, that's what I feel, and even as I take him in my mouth, I feel so alone.

He gently touches my hair and suggests we have sex.

"No way." I sit up and toss my hair in his face. I want to keep it light and easy. "You'll be the first one I have sex with when I'm thin again," I kid, turning away from him.

"When will that be?" he whispers, stroking the back of my head.

"I don't know. But I'm starting my diet tomorrow if it means having sex with you!"

But I know the reality. I'm not ready to have sex with him, or with anybody. I haven't been ready since I broke up with Bobby about 2 years ago. I don't deserve it.

I don't want to remember. I don't know how to say this; I've never talked about it before. I didn't tell my sister or anyone but Bobby and Marcy at the time.

I was dating Bobby. I wouldn't go on the Pill because of my mother having had a stroke, and my fear of the same. I couldn't manipulate a diaphragm, the bending and the maneuvering between my thighs. A search for the right position was like going down a cave without a light. I couldn't be a spelunker, a cave explorer, on a regular basis.

Bobby said he was wearing a condom. I saw him put on the condom. I didn't see him take it off, though later he admitted he had. I trusted him, and he betrayed me. He wanted me to get pregnant and stay with him. He thought he was doing me a favor.

For years, I had stopped getting my period on any regular basis, though before my early thirties, I was like clockwork. I didn't mind *not* getting my period; this body was like somebody else's anyway. This time, I didn't get it for 3 or 4 months. I never kept track. I had the worst indigestion, but I thought it was too much tomato sauce. I ate a lot of pasta, chicken, or eggplant, all from the Italian deli, all smothered in tomato sauce, which, I rationalized, was very high in acidity. I almost convinced myself that it was the tomato sauce.

Yet something in me finally said, "Maybe?" So one night, I peed on an over-the-counter pregnancy test. I was shocked and not shocked at all. The blue line appeared and made me mute. I felt empty, but for the first time in a long time, I didn't want to eat. I threw the stick away as if that would change things, and I went to bed. I couldn't sleep but willed myself unconscious.

I didn't know what I was going to do. I love children. I want children. I adore my sister's 3-year-old boy even if I overfeed him mandarin oranges and he explodes with the runs. Who knew that six oranges were too many for a toddler? I joked with my sister afterward that maybe I had portion control issues. But he was enjoying them so much. I'm really the world's greatest aunt.

The next day, my gynecologist said to me in no uncertain terms: "With your family history, with your weight, do you want to risk your health by having this baby? You will. It's your choice."

I didn't have a choice. Bobby and The Body betrayed me. I was 35 years old, and I had an abortion. I paid for it by myself. He didn't offer. I didn't want his money. I wanted a baby; I just didn't want to die from having one.

At the hospital, I wanted to know the sex of the fetus. But the nurse wouldn't tell me. She said it would hurt too much. It doesn't matter. It still hurts.

Chapter 7

I smoothly convince myself, especially online, that I'm "only a little chubby." Since I rarely meet any of the men I chat with online, it's easy. I make excuses not to meet them. My whole life is conducted invisibly, on the phone.

I spend most of my days working from my apartment, obsessing about a sale or a shipment or trying to collect a payment. I'm supposed to go out on sales calls, but I rarely do. Some days, I barely get dressed. I pull on a T-shirt and a pair of black stretch pants and wrap my uncombed hair up in a ponytail and shuffle from my bedroom to my desk.

The phone rings at 8 a.m. or earlier: "Sue? I need computer paper, Sue." "An order didn't arrive, Sue." "Can I rush—Sue?" I say yes to everybody; that's my job, and I'm exhausted.

I order breakfast. The deli delivers two everything bagels, toasted, with extra vegetable cream cheese, two slices of American cheese on top of the cream cheese, and a fried egg and a tomato. For a snack, I ask them to include a pint of ice cream or a bag of Milano cookies or a pound of macaroni salad. They know me. They know not to screw it up. If the bagel arrives untoasted, I'll get on the phone with them and let them have it.

I order lunch. I start with the pizza place. I order a pasta dish—pasta puttanesca, which is pasta with olives, capers, and anchovies with extra *extra* Parmesan cheese on the side. When I call the Chinese take-out, they know my address by heart. The guy who always answers the phone stammers in broken English, "Yes, yes—yes, yes—we know." Susan from Long Beach doesn't have to give her phone number or house address. I always order the same thing: chicken wings, steamed vegetable dumplings, General Tso's chicken, fried rice, and egg roll. I leave the downstairs door open and the money on my countertop for each delivery. I don't like to get up in front of deliverymen. I need to order from two places so I'll have enough to nibble on during the afternoon until it's time for dinner.

At 5:30 p.m., I write up my last order of the day, assuring the customer that she'll have her computer supplies ASAP, no problem, and slam the phone down. I have to scramble to make sure that her order will go out, but I make it happen, again—another end-of-day emergency handled.

My head and shoulders and arms ache as if I've been hiking uphill. I've been in my apartment alone all day. I haven't moved except to eat.

But now it's time for dinner. I used to love to cook, but I don't anymore. I don't like to go food shopping anymore; it's too much work.

People stare at me. Once, a little girl asked her mother if I was pregnant. Anyway, I don't have time to plan ahead, and I have no one to cook for but myself. I don't have the energy after a full day at work. It's not worth it anymore.

If I can walk down the stairs, I'll go for fast food. If I can't, I'll order from a different Chinese restaurant, the Szechuan one. I don't like ordering in from the same place twice in a day. I don't want them to think that's all I do—order in—that's not normal. The Szechuan place has better chicken wings anyway.

I have to eat. I debate, in or out? Tonight, I can make it to my car.

I don't comb my hair or wash my face. No one is going to see me; it's like the fat camouflages me. No one has to know the real me.

The smell of the ocean is near, but that's not the smell I'm after. My car is parked right in front, and I hurry to it. My mouth is watering even before I sink into the car and go.

I start on the main drag in Long Beach with the BK drive-thru and order a fish sandwich with extra *extra* tartar sauce and a Hershey pie. They have the best and *bigger* fish sandwiches. I drive off and eat and debate whether I'll go to McDonald's next because McDonald's is easily accessible on the left-hand side. I don't want to waste time crossing the road. Usually, I'd keep on the right-hand side of the road loop, and I do that tonight.

So, the next stop is Dunkin' Donuts. I finish the BK with gusto. I don't want the order-takers at Dunkin' Donuts to see my BK bags. At Dunkin' Donuts, I order an everything bagel with extra vegetable cream cheese, American cheese, and an egg. I debate whether I should order Dunkin' Donuts chocolate chip cookies or McDonald's (which is now definitely at the end of my loop). Tonight, I don't want to wait and order six chocolate chip cookies. I'm having a great time. I'm high. I'm blasting the radio.

Next stop is Taco Bell/Pizza Hut. How convenient that they are built together. I order a supreme personal pizza and nachos with extra *extra* cheese and sour cream. I wish that they had desserts there, but all they have are cinnamon twists, and those are just okay. Glad I got the cookies! I'm driving with one hand and eating with the other.

After I'm through with the evidence from each meal, I hide it under the seat. Other cars are hurrying home from the train station. But I'm not ready to go home yet. I'm flying. I'm buzzing.

McDonald's. I order another fish sandwich with extra *extra* tartar sauce—they have the good sauce—french fries and a McFlurry with extra *extra* M&Ms and Oreo cookies. Next, at KFC, I order only one thing: a Twister, a wrap of chicken strips with extra *extra* sauce. I have one more fast-food stop: Wendy's. I order an extra-large french fries—these taste different, more potatoey, and I like them the best—and a simple single with cheese. I'm doing good!

Before going home, I stop for my late-night snack. I pull through the Dairy Barn. There's a very overweight woman who slumps at the cash register.

I ask for my snack: a box of Yodels and a Ben and Jerry's Chocolate Fudge Brownie frozen yogurt. The Häagen Dazs Mocha Chip ice cream was what I really wanted, but I didn't want to overdo it.

Her hair is pulled back from her face. She doesn't wear any makeup. It looks like it hurts her fingers—they are so swollen, bitten down, without any nail polish—to be a cashier. She languidly takes my money and, even more slowly, gives me change. I always compare myself with her, and in my mind, I always come out thinner.

Some weeks I spend $300 to $400 a week on fast food and deliveries, but it's worth it. Tonight, I'm in that sultry, full, near comatose state, surrounded by the smell of grease, salt, fish, meat, and sugar, clinging to my skin.

I slump back in my car seat. I don't want to leave. American flags wave on porches. I try not to move at all. It's like I've just spent an evening out with my friends partying at a great party.

And it's like I have a hole in my soul.

The first stars fade into the twilight. I love astronomy. I love really dark nights in the woods. We camped out a lot when we were kids. I want to wish on the first star, and try to form the words, *star light, star bright.* I let my mind wander over other things I could eat, and I stare out into infinity in a hazy, happy calm.

If I don't want my Chocolate Fudge Brownie frozen yogurt to melt—though I like it when the brownie chunks nestle into the soft, melting cream—it's less effort to eat—I'd better get going. It hurts to move my legs or to bend my stomach and sit straight up. I do it all in slow motion, as if I need to be guided by the stars.

But before I go into the house, I clean out my car. The salt of the sea settles on the street. I manage a deep breath with a little effort. I make sure the top of the garbage can is on tight and secure and drag the can to the curb for pickup.

I lock my car.

I step away from my car.

And with that, all that I have injected into my mouth evaporates. None of what I've eaten counts. Not one bite. That's the rule, if I eat in my car. It's as if the past 2 hours, my entire fast-food loop, didn't happen. I'm empty—that hole in my soul is bigger, not smaller.

Yet my mouth opens and a laugh comes out. Somehow I think I've gotten one over on someone. I carry my Yodels and frozen yogurt upstairs. I'll start my diet on Monday.

Top Six Things I Tell Myself on My Binge Route

- Eat *anything* and *everything* because I'm starting my diet tomorrow.

- BK fish sandwiches taste better than McDonald's, but the tartar sauce on the McDonald's is better than BK's. Dilemma solved: Eat both.

- Put the phone on vibrate. No distractions. No calls from friends asking, "Hey, what are you doing?"

- Eat everything in the car; calories don't count there.

- Throw away all wrappers and containers immediately.

- Don't buy value meals. You end up with too many sodas when going through multiple drive-thrus, even if it's only a quarter more.

Chapter 8

"I'm hot and wet," I whisper into the phone. After hours online, I've found Andrew. He's from northern New York, less than an hour from me. I know Isaac isn't right for me, though I keep him as a treat. I e-mail Andrew an old picture of myself, from the body-building days. He sends me back one with him standing in the background. In it, he's very Banana Republic as far I can tell: thin, tall, preppy, and in this fuzzy photo—not really my type at all. He's in sales and on the road a lot, as far I can gather.

Andrew sounds scratchy and nasal and overeager or anxious, depending on the day. His voice isn't deep or smooth or edged with a twang, like Tommy Lee Jones, which would drive me wild. But he calls me. I like being pursued. And he likes calling me, a lot. He's punctual, too. I can expect his calls at 9 p.m.

"When I can I meet you?" he typically asks first off, as if to get it out of the way.

"Definitely soon," I lie.

"When? You sound so hot!"

"You're the one who's hot," I say, wanting to start.

"Tell me what you look like again?"

"You have my picture."

"I know, but is that a recent picture?"

"I'm a little bit chubbier now," I admit. "And I want you. I want you so bad. I'm aching. I'm all hot and wet and ready just talking to you."

"You are?" he says, his voice dropping.

"Yes," I say in my most sexed-up voice. "Talk to me. Tell me you want me," I urge, because I'm not alone if I hear his voice. "Tell me how you want me. Do you want me on top? Do you want me to pin you down? Do you want me to take control?"

He groans, "Yes."

I have him back.

"I'm wet and ready for you, Andrew. For no one else."

I'm having the safest kind of sex with him anyway—phone sex. He can't touch my body. He can't see it.

I lie back uncomfortably on my bed. I pull out my vibrator, "the bullet." I don't like to put anything inside me, and this does the trick, massaging the outside. I'm wearing a long T-shirt; I don't like to touch my own skin. I try to be creative, though I hesitate at first. He has no inhibitions. He teaches me the language of phone sex, how to arouse him by purring at him about how hot he is, how big he is, how strong he is, and how wet and ready I am—and I am.

I prop myself up on the pillows. My hand, gripping "the bullet," is stretched as far as it can go. The electricity shoots into me. My knees hurt to bend. I curl up on my side. My eyes are closed, and my body stirs as if from hibernation, warm and safe, the machine whirring between my legs. He's pounding my name over and over, "Oh, Sue," like they're the only words to a punk rock song. I imagine him next to me, kissing me, licking me, throwing me on my back, and I'm that girl in the picture, long-limbed and toned with a flat stomach and legs that could raise and bend and wrap.

He kids that I'm saving him hundreds of dollars in 900 numbers. He suggests I could make a small fortune by going into business. Andrew thinks he's complimenting me. I watch the clock. I make sure we're done by 10 o'clock so I can order Chinese delivered. I'm starving. Men come and go, but Chinese chicken wings are forever.

Lies I Tell During Phone Sex

- I'm only a little chubby.
- I can't wait to get together.

- I'm wearing a red thong.

- I just came from working out, and I'm all worked up for you.

- I'm wearing tight jeans. Size 8.

- I'd like to screw you all night. (Actually, I want to be off the phone by 10 o'clock in order to call in my Chinese delivery.)

- *Of course* that's a recent picture of me.

One night I ask Andrew: If he had a choice between chocolate cake and key lime pie, which would he choose?

"The cake," he says, not warming up.

"Brownie versus key lime pie, which one?" I say in my most sultry voice.

He chooses chocolate again.

"So you're a chocoholic," I coo. "I'm a big cookie person. Chocolate chip. With big fat chunks, hot and gooey. Real gooey," I giggle.

"Bananas," he offers. "How about banana cream pie, spread all over your body?"

"How about just the cream? I don't like bananas very much. They stick to the roof of your mouth," I say, liking this phone call more than any others.

"Whipped cream?" he offers.

"What a cliché. How about ice cream?" I whisper back, tensing with desire, and wishing that this guy was a little bit more imaginative. "What's your favorite flavor?" I know what mine is. I know what I want.

He says, his voice scratching up another octave, "Chocolate," showing his total lack of imagination.

"You know what I like?" I whisper, almost licking the phone. "I like Breyers Mint Chocolate Chip, an entire pint, softened just a bit," and lie back and let the memory of eating spoonful after creamy, sweet, chunky spoonful tighten and loosen me.

"You know you're hot," he starts. "You're really hot. Are you wet?"

"It's you who's hot," I say. I can't wait for this to be over.

He groans louder, faster, shallower, and I urge him on, saying his name over and over.

That spring, Andrew and I have phone sex at least 30 times. We never meet.

Chapter 9

The Russian. He glances beyond me as if another version of me will come through the vegetarian restaurant door.

I met him online. I told him that I'm "a little chubby," but I never sent him a picture. He works for a car dealership and drives long distances. We talk on the phone for hours while he's in the car, diving into intense conversations about nothing at all. He's never been married. He loves children. He's thinking of becoming more religious in the Jewish faith; so am I. We laugh. His deep Russian accent resonates long after I hang up.

I'd only agree to meet him at a restaurant I've been to many times before. It has armless chairs. He's there first—medium build, brown hair, an average, normal guy. I wait for him to open his mouth so I can hear his accent.

But he just looks me up and down. I smile. For a second, I imagine he must think I'm hot. He drops his eyes. He's embarrassed. He can't keep looking at the fat girl across from him.

Everyone in the restaurant stares at us, I'm sure of it. We both order the Caesar salad with salmon, my suggestion, since I'm living in a carbless world. I'm watching him eat. He's not touching the bread, so I don't. He's putting down his fork, so I do. He's leaving some salmon behind, so I will too.

I chat away to distract myself. He can't look at me. I touch his hand so he has to look at me.

At the end of the evening, he pays—a sure sign to me that this is something more. He gives me a quick kiss good night. I'm sure he is going to call me again, and he does.

He phones me on the ride home.

I almost drop my cell phone, I'm so excited to see his phone number.

"Hi," he says, despondently.

"It was really great meeting you."

"Yeah, but—"

"I had a terrific dinner," I continue, cruising down Flatbush Avenue toward the Belt Parkway.

"Did you ever like someone but know it wouldn't work out for whatever reason?" he asks sadly, and not quite hypothetically.

"What are you trying to say?"

"What would I tell my friends and family?"

"What are you talking about?" I speed the car through a yellow light.

"Your weight?" he drops on me.

"What about my weight?" All the heat in my body swells to my face. My head throbs. I'm so glad I'm alone in the car.

"What would I tell my friends? My family?" His Russian voice cracks.

"About what!?" I say, hitting the top of my steering wheel for emphasis.

"About you, Susan. How would I explain?"

"I've lost weight. I'm on a diet," I say, factually. I'm always on a diet.

"Susan, I can't see you again. How could I ever justify it?" he sighs.

I scream into my cell phone: "Once I lose my weight, which I will, you will never have a chance with me!"

The quiet of his breathing breaks in. There's nothing more to say. I hang up. I hurl the cell phone across the seat. I'm trapped in my car.

I swerve into the Burger King on Flatbush Avenue. I never hear from the Russian again. As I get bigger, my world gets smaller.

Around this time, my sister and my older brother, Mark, decide to stage a kind of intervention.

We meet at a local Mexican restaurant in the late afternoon, and the restaurant is deserted. The waiter automatically brings fresh, warm triangles of chips and salsa. My sister takes it away from me. I insist I'm on a diet, which is true in a way, and that chips and salsa are fine on this diet. Salsa is very low-calorie, I insist, digging one chip and then another into the hot, salty, pungent mix of tomatoes, onions, and peppers, asking for the waiter to bring us more even before he takes our order. I'm going to start a new diet on Monday.

My brother Mark is a barrel-chested guy with huge forearms. He has eyes with deep bags from allergies, a high forehead, and an imperfect aquiline nose.

Caroline sits across from me. She's too serious for me. She's thinking of things she doesn't say, and that's what she's doing now as she pulls the chips toward her again.

"Everyone is concerned about you," she jumps in.

"Who's everyone?"

She glares at me.

I reach over and eat more chips. "What does that mean, 'concerned'?" *What the hell does she want me to say? Who the hell are they to be talking to me about my life?! They're not thin. They could both lose a few pounds.* Caroline looks like she hasn't slept. Her skin is red and blotchy and broken out. She needs to have her hair cut or highlighted or blown straight. Her mascara is smeared. She doesn't even know how to put on makeup.

It's my father's fault. All he ever did was feed us instead of hug us.

It's our metabolism. We're big people.

I'm sure I have more muscle than fat.

My sister cuts into my thoughts with a "Susan—!" Only Caroline can ring out my name like that—into emphatic syllables that stops the tumble in my brain.

I look right at her. Her brown eyes don't blink. "What? What do you want from me? Things are going great for me. Really great."

I feel ambushed.

The waiter brings more salsa. I grab the chips back to my side. Nobody is going to tell me what to eat and what not to eat!

My sister urges me to quit my job, and to go get a real one in a real office.

"If you had a job, you'd be out of the house every day, seeing people."

"I don't need to see people."

She plays with one chip and puts it down. My sister doesn't understand. Caroline's never been a chip eater.

Once upon a time, a lifetime ago, I was a paralegal. I want to scream at her that that was another person, a person who wore business suits and high heels and who could easily walk down the street. I need my job; that's all I have.

"It's a growing business," I lie.

"All that's growing is you," says my brother.

I ignore him. He glances over at my sister as if to say to her, *I told you so.* I have a long history of fighting with this brother.

"Why don't you take some time off—go on vacation?" says Caroline.

She might as well tell me to go to the moon. I'm broke. I'm spending $300 to $400 a week on food. But I don't tell her that. I haven't left the house in at least a week except to go through a fast-food drive-thru. How could I go on vacation?

I munch through the chips. I wave the red plastic basket in the air for more. I shout at the waiter, "*Por favor!*" I'm loud and rude, and Caroline winces because she's so perfect.

We order. This is a late lunch for Caroline and my brother Mark, but it's only a snack for me. I decide on the chicken fajitas to prove to them that I'm okay. The fajitas arrive in a sizzling black cast-iron pan. I don't eat the tortillas that come with them.

I think—*screw them*—they should both focus on their careers and not mine. My sister is a workaholic, spending, like, 60 or 70 hours a week at her job in cable television, traveling all over the place. She should stay home and take care of the baby! My brother is doing what he has always done to me: giving me a hard time, picking on me, acting superior.

I dive into the fajitas. I finish eating before Caroline or Mark. I watch them eat. I could have a whole other meal, or two. I reach for the chips. I ask the waiter for more, again. "I will eat what I want!" I hiss. Caroline doesn't even finish her meal. She asks to bring part of it home. I pay for lunch, even though I'm broke. All my credit cards are close to their limits, but I want to prove that everything is fine with me, and it is.

I'm just sick and tired of them acting so superior. *Who made them my boss! I don't need another boss! I know what's best for me. Who the hell are they to judge me?* I get in my car and drive toward McDonald's.

As I get bigger, my world gets smaller.

By the beginning of the summer, I'm very weary. I stop seeing my friends altogether. I make excuses. They stop asking me to join them. I can't fit into any regular chair. I can't walk anywhere. I don't want to go in anyone's car but my own. I won't let them talk to me about my weight. I cut them off with "I'm on a diet."

I used to bike on the boardwalk, three blocks from my house, every so often. On this beautiful day, this will be the day to start really dieting. I venture out. The seat is lost underneath me. But I get the bike going. I pedal down the street, sweating. Some of neighborhood kids see me and start following me, yelling out after me, "Fat ass!" I turn around, and bike home as fast as I can. When I get home, my tires are almost flat. I don't want to leave the house at all.

For the first time in my life, I feel old. I'm 38 years old. I try not to think of anything but what I will eat next. As soon as I wake up, I start planning what I'll eat. Eating consumes my day—pun intended.

I've started timing my eating. Every half hour I have to have something. Now, I'm waiting for a pizza place to deliver. The Chinese place is always quick; a delivery gets to my house in less than 10 minutes. But I've already ordered and eaten the Chinese, and the pizza isn't here. I'm usually careful not to have this happen. I hate waiting. I stare at the television, but what I'm really doing is jonesing for the food. I scratch my arms and pull them into my 5X man's T-shirt. I make up a game to keep my mind off the time. If I watch one television show over another, the food will get here faster. I laugh along with the sitcom's laugh track. It hurts. But I'm not allowed to turn the channel. I'm waiting for my food fix.

This night it takes the pizza place 42 minutes to rush the three blocks to my house. *I said rush, didn't I?!* It's 10:30 p.m. The old man delivers my order. I hear his heavy steps, his curses in Italian as he trudges up the stairs. He finds his money and leaves, and I go out of my bedroom to retrieve my food.

By 11 o'clock, I'm completely comatose. I'm in a haze. *If I took drugs, it would feel like this. Good. Real good.*

My bedroom is littered with empty Chinese cartons and pizza boxes and diet soda cans. I'm in my bed. The bed smells like cheese and oil.

I can't think. I can't sense anything, but it's good. I want this feeling of *not feeling,* of numbness, to last. Some people would call it being dead. I drop asleep.

As I get bigger, my life gets smaller.

I hardly sleep through the night anymore. I'm having a lot of trouble breathing. Light-headed and woozy, I finally decide that I should go see my general practitioner, just for a checkup.

At the doctor's office, I can't fit into any of the gowns. "You should be able to accommodate a person who has to lose a little weight," I say in a snarky tone to the nurse. But I make do by using two gowns, one for each side of my body, and tying them together in the middle.

The doctor comes in, young, trim, efficient. Following protocol, he says, "Let's get on the scale."

"I don't want to get on the scale."

"You have to," he says, peering at the chart, not looking at me.

"I don't want to." I don't remember the last time I got weighed. I wouldn't let the nutritionist weigh me. Why did the doctor need to?

"You have to get on the scale, or the exam is over," he orders, glaring at me now.

I get on the scale.

I'm shocked, literally speechless, holding onto the scale so I won't fall down.

"Is that right?" I say, my heart beating. "Do I look that heavy?"

The scale read 444 pounds.

"You don't look thin," says the doctor with a flat expression.

I want to hit him. Taking my blood pressure comes next. He has to call the nurse to get an extra-long cuff. It doesn't fit my upper arm. He looks annoyed. The cuff fits, barely, around my lower arm.

He studies the gauge. He looks at my veined, swollen feet. He glances at his watch. He looks everywhere but at me.

"I'd like to put you on blood pressure medicine," he finally says.

"Why do I have to be on blood pressure medicine?"

And then he says the words that rock my world: "Because you could walk across the street and have a stroke."

He could have said anything else: *You could have a heart attack, you could get diabetes, you could die, Sue.* But he said what I feared most in the world because of my mother: *You could have a stroke.*

I didn't want to end up in the bed next to my mother, eating mush and waiting for someone to change my diapers.

I expected him to say more to me, to ask why I had gained so much weight, to probe a little, to look at me. *I haven't always been heavy,* I want to say. *If you ask, maybe I'll tell you: I want to get my life under control, though eating is the only thing I can control.*

But the doctor doesn't look at me. He busies himself with my chart, and says, "I'm going to make an appointment for you to see about gastric bypass surgery. Okay." This isn't really a question from him.

"You want to do what?" I say, my voice trembling.

"Let's see if you even qualify. Okay? You may have to lose some weight first." He doesn't look at me. He closes the file and hurries to leave.

"Don't bother making that call," I say, my voice rising as I pull the two gowns around me. "Save your quarter!"

He finally looks at me—a look of total disregard—a look of dismay—a look that goes right through me. It's as if he has nodded his head and told some people to go right and me to go left, some people to live and me to die.

He leaves without another word to me. He's done his job.

I stomp out of the examination room. I don't want to start with surgery as the first option. I don't want it to be the only choice. I don't want to be opened up, sliced up, cut up.

The doctor didn't even give me a chance to discuss other options. I was athletic all my life—well, for some of my life. I know I can be thin again. I just don't know how.

My car is parked on the street across from a park with a gazebo. It's midmorning and a gorgeous spring day. Kids are playing in the park, climbing on the bright-colored monkey bars. I don't start the car. I don't know where to go.

I call my father and pour out my news about the high blood pressure and the prescription. He knows what it means to me without me having to say it. It's all about my mother and my fears. I break down and cry hysterically.

At first, my father is brisk and short with me. He has a gruff I'm-from-the-Bronx-so-don't-even-think-of-it bark. I'm the daughter he has to worry about all the time. I'm the one who took forever to finish college, who's not married, who's always short on money and long on plans. I expect him to yell at me.

Instead, he says in his version of a gentle voice, "Enough with the eating, Susan," as if that is all I need to hear to change 8 years of bingeing and dieting and lying.

I'm the one who doesn't listen.

I know that my weight isn't at all about how much I eat but about *why* I eat. I've been through therapy. I cried and ate my way through 4 years of therapy. *I know why I eat. Food is my heroin.* Food obliterates everything else. I don't have to feel anything but that Whopper sliding down. I know it's not normal.

I'm screaming into the phone, "What should I do?" I'm holding my cell phone so tight that I think it'll break. I'm hyperventilating. I'm saying all this and, yes, all I can think is that I need food. I'm missing lunch.

"All I want to feel is normal. All I want to do is look normal. But I don't know what to do."

"We'll figure it out," says my father, sounding far away and helpless.

"How am I ever going to meet someone?"

"You'll meet somebody."

"How can I ever have kids? I won't have kids!" I look over at one happy little girl playing in the park. "I don't even get my period."

He says nothing. I never talk with him about The Body.

"I can't have kids if I don't lose weight. The doctor says it's too dangerous."

"So you'll lose the weight. You'll just lose it."

"I can't do it in Long Beach. I'm killing myself here."

I'm waiting for him to yell at me. I'm so sick and tired of being a disappointment to him. But he doesn't even raise his voice.

"Come home," he says. What he means is run to him in Florida. He lives in a one-bedroom apartment in a 50-plus development. That isn't home. And I can't run.

We talk for 3 straight hours. Mostly, my father says that he doesn't have any answers. He doesn't know what to say, and he admits it, and I panic even more until I realize that what he's saying is that *I'm* the only one who can change me. I'm in control—no one else—and that realization, though murky and half-formed and hurting my stomach, somehow helps.

He does say this, in his frank, no-nonsense way: "Susan, you're not alone. You have me, you have your family, and you always will."

"I'm going to do it, Daddy," I say with just enough shaky confidence to get off the phone with my father. But I don't know what "it" is.

I hang up and call ahead to a Persian restaurant, a standby of mine near the doctor's office. I order my favorite: salmon kebab with basmati rice and potato salad loaded with mayonnaise and pickles, grape leaves, and eggplant salad. The svelte couple behind the counter hands it over to me in a huge roasting pan. I hold it carefully with two hands. There's enough for a family of four.

I eat it all in my car, parked outside the restaurant, a trough of food. I don't know how I can finish it all, but I do, and I resolve, *This is it. It's over. I'm going to close that hole in my soul.*

Chapter 10

My father's big arms carried home half-eaten boxes of store-bought pineapple coffee cake or round loaves of fresh bread from the Portuguese bakery in Mamaroneck. We'd break the loaves in half and eat them from the inside out—mounds of white, warm insides—and then devour the crusts. Crumbs fell everywhere.

My father was a salesman, always on the road. He sold cookware, fancy pots and pans—first for other people, and then he opened his own company where he imported and exported what else? Gourmet cookware.

My father kidded that he got a deal for us—four kids, all economy-sized. We were fit. We spent hours on bikes and running games and no one worried about our weight.

For a while I had a pet rabbit, Nutmeg, and my father procured piles of old lettuce and greens free from the vegetable manager at Waldbaum's. Nutmeg lived in a two-story condo-type rabbit hutch that my father built for him, and we fed him piles of food until he had a heart attack one day and died on a bunch of carrots.

I think of everything, including this, as I realize it's over. I can't live in Long Beach. I can't keep my apartment or job. I can't stay and have a stroke racing around the drive-thrus. I can't stay and lose the weight here.

But what the hell am I going to do? How am I going to do this? How am I going to start? Who's going to help me?

At home that night, after the doctor's visit, with my new prescription of blood pressure pills on my countertop, I start researching on the computer. I spend all night searching key words like "fat" and "fat farm" and "weight loss," and I face a million entries, every type of "cure" and pill and surgery and clinic.

There is a reason for everything. In the back of my mind, I remember a date once mentioning a place, the Rice Clinic, and I look it up. There are no massages, no special promises, and no cures—only a program that's been in operation since 1939. I call and speak to the director. She urges me to come down to Durham, North Carolina, to see for myself.

It's August. I tell my sister that I'm going away for the weekend. I let my father know the truth but make him promise to keep it to himself. I didn't want to tell anybody, but God forbid I should have a stroke or heart attack on my way down.

On a Thursday, I leave for Durham. I haven't had a vacation in years, though I don't consider this a vacation.

I don't even *think* of flying to Durham. The last time I flew anywhere was to visit my father in Florida, and that was a year or two before. I had an aisle seat so I could stretch my legs. I prayed that no one would sit next to me.

I had to trudge into the plane sideways. I couldn't fit through the door or down the aisle. I couldn't fit in the seat if the armrest was down. "We're just going to keep this up, thank you so much," I said to the skinny Indian businessman jammed in the middle beside me.

He shifted, straightened, probably willed himself to take up less room. My stomach almost extended to the seat in front of me. I was sweating down my sides from the effort to get on the plane. He stared straight ahead.

I hid my lap with a sweater, something I knew I didn't need in Florida, praying that the flight attendant wouldn't ask me if I had my seat belt on. Of course I didn't. The Indian closed his eyes. I wanted to disappear.

When the flight attendant came around and whispered, "Do you need a seat belt extension?" I wanted to scream "No!" but forced myself to say yes.

I arranged the seat belt extension, hoping that no one would see what I had to do. I felt exposed. I was that fat person on the plane whom no one wants to sit next to. Even with the extension, the seat belt squeezed around me. Forget about getting something to drink. I couldn't hold it anywhere. The tray wouldn't flatten over my stomach.

The plane took off. It was a clear, beautiful day down the Eastern Seaboard. I shuffled out of the plane sideways.

That Thursday in August, I load myself and a weekend bag into my Altima and head south. I know nothing about Durham except that it's about 10 hours south and west. I'm scared to death. I eat bags of Funyuns, one of my favorites, all the way down, and the car smells like salt and onions.

The next morning, I meet Laine, the Clinic's director, at a food store across the street from the Clinic. While I wait for her, I buy three almond butter and jelly on whole wheat sandwiches and a diet Snapple and gobble them up in my car. I don't want her to see me eating.

When Laine finally arrives, I'm relieved. She has short brown hair, glasses, and a lot of energy—and she's heavy. She won't judge me. She can't.

I climb into her spacious SUV. I'm happy that she doesn't wear a seat belt because I can't wear one. Laine's going to show me around Durham, and all I can do is remember what happened to me last fall when a New York City policeman stopped me. I had no idea why I was being pulled over—I had just driven past Gray's Papaya on the Upper West Side, one of the most famous hot dog places in the city, though I hadn't gone in. I would have had to park and walk in and I wanted to conserve my energy for the night—it was a Saturday night, and I was going to a singles dinner event.

"What did I do?" I asked the policeman through my window, really clueless and trying to be flirtatious, which wasn't hard. He was young and cute with dirty blond hair and piercing blue eyes—the kind of guy you want to be a New York City policeman.

"You don't have your seat belt on," he explained, standing at the side of my car.

I knew I wasn't wearing a seat belt. I couldn't wear a seat belt. I had to admit that the reason I wasn't wearing my seat belt was that it didn't fit. I had to show him that I couldn't put it on. He had peered into my car, looking buff and sharp in his uniform.

He looked down at my stomach. I wanted to disappear. I made some more excuses about making sure that I'd get this "situation fixed."

He backed off. "Okay, no problem," he said, with that familiar look of shock and disbelief and half-hidden disgust on his face. That night at the dinner, there were tables set for 10, but mine had only nine people because

I needed two places to fit. The embarrassments of obesity are small, never-ending, soul-burning.

Durham is a city that was built on the tobacco industry. Old, red tobacco warehouses near Duke University are now apartments. The Duke family, which made its fortune in tobacco, built up Duke University, with its red Gothic towers. I'm glad I don't smoke and never have. I'd probably be dead.

Now, Durham calls itself the "city of medicine." Fat, or specifically, obesity, seems to be big business here. The Clinic is only one of several similar places in town.

As we drive, there's nobody around. I'm used to the jam-packed New York City sidewalk—or, more specifically, I'm used to avoiding them. Even Long Beach has sidewalks, which in the summer are crowded with people pushing toward the boardwalk. Durham is a city largely without sidewalks. I could be invisible here.

I'm not paying attention to where we are going until we turn down a main street. And there they are: Wendy's on the right, Burger King on the left, Taco Bell, KFC, Bojangles, the Cookout, the Doghouse, Miami

Subs, Arthur Treacher's, Waffle House, Subway, Dunkin' Donuts. My heart leaps.

"Oh my God! What am I going to do?" I panic.

"These places aren't going away," says Laine, impatient for the light to turn.

"I can't drive by this every day." Almost every one of my old fast-food places greets me, along with a few new ones.

"You're going to have to deal," says Laine, matter-of-factly.

I'm stunned. I want her to turn the car around—or just go through one fast-food place, just one of them, right now. There's BK. I need a fish sandwich.

"What do you mean! I'm addicted to this," I argue with her, pointing at BK, the place I want to go to right now. I consciously drop my finger. I send her mind signals: *Turn. Turn. Turn.*

"Susan, deal with the fact that these places aren't going to go away."

She's being honest. I like it and hate it. She's right. But being right and honest isn't helping me.

The light changes and she shoots down the street. Fast-food and family-style barbecue places compete on both sides of the street. I try not to linger over each one. I salivate. I have to swallow hard. The lump appears at the back of my throat. My blood sugar drops. I'm woozy. Grilled beef and pork saturate the air.

One part of me knows that Laine is right. I have to control myself. The other part me says, *Wow. I can't wait to leave her and eat.*

I'll find out that others at the Clinic call this stretch of road "Sin City." I'll end up calling it "Murderer's Row."

We go for lunch at the Clinic.

The Clinic is set off a quiet street, almost in a bowl of a dirt parking lot. It's a low-slung white clapboard building. Roses are planted out front. When I hobble through the door, my first thought is of Girl Scout camp, and I should know. I went to Rock Hill Girl Scout Camp in Mahopac, New York, for three summers.

The Clinic opens up to an alcove stuffed with flyers for room shares, exercise programs or gyms, and a list of emergency numbers. There are two main rooms. To the right is the Inspiration Room, where seminars are held. In front of me is the dining room. Half a dozen bare brown folding tables stretch side by side. At one end is a group of wide leather couches around a stone fireplace.

I'm shocked that it's a house—rustic, wood-beamed, and wood-floored. An upright piano in one corner and a computer in the other add to the homey air. I had expected it to be more institutional (every bad vision of my mother's state hospital flooded back to me).

On one full wall are the food choices, marked with colored pen. The different colors outline Phase 1 and Phase 2 foods, Laine explains.

Red for starches, and you can only have one, and black for everything else, which includes vegetables and fruits, and you can have two of those. I don't see any meat on the wall, and I'm aching for a hamburger.

I can eat one of everything on the wall. Make it two.

Straight back is the kitchen. Teenagers serve food to the dozen or so people in the dining room. It's a very humble place. Nothing "fancy-schmancy," as my father would say. This could be the right place for me. Maybe. But how would I survive on this food?

"Why don't you try Phase One?" said Laine gently.

I'm seeing rice and fruit on the board, but I'm thinking of Burger King, Wendy's, and KFC, all of which I promise myself that afternoon as a reward for getting myself to the Clinic.

I sit at the end of one of the brown tables. I don't want to be near anybody. I don't want anybody to hover over me. I don't want to be in the proximity of anyone fat, as if it could be contagious.

I eat as slowly as I can: white rice, pineapple, and cantaloupe. But it's almost impossible. I could be eating anything. I'm done in a minute.

Laine encourages a woman with a Dorothy Hamill haircut to come talk to me. She's around my age, very short; she carries all her weight in her legs and butt, but she's clearly losing it. "This program will change your life," she chatters at me, and a whole lot more. But I'm dizzy from staring at the white, yellow, and orange on my tray, so I forget what she's saying right after she says it.

I want a diet soda, but there's only water, herbal teas, decaf coffee without milk, and bowls of lemons. I rarely drink water, even though every diet tells you to do so. After a minute, my spoon clinks around an empty bowl. I need more.

A man in his sixties whose stomach almost reaches his knees concurs with Dorothy Hamill. He has a Texas drawl. He explains, in a very straightforward and logical way, that weight loss is a mathematical equation. I suppose my previous efforts to lose weight—low carb, shakes, obsessing over calories—should have taught me all of this. But somehow, sitting in the Clinic in Durham at the end of a beat-up foldout table, it finally makes sense as he lays it out.

Texas speaks slowly, calmly, and methodically, with deep kindness in his eyes and a direct stare. "It's calories in versus calories out. I've figured out what I need to do to lose 3 to 5 pounds a week, Sue, and so can you."

Texas and I are in intense conversation for at least hour. Yet, for most of the time, I stare down at the floor, hoping that no one is watching us talk. I hate to be seen with fat people, and I hate myself for even *thinking* that.

Texas makes so much sense, even if what he's saying isn't new or radical—even if it's vaguely familiar. And though I listen to what he's saying, what I really hear is that this place is safe—that they will help me take care of *me*.

"When are you coming?" he asks, and holds his stomach up. He has so much skin that it's like Play-Doh around his middle.

"In 2 months," I reply, and with that, I decide that I'm going to try to save my life here.

"Exact date."

"I could move here by October 1, if everything falls into place."

"Make it fall into place."

He lets his breath out slowly. His stomach rolls forward. Texas looks me straight in the eyes and drawls out, "You're killing yourself, Sue, slowly and surely. I know. You have to change your life."

I leave the Clinic around 2:30 or 3 p.m. I head straight for Murderer's Row to celebrate my decision.

I can smell the meat even before I turn down Hillsborough Drive. I'm aiming for the Cookout. The thrill of a new discovery makes my heart beat faster. The Cookout pumps out the smells like I'm a blind and deaf, long-lost friend and my only working sense is smell. My body reacts almost independently of my mind: my heart races, my mouth waters, and my throat tightens as I drive up to the take-out window. It's as good as any sex I've ever had.

I ask for pickle, coleslaw, and extra ketchup on my hamburger. My hands sweat over the new and unexpectedly wonderful choices as I order. The crispy, large cheese french fries come loaded with cheese. The onion rings are solid, crunchy, but oily. The hamburger is real meat, juicy, grilled. It's the best hamburger that I've ever eaten. What makes the shakes extraordinary are how many things I can add to one—Heath Bar crunch, toffee, and peanut butter cup—and how thick and full of real cream they are.

Over the next 2 days, I find an apartment. I tell Laine that I'm definitely going to return. With that decision, I give myself permission to go on a wild binge—after all, in a few weeks I'll be eating only at the Clinic.

I visit the Cookout four more times over the weekend, devouring the same meal as my first. My last Cookout meal is on the way out of town—something substantial for the way home, along with my other snacks. I slurp down the last Heath Bar–toffee–peanut butter cup shake before I drive past the Durham city line. I leave the city of medicine and tobacco feeling saved, and I eat for the entire 10-hour trip back home.

The first person I tell about my Durham experience is my sister. I'm extremely nervous. I go over to her house. I haven't been there in weeks, since she had a pool party and all I could do was sit on the edge of the pool dressed in my black stretch pants and my black T-shirt and splash my swollen feet in the water.

Even though it's August, Caroline makes a cup of hot tea. She has to find the right mug and pick her tea; she has a dozen kinds. She has to pour the milk in first. The teapot boils. She almost seems to count before turning off the flame, pouring the water out, and dunking the tea bag. My sister drinks cup after cup of tea all day.

Caroline is 2 years older than me, but her life is much more set. She married at 22 years old and has stayed married to the same sweet guy for more than 20 years. They still hold hands. My father is certainly proud of her.

We sound like sisters. We look like sisters—shoulder-length chestnut brown hair with highlights, brown eyes, clear skin, and curvy figures—except I'm funnier, louder, wilder, taller, and fatter. And my legs shake from the effort of standing.

I've never admitted to her that I binge, that I have a problem with food that goes beyond a few extra cookies. I'm on a diet; that's what she knows. I'm always telling her I've lost 10 or 20 pounds. By going to Durham, I'm admitting that I have a problem that I can't deal with by myself to someone who deals with every problem in a no-nonsense way. I don't trust how she'll react. She'll laugh at me. She'll tell me that I'm being silly or that I'm overreacting again.

She probably thinks that I'm going to ask her for money, which wouldn't be unprecedented. But I'm not. Somehow, in the last 6 months, I've managed to save some money for the first time in my life. Ever since Caroline and Mark's intervention, I'd felt a need for money in the bank. I didn't know why—to escape, maybe.

I tell her.

"What I care about is that you don't end up in the bed next to Mommy someday," Caroline says. She splits me open, exposes me. She clutches her tea with both hands. I never told her about my visit to the doctor or the hypertension medicine. "I don't want to visit you in a nursing home."

She is going to hug me, and I want to cry. But she doesn't, and I can't.

"When are you going?"

"October 1."

"The sooner, the better."

Next, I tell my father.

"You're doing it, toots," he says confidently.

I wish he would say that he's proud of me. Instead, he asks, "When are you going?"

"October 1."

"Good. The sooner, the better."

The sooner, the better. Try to leave now. Try to leave today if you can. You set October 1 as the date. Go.

But going is hard.

I've lived in Long Beach, on the second floor of this house, for 10 years. My boss owns the house. He's planning to sell it when I move. *Good,* I think. *Burn it down.*

But I can't pack. I can't bend. I can't pick up a box. I can't do anything. I order Chinese in, a double order of wings. I'm going to eat as much as I want because I have that October 1 deadline.

I have a hump of fat growing on my back.

I have a double closet of clothes, and more stashed up in the attic. Complete wardrobes from size 10 to 34 are stashed throughout the apartment. Thirty or 40 pairs of jeans are included in the piles. I haven't worn a pair of jeans in 6 years.

I have a favorite brown pair that I put on a pile to keep. It's a size 18; I can't be more hopeful than that.

A row of business suits comes down out of my closets, in sizes ranging from 12 to 26. After size 26, I stopped buying suits. Now, I'm giving them all away.

At one time, I was on the advisory board for Styleworks, a group dedicated to helping women in need with clothes and skills for the business world. I worked with Malaak Compton-Rock, Chris Rock's wife, who founded the organization. I had bought a new suit for one of the board meetings. But when the date came up, the suit didn't fit. I had to wear my black stretch pants and turtleneck, and worse yet, I wore dark brown work boots because I didn't have a pair of shoes that were sturdy enough to support me. I'll never forget the shock on Malaak's beautiful face when she looked down and saw those boots. I soon quit. I couldn't help myself very well—I had no style—and I couldn't really help others. When I find the work boots, half fallen apart, I throw them away.

Ten 50-gallon garbage bags are packed up with clothes, and I'm not through yet. My sister and brother-in-law put the bags in the back of their minivan and drive off, intent on stuffing everything into one of those used clothes donation boxes. Caroline asks me again when I'm leaving.

"October 1," I say wearily.

"That's in 2 weeks."

"I know," I say, the hump of fat on my back feeling large and heavy.

My friends give me going-away parties. The first is in September with Marcy and Lena, among others, at a restaurant in Croton-on-Hudson. It has a beautiful, huge fireplace, very warm colors, and expensive chairs. I haven't seen my friends in months.

I feel like I'm "out." They all know why I'm going to Durham. This dinner is our last together for a while, so I order anything I want to order. I'm going away—almost a jail sentence, I kid.

"When you come back," says Lena, whom I've known since high school, "we want the old Sue back." Lena is a warm person. If Lena were a color, it would be gold or yellow. She's striking, with long, wavy, brown hair and a Julia Roberts smile. Lena's also a nutritionist, though I've never asked for her help. I always felt that I knew how to lose weight. I was always on a diet.

"To the old Sue!" rocks the table.

I cheer, raising my roll in a salute.

I eat all the bread I want, and I don't hide it from anyone at this dinner. I sop the crust in silky olive oil. I ask for another bread basket when the first is finished. Pasta comes dripping in a cream sauce. We all order dessert. Everyone else splits their dessert. But I have my own, a really huge piece of ice cream cake.

Marcy gives me a plaque that says, simply, "Courage."

She also hands me a frame with three pictures of the three of us: The first photo is of Marcy, Lena, and me in high school. I'm wearing my favorite lipstick kisses T-shirt. The second picture is of the three of us in our late twenties, me at around 165 pounds, bodybuilding, and hugging the both of them. The bottom picture shows a whole group of us at Lena's bachelorette party—me at 35, bloated and hiding in the back, only a head, the rest of me hidden. The old Sue is dead.

My Long Beach friends, headed by Laurie, take me out for another going-away party. We go to a steakhouse in Oceanside, the best steakhouse ever. Oceanside is on the south shore of Long Island. The steaks are oversized, and when you slice one, you say, "*That's* a steak."

I order a 26-ounce rib steak—rare. Everything's à la carte, and we order it *all*—mashed potatoes, spinach in garlic sauce, mushrooms in white wine sauce, bread and butter on the table.

These friends never knew me when I was skinny. I've eaten a hundred meals with Laurie. She's never judged me. We've never discussed weight really seriously. Sometimes I'd casually say, "I have to lose weight" or "I'm on a new diet," and once we went low-carb together. But we had great times on that diet: We went to the local pizzeria for the gyro salad with extra cheese and meat and yogurt dressing; we ate Chinese chicken wings. . . .

One night, Laurie came over to my house because I kept talking about how great my chicken wings were. This was the first and only time I ever cooked chicken wings for another person. I bought a family packet of chicken wings for the both of us, added Tabasco sauce and ketchup, and broiled them in the oven for 20 minutes exactly. I served them with blue cheese dressing, and she pronounced them some of the best ever. I knew I had a kindred spirit—even if she was only yo-yoing around 200 pounds. That night, we couldn't finish the wings—or I didn't want to finish them in front of her, even though she was my eating buddy. I ate them after she left: cold, greasy, red with sauce and slathered with blue cheese dressing.

At the going-away dinner, we order dessert, too, of course. A wedge of German chocolate cake. I don't share at this meal either.

The middle-aged waitress with too much blue eye shadow asks, "What's this for? What are we celebrating tonight?"

"It's a going-away for me. I'm going to a diet center."

"Oh yeah?" she says in her heavy Long Island accent that says *You gotta be kidding* without saying it.

"When are you leaving, honey?"

"October 1. The sooner, the better, right?" I grin, biting into the cake.

I don't tell any of the guys I know that I'm leaving. I don't tell Bobby. I don't tell Andrew from White Plains. I don't tell anyone I'm flirting with online. I don't tell anybody except Isaac.

"You're going to be the first person I have sex with when I get my body back," I say to him, after telling him I'm going down to Durham. I haven't had full-on sex with anyone since Bobby, 3 years before. I couldn't bear to think of having sex with anyone, but I give Isaac the sweet-as-pie Susan smile.

"You promise?"

"Yes."

"Good. I'm happy for you."

"And, Isaac," and here I hesitated, "I just want to thank you for being so kind to me when I haven't been so kind to myself."

"You're a really special girl, and you're going to do great. And I'm going to keep you to your promise."

The last person I say good-bye to is my mother. These days she's in a clean, bright, well-maintained nursing home about 2 miles from my house.

I find her parked in her wheelchair in the hallway, in front of the television. She's in a yellow dress with fake pearls around her neck. I come with a large coffee, decaf with milk, no sugar. I place a straw to her lips, and she drinks it happily.

"Mommy, I'm moving to Durham, North Carolina, to get skinny," I say cheerfully.

"Really?" she says, in her innocent way. I'm sure she has no idea what I'm saying.

"I'm going next week."

"Really?" she repeats, the words mumbled in her mouth.

"I don't want to be in the bed next to you, you know, Mama-luke," I say, using my pet name for my mother.

She doesn't react to this except to smile at me.

I hold her good hand. Her skin is scaly and dry and her knuckles are swollen. She has large hands that once briefly held four children. If she could stand, she'd be a tall woman. Once, she had thick, chestnut brown hair, painted in oils, typed 100 words a minute, and loved to dance. Now, she slurps the last of the coffee, and she's happy.

I don't tell her nurses that I'm leaving, even though they're used to seeing me a couple of times a week. I don't want them to think that my mother is alone in the world. I make my sister promise to visit more often, even though I know she'll never visit as often as I have.

"I love you, Mama-luke," I say, reluctant to let go of her hand. I'm afraid to leave her. "You're going to see a different me in a few months, I promise you."

She watches me, and smiles. "I love you too, angel."

ctober 1 comes and goes, and I'm still in Long Beach.

My boss asks me to stay. Four rooms are cluttered with computers, printers, fax machines, filing cabinets, hundreds of catalogues, a thousand pens, paper clips, packing envelopes, a million stacks of marketing and product ideas that never worked. I don't know how I lived like this for 10 years.

I'm angry. I'm rage-full. I want out. But I stay. I'm loyal.

My sister calls and asks me *again* when I'm leaving. I tell her it looks like November 1 now. She sounds exasperated, impatient.

"What's holding you up?"

"Everything, okay? Fuckin' *everything.*"

I'm ready to hang up on her, but Caroline lays a bombshell on me. She's quitting her job. She's walking away from her high-powered, all-consuming job as head of marketing for a cable television company, a job she's grown up with for more than 14 years.

Now, the second shocker from Caroline follows: She offers to drive down to Durham with me. My first thought is, *She can't. I won't be able to eat anything on the way down.*

Yet, I want her to be in Durham with me, but I don't want her to drive with me. I'm looking forward to 10 hours uninterrupted in the car. But I don't say this to Caroline. I just thank her. I think she believes that I may not go unless she makes sure that I actually arrive. Maybe she's right.

Chapter 11

It's the second week of November, and I'm finally ready to exit Long Beach.

Caroline and I are supposed to leave very early on Friday, November 14. The day is clear and brisk and cloudless and the smell of the ocean is sharp and near. I'm already late.

My car is stuffed with my computer, an abstract oil painting signed by my mother, my jewelry box, my makeup case, my pillows and comforter, and whatever else I couldn't pack in time for the moving van. The second floor of the house is swept clean. I leave just enough space for my sister to squeeze into the front seat next to me.

This is totally surreal. I can't be leaving. Susan lives on the second floor of that house. Susan knows all the numbers for delivery by heart. Susan has her loop of fast-food drive-thrus. Susan knows every 24-hour deli, pizza place, and fast-food outlet within 30 miles.

I drive away from the sea. Is this really happening? Am I really doing this? Is there anything I should eat before I leave? I drive past Burger King and think: *I don't have to stop; there are Burger Kings everywhere.* The Italian deli is closed; the pizza place and the Chinese take-out are, too. I go totally out of my way to go to the Oceanside 24 Hour bagel place for a tuna fish sandwich on an everything bagel, three chocolate chip cookies, and a coffee for the 20-minute ride to my sister's.

"I want to drive straight down," I say to Caroline when I get to her house. She's ready and waiting for me.

"What does that mean?"

"Only bathroom stops."

"It's a 10-hour drive."

"We can make it in 8."

"No. I need to stop."

Caroline had wanted to make this a little vacation—stop overnight in Charlottesville, Virginia, because she wants to see Monticello. I didn't even know what Monticello *was*. When she explained that it was Thomas Jefferson's house and that it's on top of a mountain, I said no. I had to get down to Durham.

"We're stopping for lunch, Susan."

"I don't want to stop."

"I'm stopping and having lunch," she says chidingly. "You can sit in the car."

"Okay, we'll stop for lunch," I say, not wanting to go into all the reasons why we can't just stop for lunch. *Will I fit in the seats?*

Now that we're finally on our way, now that we're leaving Long Island, going west on the Southern State, west on the Belt Parkway, over the Verrazano Bridge with the sun at our backs, I wish I could eat. My feet are so swollen that it hurts to press down on the gas. For the first time, my car is claustrophobic. I should be eating something.

We talk about nothing and everything.

Caroline keeps looking at my stomach. My world closes in.

She tells me for the first time that she wants to have another child. She'll be 41 years old in 2 weeks.

If I ask Caroline to stop staring at my stomach, she'll deny it. I drive faster.

I want to turn on her and say, "What are you looking at?" But I don't. I keep my eyes on the road. I just want to get there.

"I think I may come up to New York for New Year's Eve," I venture. "But I have to borrow some money from Daddy to do so."

"I thought you were going to stay in Durham."

"I plan to come and visit once in a while. Don't you want to see me?"

"I want you to focus on *why* you're going to Durham."

We drive in silence—only 9½ hours to go.

"I thought you had money," she snaps.

"I do. But this way I'll have *enough*."

"You said you saved money."

"Enough to pay for the Clinic. For a year."

"I thought you were starting over."

"I'm going for 1 year to lose weight. That's all that I'm doing!"

Caroline stares out the window.

Only 9 hours and 15 minutes to go.

We're out of New York. We're someplace in Jersey, driving down the turnpike. She wants to stop. I ask her if we can keep driving.

Around lunchtime, my sister insists that we stop and get out of the car for lunch. She can't just go through a drive-thru. She won't. She can't make it easy on me.

She suggests that we break in Baltimore and find a place to have seafood. She has something specific in mind: crab cakes.

"Let's have a nice normal lunch."

That's what I want—*to be normal*—so I reluctantly agree.

I pull off the interstate and head down to the water, to the tourist area. *I'm not a tourist; I'm an alien from the planet of the morbidly obese.*

The first thing I notice about Baltimore is not the harbor or the aquarium, but that parking is blocks from the seaport area. We valet park. "With so much stuff in the car," I say, "I don't want it broken into."

I don't want to say to my sister, "I can't walk." I don't want to go into a restaurant I haven't eaten in before—who knows whether I'll fit in the seats.

"What's the big deal?" she says, but she lets me valet park.

I plod after her. She's been to Baltimore before, and she knows where she wants to go. But I stop a few steps beyond the front door of a restaurant, peer in, see the wide seats, and pronounce: "This is nice."

She's looking at me, at my stomach, again. I'm going to cry. I'm so exhausted. I have to eat. I'm ready to storm in without her. But she agrees, and we're ushered into a restaurant with a dark wood nautical interior, pretty white and red checked tablecloths, and a full view of the harbor.

While my sister is in the bathroom, I eat all the bread in the basket and ask the waiter to refill it. He's a great waiter. He scoots down another bread basket before my sister returns. Caroline orders crab cakes, a Baltimore specialty, and I do as well. It sounds good; anything sounds good.

I wish I could calm down and enjoy the meal, enjoy being with my sister. I wish I could feel normal. The bread breaks in my hand, and I push it into my mouth.

The crab cakes arrive, thick and succulent and served with fries. Caroline is watching me—*the fat sister, the failure*—eat.

Eleven and a half hours after we leave Long Island, we arrive in Durham. I'm exhausted. All I want to do is eat. We check into separate hotel rooms. I thought we'd need a break from each other. And if I do have to eat, I don't want to have to okay it with her.

But she surprises me. "Let's go get something for dinner," she suggests. It's a perfectly normal thing to say: It's dinnertime, and people—even my sister—eat dinner.

We discover a Mexican restaurant in the strip mall next door.

"Good thing I'm starting in a week—I can eat what I want tonight."

Caroline gives me that long, disapproving stare and carefully says, "Okay."

The restaurant is safe—the chairs are wide and the tables well-spaced. In fact the place is almost empty. We order nachos grandes and share.

"Do you want more chips?"

"No. I'm going to start cutting back," I say, though of course I want more chips.

We each order fajitas. Caroline has a beer. I have a diet soda. We barely look at each other.

In front of her hotel room, I say good night and assure her, "I'm going right to sleep."

But I don't. I peer out my door to see whether Caroline has gone outside to get a soda or ice or even gone for a walk. *What would I say if she knocked on the door and I wasn't there?* I'd tell her I just wanted to go for a ride, I couldn't sleep, and I wanted to see the apartment. I would have come up with something other than the truth.

The truth is, I want to eat. I can't breathe in the hotel room. The lump in the back of my throat chokes me. I have to go.

I have 1 week left before I go cold turkey. I slip out. The night covers me, and I'm hunkered down in my overstuffed car as fast as I can get there. I'm excited. I'm going on a joyride in a new city.

I go looking, creeping, searching for something to eat. I have to find that strip of fast-food joints from my first trip—Murderer's Row.

After 15 minutes or so—I have an excellent sense of direction—I find the Cookout and all the others, on the street corners, waiting for me. It's not 11:00 yet, and they're all open. I feel triumphant. I feel cool. My sister, surely sleeping back in the hotel, will never know, and that's part of the excitement. *This is my secret.* In my packed car, I dive into the smell of grilling hamburgers and order it up.

In the morning, we look for a place to eat breakfast. Caroline's ready to walk in the Waffle House.

"Wait; let me see first." I peer in. "Only booths. Forget it. I can't eat here. I won't fit in the seat."

For the first time, I realize that this has become a normal thing for me to think, and now I've said it.

I wait for my sister to make a remark, but she just nods her head. I drive on.

We have breakfast at Cracker Barrel. The chair wobbles, but it doesn't have arms, so I'm happy about that. The Cracker Barrel is filled with plus-sized couples. The tables are widely spaced, the menu oversized, and the generous-sized waitresses middle-aged and doting with pots of coffee. All of this is new and strange to a New Yorker.

I order pancakes with extra butter. The waitress brings me maple syrup in little bottles. I ask for three more. Caroline orders toast, eggs over easy, and hash browns.

"Stop watching me eat!"

"What?"

"You've been watching me ever since New York."

"No, I haven't."

"You have."

"I want to enjoy breakfast, too. So let's enjoy breakfast."

I don't care about enjoying breakfast. I just want her to eat and not watch me.

I also want her to leave. Yet I don't want her ever to go. We finish breakfast in silence. We have to meet the truck at my new apartment.

There's a problem with the apartment; Caroline sees it immediately. In order to get from my apartment to the Clinic, I have to drive past a string of fast-food places, another Murderer's Row. There's no other way to get there. I tell her that it won't be a problem.

"I think it's a *big* problem," she says worriedly, slumped in the car.

"These places are everywhere."

"But do you want to have to drive by them every day? What if you feel tempted to have a hamburger?"

"I can handle it! I have to learn to handle it! These places aren't going away!"

"But do you have to put them in your face every day? It's a mistake!"

Townhouse apartments and pickup trucks ring the complex. I was told that a lot of singles live here. I don't know what singles in North Carolina drive. A pool and a clubhouse round the corner. Someone bangs out country music. The apartment is much smaller than in Long Beach, with narrow windows and no morning sun. Chlorine rises in one room and ammonia in another, but I'm excited. The kitchen isn't new, but I'm not planning on cooking. I stomp into the leasing office alone.

Someone is looking out for me, though I don't realize it at the time.

My signed lease has been lost. There's no record of it. I can't move in. I'll have to get my credit report re-faxed to them; it'll take a day or two, but I should be able to straighten it out. My sister has other ideas.

"This isn't New York. I bet we can find another place today," she says in her take-charge way.

I can't move. This enormous truck is blocking the driveway. It's my moving van. The drivers are eating sandwiches; it's 10 a.m. My stomach turns. I need to eat, but I can't since my sister is here. She won't eat before lunchtime.

"There's another complex that was mentioned. It's more expensive."

"How much more?" asks Caroline.

She does the math quickly. With the promised first month of rent free, it actually works out the same.

"Okay, let's go there," she says, "and just look at it."

I tell the truckers. The driver opens the door. I almost swoon. The inside of their cab smells like chocolate chip cookies. His partner, who is younger, smiles a toothless grin at me when I tell them to follow me.

We find the other place. It's a mile from the Clinic. There are no fast-food places on the way from the Clinic to this apartment complex. This apartment is on a hill with wide spaces of grass and wildflowers. A farm with a cow spreads out at one end. A lot of comfortable four-door cars, the kind retirees like to drive, are parked here. It's so quiet.

"I can only rent a first floor," I puff.

"Why?" says Caroline, annoyed, critical, short-tempered with me.

"I can't walk up and down steps every day anymore."

We learn that there's only a two-bedroom apartment for rent at this place.

The leasing agent says, "The apartment is right down here," and points to a building that's almost right in front of us.

I look at my sister and say, "Let's drive." The thought of walking is too much for me.

The apartment is on the first floor. It's bright and airy and clean and has a small patio that overlooks a hill dotted with trees. At any other time in my life, I would have loved the kitchen, a nice-size galley space with practically new, shiny clean appliances. I don't plan on cooking, or even storing, food in the kitchen. I agree to take it—there are no steps to my front door—if they agree that I can move in today.

I don't think this is usually done in Durham—the leasing agent looks so amused—but I'm in.

The truck unloads. My sister helps me unpack the car, and that's all we unpack. I have to stop repeatedly just to sit and catch my breath. We don't unpack anything else.

It's dinnertime—my last dinner with my sister. We drive down to the main strip, looking for a fun place. After about 5 minutes, my need to eat rising in my throat, I point to a picture of a cow and say, "That looks good."

Inside, we find big, round, dark wood tables; well-trod carpets; and a crowd gathering for the early-bird specials.

"Do you really want to eat here?" asks Caroline, eyeing the heaping plates of ribs passing by.

I have to eat. "Sure. It looks like a lot of fun."

I order the beef ribs, a huge slab, a full order as opposed to a half-order. A cold, boiled or broiled or barbecued (it's hard to tell which) mass of bones arrives with a side order of soggy french fries. Thank God this isn't my very last meal, or I'd be pissed. This isn't Oceanside. "Fuck," I say, dangling one thick, cold rib, and laughing.

Caroline squints and rubs her forehead and looks like my fed-up tenth-grade geometry teacher. "Do we need to have that language?"

"You never curse?"

"Rarely. Haven't you noticed?"

"Just on this trip," I say, looking for our waitress, who appears in a short skirt and ruffled top. I ask for the ribs to be taken back and heated up.

"Aren't there other ways to express yourself?" she says, playing with her piece of bread.

"This is how I express myself," and I stuff a roll into my mouth. "People seem to understand me."

She doesn't laugh with me. I've spent enough time with my sister.

At least she doesn't say anything when I order dessert: a chocolate seven-layer cake, heavenly. It's the only good thing about the whole meal.

The next day, I can't wait to drop Caroline off at the Raleigh-Durham International Airport that afternoon. I want to eat. I want her to go. At the departure curb, Caroline half hugs me. Her arms linger awkwardly around my neck. I think of my nephew, the 3½-year-old who once said, "You're too big to hug all the way around, Aunt Susan." I want to be hugged. I want her to be proud of me.

"Everything's going to be okay," says Caroline, taking a step back, taking on her role as big sister, as caretaker. "You're going to be okay? Tell me you're going to be okay."

Am I going to be okay? Suddenly I don't know. *I'm not okay.* I don't want her to leave.

"I'll come visit; don't worry," Caroline says, as if I'm going away to do time instead of to lose weight. But I know she means well, and I hang on to her. Now I really don't want her to leave.

But finally, she does. And I'm terrified—more terrified than I've ever been in my life. Everyone is a stranger; accents as foreign as French swirl around me. I'm alone. No, even more than alone, I'm abandoned, left behind, left to find my own way, motherless, friendless, angry, sad, frightened, full of rage and fear.

Shit. Fuck. Shit. Fuck. Fuck. I can't do this all alone. Triple fuck. I want to go home. I want to get in my car and go back to New York.

In my car, I'm crying hysterically.

I call my father. "I just dropped Caroline off—" I can't even finish talking.

"Everything is going to be okay now." He emphasizes "now."

"How can I do this?"

All the shame is out. Everyone knows I'm down in Durham to deal with my problem.

"You can do this," he says.

I have to drive away. I'm parked in a 15-minute drop-off zone and a security guard waves me off. I'm in my car, sobbing, alone. I have no choice. This has to work. I have one chance. I hate myself. I'm so exhausted. I'm so tired of feeling tired all the time. All I want to do is—

I hate myself.

At that moment, it hits me. At that one moment, I know it's not just about losing weight. It's about getting my true self back. It's about finding a way to love myself.

I drive away from the airport, crying.

I have to make it work. This is my one last chance. This is it, or I'll end up 500 pounds, or worse, I'll end up with a stroke.

But it's all on me, and I'm scared to death.

Yet if it's all on me, I know I can make it work. I know I can. I reassure myself that I've found a place that's safe, that's medically supervised, that can help me. I know I can and will lose weight because *I can't turn back*.

At my apartment, I sit on the bed, the box spring cracked, not from the move but from my weight. *I want my life. I will have my life. I know I can do it.*

But I don't have to start today.

Other people have last meals; I have a last week.

I give myself a week to get settled into Durham, to set up the apartment and my new home office. I start at the Clinic on Monday. I don't bother unpacking any boxes.

I'm finally by myself. I'm relieved that Caroline is gone. I can go out and troll for food. I have a full week to eat what I want—all in a very methodical way, of course. I hit every drive-thru on Murderer's Row. I eat from the Cookout three times a day: hamburgers, french fries with cheese, large onion rings, and shakes loaded with extras. I hit the Burger King, Taco Bell, Wendy's, Miami Subs, McDonald's, and KFC drive-thrus every day. The day starts with breakfast at Dunkin' Donuts, and ends there, at the same store, with Baskin-Robbins. This is the cycle of life for my first week in Durham. Sometimes, I wonder what would it be like to turn my day upside down: Start with ice cream and end with doughnuts. But I don't. At night, I order a brownie sundae with mint chocolate chip and chocolate peanut butter and extra chocolate sauce. I order the same thing every night that week. Outside, the air is cool, and there are tall, towering pines. But I can only smell one thing: the next drive-thru.

I don't want to change my routine during my last week. I want it to be ritualized. I want the comfort—and yes, pleasure—of eating until I'm calm, until I can't think, until I'm floating in my food coma. I could be anywhere in the world.

For my last week:

I don't exercise.

I don't unpack.

I don't put on makeup.

I shower and eat and sleep, and count off the days, and each day I want to eat more. And I do. By Thursday, what am I *not* eating? I get two hamburgers at the Cookout instead of one. I sample Arby's for the first time: a fish sandwich (to compare with BK's and Micky D's; not bad) and jalapeño poppers filled with cheese—large, of course. I discover a drive-thru Chinese fast-food place: spring rolls, fried rice, lo mein noodles. I don't even have to call and wait to have it delivered.

Just before closing, when I think no one will see me, even though I don't know anybody, I make it into Pizza Hut. Covert—*a spy on a mission to have all the fast food in Durham!*—that's my plan. This is the only place I go into. I park right next to the door. I order my favorite, a medium supreme pizza. The pie, enough for a family of four, doesn't even make it out of my car. I finish it before I get home.

Anything I can drive-thru, I do. By the end of the week, my sense of mission falls away. I'm stumbling through an exotic drug bazaar. I only want to stay high.

When they call—my sister, my father, my brothers, Lena, Marcy, Laurie—I let them know that I'm doing great.

Laine calls and asks whether a German television crew can tape my first day at the Clinic. They are doing a piece on obesity in America.

"Sure. Why not?" I've never been on television before, but I don't care. My whole life feels like someone else's life, not my own. "Whatever you want me to do, I'll do." *Just let me eat.* I don't say this last part to Laine. I'm on my way through a drive-thru, some disembodied voice is asking me, "Can I take your order?" someone is handing me food with a smile and a "thank you" and asking me if I want more ketchup, and of course, I do. "Sure, I can be on German television. It'll be a blast."

The Cookout is my very last meal of my last week—at 9 p.m.—on the Sunday before *the* Monday. And I can't wait to get there. My throat is tight. A roar rushes through my head although the streets are eerily quiet, as if everyone else has somewhere else to be but me. The stars seem brighter, the night colder than on a normal night.

A hamburger with pickles and coleslaw, and fries with cheese, and onion rings and a shake slide into my car. Everything rests on my lap. I eat as fast as I can. I want it inside me. I need the calm, the numbness, the dulling.

It's delicious; it's tasteless. It's gone before I know it. I want more.

Just two more hamburgers, I argue with myself. *Two more and that's it.* I negotiate with myself. *One more, that's all. If you eat one more in the car, you know it won't count.* Instead, I drive away.

It's finally Monday morning, November 24, 2003, and I'm due at the Clinic at 8 a.m. to get weighed in and have blood drawn. I'm exhausted. I couldn't sleep. My first thought is, *I can't go. I should take one more day. I'll start on Tuesday.* But somehow, I pull myself out of bed.

I almost drive past the Clinic. Not a half-mile away is what I really need: doughnuts, bagels, and coffee. I feel like an addict. I need that fix.

My car hits the gravel driveway of the Clinic. I'm there at 8 a.m., and I haven't eaten since midnight. I'm 8 hours into this and I'm ready give it up. But I'm here. I could barely fit my feet into my shoes this morning. My ankles are the size of an average person's calf. I can't get out of the car.

*G*et out of the car, Sue. Open the door. Get the foot out. Get the ass out. Go in, Sue. Do it, now. Do it, or die.

I heave myself out of the car.

First, I'm scheduled for a full medical checkup at the office, a separate cottage up on a small hill. I've parked in front of this building. Julie, the physician's assistant, leads me into the examination room. She is soft-spoken and motherly.

I immediately start sobbing in disbelief. *How did I get here?* I can't move. I can't walk. I don't even know my weight yet. I change into a robe. *At least here they have the 5X ones that fit me.*

How am I going to do this? I've been sobbing every day of my life for the past 10 years, and I don't want to cry anymore. I try not to cry. I hate myself for crying. *I'm going to die.*

How did I do this to myself? And I don't mean all the fast food I've eaten this week. I don't mean all the family packs of chicken wings. I don't mean all the pizza and Chinese deliveries. I know what I ate. Even I don't know what I mean, but right now all the pain and humiliation and shame is welling up inside me. And I hobble to the exam table, and we begin.

"You're going to be okay, Susan," Julie says soothingly as she takes my blood pressure. She doesn't have to go looking for an extra-large cuff; she has one right here. But it doesn't fit around my biceps, so she wraps it around my forearm. I wait for that look of disgust, but I don't see it. She draws blood. She listens to my heart. I wait for her to tell me she can't find it under all that fat. But she doesn't say anything.

The doctor enters. He looks like an old country doctor with white hair and round glasses. He has a very quiet and calm voice.

"You're doing the right thing, Susan, staying for a longer time," he says. "For a year, right?"

"Only if this place works for me," I say, challenging him.

He prods my rolls of fat. He's not going to be able to find anything. I'm a shell. He smiles a beautiful smile, wide and large for such a slight man.

"We'll take you off your blood pressure medicine."

"I'm scared to do that," I say.

"There's nothing to be scared of," he says with confidence.

"Are you sure?" I demand.

"You're going to be okay."

I believe him.

I trudge over to the Clinic with Laine, about 50 yards. I have to stop five or six times to rest.

I'm terrified.

But the first thing I do when I enter the Clinic is look to see whether there is anyone bigger than or as big as I am. I search the faces—laughing, smiling, bent over oatmeal or cereal and fruit—hoping to see someone wider than me. There's no one. I'm the fattest.

The German camera crew waits for me in the Inspiration Room, where I weigh in. An incredibly hot, dirty blond, muscled camera guy; a sound technician; and a high-energy, focused, willowy producer introduce themselves. I'm so exhausted. I can barely raise my hand to shake theirs. *What was I thinking about saying yes to a camera crew on my first day? I'm an idiot. I wasn't thinking.*

"Laine, I'm scared," I say.

"What is that, Susan? Can you say it again for the camera?"

I say it again, because it's true, and I decide: *I'll lock away the part of me that's really scared, and I'll perform. I'm a liar and a fake anyway. I can get through this. I can get through 1 day, and then I can decide whether or not I'll go home.*

I take off my shoes; they must be at least 5 pounds each.

I step onto this oversize medical scale. I'm 468 pounds. "I thought I'd be over 500," I say to the nurse and the cameras, half-kidding.

"No, you're 468.1 pounds."

"At least I'm not over 500 pounds," I joke, but no one is laughing.

The cameras follow me to breakfast. I'm so glad the chairs don't have arms, though my butt is half off the chair. The first thing I have to eat is oatmeal with cinnamon and a bowl of cut-up cantaloupe. I make a joke to the camera crew about my back fat, the hump on my back that makes my neck protrude forward. I hope they're not taping that, but they are.

Maple syrup and small raisins arrive in a pill cup. Laine explains that these are "free," which means I don't have to count them against my portions. I quickly realize that there's a system to this food, and I'd better learn it if I'm going to stay.

Ray, the head cook, swaggers out to greet me. "Welcome! We'll take care of you here," he says in a Boston accent. He gives me a bear hug, enveloping me in his white chef's coat. I smell garlic on him. A man hasn't embraced me without wanting something in return for so long. He almost breaks my heart, and breakfast isn't over yet. I don't care if the hug is for the cameras or for me.

I try to eat slowly.

"They had to bring over the cute guys to tape me?" I say to Gunther, the cameraman, pushing my spoon around the bowl, conscious that people are watching me eat.

"Me?" he says, swinging the camera around me. "You think?" He laughs playfully.

I give him one of my best Susan smiles, wide and friendly and teasing. I'm playing at being the fun, outgoing, I-can-do-anything Susan right now.

"You'll want me when I'm thin, you watch."

"Yeah, yeah," he teases.

At 9:30 a.m., I'm finished with breakfast and now have nothing to do until lunch. I go home to sleep off the morning—without the camera crew.

I eat lunch with about 15 other people who are currently at the Clinic. After lunch, the Germans ask me to film one segment over and over.

"I know you're staring at my ass," I crack at Gunther.

"Can you do it again, Susan?" he asks again. "Just get out of the car and walk up to the door."

"Now walk in," says the producer. "Now walk out. Do it again. You're doing great. Do it again."

Gunther grins. He's shooting my ass. My big, fat, wide-body, jiggling ass, and I can't get in and out of my car one more time.

"Enough," I say, planting myself on a seat inside the Clinic. "I can't do it anymore. It's too much."

"I think we have the shot," says the producer carefully.

That night, I think, *I can't go back to the Clinic.* I have to go home or back to New York. *I can't do this.* It takes until Wednesday to think, *I could do this, maybe.* And everyone's talking about Thanksgiving. It's my first Thanksgiving away from my family.

At breakfast, I can smell them cooking it—a big turkey, cranberry sauce, salad, vegetables, muffins, sweet potato pie—all low in sodium, low in fat, high in healthy carbohydrates, and within the program. It's the only time of year when meat is served.

I ask the nutritionist what I can eat. I'm on Phase 1, which means grains and fruit. But I think for sure that she'll make an exception for Thanksgiving.

"You'll have *other* Thanksgivings, Susan."

I'm devastated. Even here, I'm treated differently. Even here, I'm the fat one.

On Thursday, dinner is early. White tablecloths are laid on the foldout tables. Instead of the tables being in lunchroom lines, Ray sets them up in a horseshoe. It's buffet, another unusual setup, because food in preset portions is usually delivered on a cafeteria tray to each person.

I almost don't go to the Clinic this day. I can find my own turkey somewhere in Durham. But I do show up, and I am served rice and fruit.

I drink one glass of water with each meal until the doctor instructs me to drink four. Four huge glasses line up in front of me before each meal. I stare at them. *I can't drink that much water.* Sipping doesn't work. I have to gulp each one down, all four at one time, before I allow myself to start eating.

And I pee it all out, an endless stream of water. I'm in the bathroom 8 to 10 times a day. My "cankles" drain like there's a spigot on them. I pee more, if that's possible. I'm in the bathroom for longer and longer. I'm there for hours.

I read through every women's magazine, gazing at haircuts to flatter my face, remedies to clear up my complexion, tricks to organize my closets or to lose 10 pounds in 10 days. I'm literally being drained. The first month, all I'm capable of is sleeping, eating at the Clinic—and only at the Clinic—and peeing.

Yet I also have to work. I'm already worried about what will I do after a year in the Clinic. I'll need a job. I work the phones between sleeping, eating at the Clinic, and peeing. I have enough to pay the rent and the

Clinic with little to spare. I accumulate debt on my credit cards. But I know this is the right decision for me. Other people spend money on hefty mortgages, on expensive vacations, on humongous SUVs. I'm spending it on saving my life.

I'm afraid, every day—and every day, I return to the Clinic. I'm going to do it for 1 year. *This diet has to work.*

I lose 21 pounds that first week and 42 pounds in the first month.

Chapter 12

One week into the program, and I'm absolutely stripped-down exhausted. The rice, oatmeal, and grits along with kamut, quinoa, and black pearl medley rice stick in my throat like pebbles.

I plop down next to David. This is what I know about David so far: He's been here since the summer and has already lost around 60 or 70 pounds. He's a Canadian in his early fifties with straight, black Beatles hair. He always looks like he could use a shave or a shower. He's not married, and he has never been married, and he has a twin, but that's as far as we get. He's used his entire life savings to come to the Clinic.

I stare down at the rice. It's breakfast or lunch or dinner; it doesn't matter. I'm eating so much rice that they should be hooking me up with Uncle Ben. It's bland. Tasteless. In the first 2 weeks, I'm eating only the minimal amount of natural sodium found in fruits and vegetables. My body is shocked, battered.

Fast food is loaded with salt—*loaded*. I was used to half a bottle of Tabasco sauce and a half a bottle of ketchup on my family-size wings pack, topped with almost an entire bottle of blue cheese dressing—for a snack.

I'm not dieting. I'm withdrawing.

I plead with David, only half-jokingly, "Do you think I could have 1 teaspoon of Tabasco sauce?"

"No."

"How much do you think I have to bribe Ray for Tabasco sauce?" I repeat at breakfast, staring at my separate bowls of oatmeal and cantaloupe.

"Do you think I could sneak in a teaspoon of Tabasco sauce?" I say to him at lunch, moving my bowls of rice and grapes around like three-card monte, except there's no Tabasco sauce for the winner anywhere.

"No."

"Do you think I could slip some sauce into the bathroom and go get it during one of the meals?" I ruminate. I've spent enough time in the bathroom this week to know that I could sneak a bottle of sauce in my pants pocket.

"Are you kidding?"

"No."

"You'll be okay without the Tabasco sauce," David assures me.

"No, I won't."

For the first 2 weeks, all during Phase 1, I joke with David at every meal about how I could sneak in the Tabasco sauce. I never do. But he's right: I'm okay, and I'm surprised that I'm okay.

David and I don't talk about our personal lives or our family. His seriousness about the program draws me to him. We fall into a rhythm: salt and pepper, without the salt.

"I thought I'd be dead the first month, Susan."

"Why?"

"Because I'm in severe congestive heart failure. Only 13 percent of my heart works."

"That really sucks," I say with a smile.

He laughs. "I know."

I've found a friend.

Other people I meet that first week: Tennessee Tim, who's in his early fifties; he's lost 80 to 90 pounds and wants to be Bruce Springsteen. One of the lead singers for a major pop band, a sexy, bighearted girl, is here. Lorraine "My Son Is a Lawyer" immediately relates in a heavy New Jersey accent. Her advice is, "Stick with the positive people." Eddie and his wife from San Juan—they're both on the program and she doesn't speak English—eat alone together. I love Gina, a brassy, ex–New York City school nurse. Everybody complains about the food, though they eat every bite. So much for sticking with the positive people.

But most of all, I depend on the two doctors. I never trusted doctors before, with everything that happened with my mother, but now, I say: *You tell me what to do, and I'll do it.*

You want me to eat lima beans? I'll eat lima beans (and I hate lima beans).

I put my white flag up. *Tell me what to do. I've lost this battle.* And I do what I'm told—most of the time.

The day's routine is like this: Wake up at 8 a.m., get to the Clinic, weigh in and have my blood pressure taken, then eat breakfast until 9:30 a.m.; sit, wait for a class to start, maybe yoga; wait for another class, on nutrition or behavior; then go home. I often nap between breakfast and lunch, arrive for lunch around 12:30 p.m., wait for another class to start, then wait until dinner starts at 5 p.m. I'm doing what the doctor tells me to do. I'm watching the clock. I'm trying to survive.

In the afternoons, somehow I manage to answer all the messages from customers on my cell phone. But I'm going through the motions, watching the clock until it's time to eat again.

After the first 2 weeks in Durham, I fall into a regular eating pattern. I eat between 8 and 9 a.m., always at 11 a.m., between noon and 1 p.m., always at 3 p.m., between 5 and 6 p.m., and always at 8 p.m. Before every meal, I drink water first—four large glasses.

Two weeks in, I've made it to Phase 2. Now, for breakfast, I usually eat two boxes of shredded wheat cereal, half a cup of mandarin oranges with extra juice, half a cup of grapes, a tablespoon or so of maple syrup, cinnamon, and 2 to 3 tablespoons of bran. Here's where I break from the program: I save part of my fruit for my snacks at 11 a.m., 3 p.m., and 8 p.m.

Now that I'm past the rice, for lunch, I eat three-quarters of a cup of pasta. I only like long spaghetti. I ask the cooks to make it for me special. I also have to have it in a big bowl. I make a big thing of it with the kitchen staff. I don't like short pasta or round pasta or baby shells. I don't like small bowls. I also don't like the way their tomato sauce is made at all, so I ask for plain heated puree.

I'm also the condiment queen: garlic powder, red cayenne pepper, red pepper, and black pepper. Since I've stopped using salt, I need my food to taste sharp and real. I don't know how others can eat their pasta bland. One girl admits that she used to pour ketchup on her spaghetti. I shudder.

I used to make my own sauce. I used to love to cook. But I didn't think it was worth my time cooking for one. It was easier to grab something, easier to hit the drive-thru, and eventually, as I got bigger and my world got smaller, easier to order in. *I* wasn't worth my time to cook for every day. I got here by not cooking. The poor excuse for tomato sauce makes me think of my tomato sauce and of how I used to love to cook.

But I eat at the Clinic, three meals a day, every day.

In addition to pasta for lunch and dinner, I have either a tossed salad or a vegetable and a fruit. Every day, I eat pasta, twice a day, except for Saturday. Saturday is fish night.

I continue to save the fruit at breakfast and now at lunch. My snacks at 11 a.m. and 3 p.m. are not condoned. But I hold the fruit aside anyway. I know my body. I need a snack. But as long as I'm losing weight most weeks, I modify the plan.

Any diet works. It's ultimately about calories in versus calories out. But I've learned one other thing. I have to repeat it to myself because it hasn't sunk in. *This isn't about dieting. I'm going to live this way, at least for a year.* I try not to think of that too much because I can't think of forever. I can only think of today.

Eat more slowly. I'm told this. Classes are held on this subject. We practice pausing.

Before, if I'd drop my fork or sandwich or gyro during a meal, it would be like losing a step during a run. I ate everything all at once. I ate without thinking of the food or what it tasted like. I'm one of those people who should have entered a hot dog–eating contest. I shoveled the food down, as if someone would take it away from me, as if I had memories of a concentration camp—except that I'm over 400 pounds, and my memory of camp is my father showing up on visiting day with brownies.

I'm eating long spaghetti in a big bowl. My hand falls or, at first, is forced down by my other hand. I've placed my fork down while there is still food in front of me. I stare down at it like it's a mirage, except the black pepper flares in my nostrils. I don't touch my fork. I practice pausing.

I've come up with my own recipe for tomato sauce. Here it is:

SUSAN'S TOMATO SAUCE RECIPE FOR ONE

1 large shallot, finely chopped
2 teaspoons olive oil
1 large Roma tomato, chopped
Half a 14-ounce can of no-salt, diced tomatoes
Garlic powder to taste (make sure this is garlic powder only; no salt)
Ground black pepper to taste
1 tablespoon sun-dried tomatoes (check label for sodium content)
Sprinkle of finely chopped fresh basil

1 In a medium frying pan over medium-high heat, sauté the shallot with the olive oil until brown.

2 Add the fresh tomato and diced tomatoes.

3 Add garlic powder and pepper to taste.

4 Reduce heat to a very low flame and simmer until boiling.

5 Serve on top of your favorite pasta.

6 Top with sun-dried tomatoes and basil for an added treat.

Enjoy, savor, pause.

This recipe is for a single serving.

Please note that there's no salt in the water boiled for spaghetti. I make myself one serving of spaghetti at a time—about 2 ounces or approximately 1½ cups. Also, there's no cheese on my pasta. Start to finish, including the pasta, this meal takes less than 30 minutes to prepare, and the feeling that you're taking care of yourself lasts all day!

Chapter 13

One day, 3 to 4 weeks later, in December, I'm craving all day. I can't sit still. I'm shivering. That lump forms in the back of my throat, and I can't swallow it down. Cold and hot sweats crawl through me. I stay at the Clinic as long as I can. But I'm home by about 6:30 p.m. My shadow takes up half the wall. I turn the television on and off; nothing but stupid sitcoms. Unpacked boxes crowd the apartment, but I can't bear to open another one. I can't stay there. I pace. I open empty kitchen cabinets. Slam them closed. I grab my pocketbook and then drop it.

If I leave the house with my purse, I'm in trouble. I can't take money with me. If I take money, I'll be searching for a food fix. If I take my pocketbook, I'll be going to Wendy's. I crave Wendy's. I want their hamburger and french fries. I want a fuckin' Frosty!

I'm pacing the apartment, kicking the boxes marked *Office* and *Kitchen*. I chew on my knuckles. I want my fix.

I have to get out. I can't do this. It's too difficult. It's too much weight to lose.

I grab my keys. I leave my bedroom. *Just get past the kitchen.* My pocketbook is on the kitchen countertop. I come out of the bedroom, past the kitchen, my hand extends to the counter, and I grab my purse. I want to be able to do what I want.

I slam the front door behind me.

In my car, I know what I've done. I'm shaking. Terrified. *I promised myself to just get out of the house without my purse. I'm not normal. Something is seriously wrong with me.*

I start the car.

Please God, get me to the Clinic. Let me not pass the Clinic. Let me make a left-hand turn into the Clinic.

I'm driving, zombielike. I know what I want: Wendy's.

I also know that if I give in at this moment, every day from now on will be a harder struggle. This is my last hope. Other than this, I don't even want to consider what will happen to me. Turning left is having sex again, turning left is getting married, it's having children, it's normalcy. I can't do this alone. I have to be where it's safe.

Yet, the wheel tugs. The tires skid. The car swerves like a wild horse. This 1-mile trip is the ride of my life.

I force myself to make the left turn into the Clinic.

The kitchen is closing down; it's 6:50. The kitchen closes at 6:15 p.m.; they clean until 7 p.m. I've learned the routine.

Jacob, one of the cooks—he's 500 or 600 pounds—squats at one of the dining tables barking orders to the teens cleaning up. Fragile and in a daze, I'm pulsating. I'm bruised. I'm wanting. I know what Wendy's would feel like: a high. I want to obliterate myself—and all these tangled-up, jacked-up, choking feelings—more than anything else at that moment. But I made the left turn. I'm here. *Help me,* I want to scream, but I'm weak. I'm tired. *I can't do this. I don't want to think.* I'm missing my old friends, Wendy's, BK, Micky D's. *Dead, I want to feel dead. Let me go*—

"Can I have a banana?" I ask in a soft and a shaky voice.

"You know, Sue, I can't give you a banana," he says like I'm joking.

"No, I'm really hungry."

"You had dinner, Sue—"

"I know what I had! Give me a banana!" I scream. "I know what I had! Please give me a banana. I need a banana." My face is bright red. The tears stream down my face. My mouth is open wide, gaping open. I'm empty. I have nothing left.

"Why don't you go home?"

"I can't!"

I'm crying, not only because of the banana but also because I'm safe from myself if I stay here.

Jacob yells to a teen, "Paul, get me a banana."

A banana appears in my hand.

"Come on, let's talk. What's going on?"

Jacob walks me into the Inspiration Room and talks to me for 45 minutes. He talks me down. "This is going to be the hardest thing you do in your life, Sue."

I keep saying, "I don't know if I can do it. I can't do it."

"You're going to do it. We're going to take care of you."

He gives me his cell number and tells me to call him when I get home. We're the last people out of the Clinic. It's 8:30 p.m. when I get home—and I go directly home. I call Jacob to tell him that I got home safe. "Safe" doesn't mean that I wasn't in a car accident; "safe" means that I didn't stop at Wendy's.

Chapter 14

Soon it's New Year's Eve: December 31, 2003. And it's time for a party. Gina—my partner-in-crime at the Clinic—and I organize one. A local hotel agrees that we can hold it there, at no charge, if we have it in the pool area. We print up flyers and distribute them to everyone at the Clinic, and we bring them over to the two other weight loss centers in town, too. We're psyched. This is like camp, or college with competing sororities and fraternities, all getting together.

"Are you sure we don't want to get a little something extra?" nudges my flamboyant Queens friend. She means, of course, a little something more to eat.

Our menu consists of sparkling apple cider, coffee, and fruit, along with inedible bubbles and balloons, and I was keeping it at that.

Gina reveals to me that, years ago, there used to be a party called Crisco Disco where all the fatties from all the diet clinics in the Durham area would get together. They were hot, and literally heavy, parties, all about sex and more sex. She hints that maybe our party could be something more, but I'm keeping it to the straight and narrow, though I add hats and streamers.

I haven't been out on New Year's Eve since—I don't know when. I've spent more New Year's Eves on the couch than I can count. In the last few years, though, I didn't even make it to the couch, I just stayed in bed. No one wants to be with a fat chick on New Year's Eve, not even me. But now it's different. There's safety in numbers in Durham.

I haven't even been to a real party in years.

My last effort at meeting new people was an almost out-of-body experience. Out of desperation, I went to a party sponsored by a group of big women, and I don't mean big in the prestigious sense of the word. This was an organization, which will go unnamed, dedicated to oversize women and the men who like them. I was desperate. I was lonely. It was at some bar on the far west side of Manhattan, not the cool Meatpacking District. These women could have *been* meatpackers.

Marcy and Lena encouraged me to go. I'm sure they were tired of me whining about not meeting anyone normal. I'm sure they thought they were helping. Of course, they didn't come with me. They didn't qualify.

The women were all different types, but one thing characterized everyone in that bar: They were big and they were all showing skin, a lot of it. It didn't matter what size; everyone, except me, was stuffed into low-cut dresses or high-cut skirts. Everyone was flashing boobs or thighs or both. Everyone had a sign on them: *I want to get laid.*

I dressed in a pink turtleneck, pearls, and of course, my black stretch pants. My pearls were tight around my neck. When did my pearls, a beautiful white set of real pearls, get too small on me? How do pearls shrink? It didn't matter; this wasn't the kind of crowd that wore pearls.

I felt like fresh meat. Everyone, male and female, eyed me. Disco blared. I fingered my pearls. Hip-hop dance music roared. Not many people were dancing when I arrived. Soon the girls got up by themselves and started dancing and shouting, "It's raining men!" All I could think is, *If I don't lose this weight, this will be my life, trapped in a John Waters movie.*

On the other hand, the guys, a lot of blacks and Hispanics, were all normal sizes, though they whistled and commented and called out the most scantily clad and biggest of the women dancing together—big girls gone wild. "Hey, mami! Hey, sugar! Hey—"

I wanted a quiet corner and my hand held. Within half an hour, I left, totally depressed and angry with myself. *What was I thinking?*

I drove east and north to my pizza place on First Avenue. I ordered an eggplant and ziti slice, sprinkled a layer of garlic powder, hot pepper, and extra Parmesan cheese on top of the 3-inch-high tower of pizza, along with a large diet Coke, and carried it to the car. Before I hit the

Triborough Bridge, I stopped at a deli and bought a bag of Pepperidge Farm chocolate chip cookies for the rest of the trip home.

I felt neither big nor beautiful.

On New Year's Eve in Durham, around 15 people show up at around 8 p.m. The bubble machine ends up not working. The pool is open, though no one goes swimming. Chlorine is sharp in the air.

I'm dressed up in my light blue turtleneck and black stretch pants. There's no skin shown here. The party is not quite the rockin' affair for the overweight that I had hoped it would be.

By midnight, the chlorine from the pool overwhelms us. It's too hot for us oversize folks by the pool. We debate moving into the main bar area—even though there's tension about the bar food, the free pretzels and peanuts, a panic almost.

I intercede: Just think how many germs are in those bowls, how many people go to the bathroom and don't wash their hands and then put them in the bowl? We can do it. We make our way together to the bar area, more like a school group than like New Year's revelers. Fifteen fat people are less noticeable than one. We camouflage each other.

I want those peanuts as soon as I see them.

I gather us all together in the lobby off the bar. We take over the couches and pass our watered-down sparkling apple cider around and cheer in the New Year.

I'm the loudest.

I'm well on my way to losing the first 100 pounds.

By late February, I can walk.

I trek from the medical office to the Clinic without stopping; that's the 50 yards I couldn't do on my first day.

Once I'm able to do that, I hike with David every morning after I have breakfast.

We're both slow. We're turtles. We pace each other. David's very deliberate in his steps.

I tease him, "No dying today; there's no way I'd be able to run back and tell anybody."

He laughs with me. We've walked about 50 yards.

"That's enough for one day, David."

David and I walk from the cottage to the Clinic, then we make a right and pass a church on the right-hand side, where we have to cross the street. We look five or six times because we can't run if there's a car coming. One day, we make it to the red house. The next day, our goal is to reach the blue house. There's a dead end at the end of the block and a slight slope down to it. We're aiming for that dead end. We don't make it, but we're halfway there. I give David a big high five. I'm elated. We look at each other.

"Now we have to make it back," I say. It's close to lunch, and we want to get back. The road rises on the way back. We take it slow. We talk about what we're going eat for our midday meal. I'm obsessed as much as anyone about what food will be served, what vegetables, what fruit. I may be eating pasta twice a day, but it's what goes on it that makes it bearable.

Today is a good day.

For another 4 weeks, we have our daily hike, until one day, we conquer that dead-end street.

very Monday night at around 6 p.m. is the senior doctor's fireside chat in the Clinic's dining room. I make sure I'm up front, in one of the deep leather couches, as close as I can be to the senior doctor, who'll sit on a one of the dining room chairs in front of the huge fieldstone fireplace. I wait for the chat to start.

The senior doctor is in his sixties but looks much younger. He has black, curly hair, like my father. Wrinkled shorts and flip-flops are common attire.

I'm a sponge for information. About 10 other people are there with me, but to me, it's really only the doctor and me.

"So, what's on everybody's mind?" he starts.

And I dive in:

"What's the deal with salt? Why can't we have some salt?"

"Why am I peeing all the time?"

"How can I keep focused?"

"Why can't I have Tabasco sauce?"

Someone else interrupts with: "Is the Clinic closing?"

I turn to the doctor. *It can't close. I need to be here.*

"There's not enough of us here to sustain this place," says this know-it-all.

"What do you mean?" If I could, I'd leap up.

"You don't have to worry about that," the doctor reassures us. "If I have to go in the kitchen and make the food myself, we'll keep the doors open. Okay? Other questions? Ask me anything."

"What about Tabasco sauce? Can I have it occasionally?"

"No," he laughs. "Next?"

Every Monday night, the senior doctor holds these group discussions.

I feel connected to a community. I feel, again—and I can't emphasize enough how important this is to me—I feel safe.

Why I Crave Tabasco Sauce

- I crave Tabasco sauce because I crave salt. And I've learned that salt makes me crave more—more of everything. It's a vicious cycle.

The bottom line here is that salt makes me crave. I've greatly reduced my intake and am thinner and healthier. I aim for between 500 and 1,000 milligrams of sodium a day. If I don't limit my intake of it, I feel it in my ankles first, and I see it on the scale within 24 hours. Yet, I'll admit, my lips still burn and my throat tightens at the thought of Tabasco sauce, that red liquid fire.

alking with David is part of my daily rhythm during those first few weeks. But by the end of January, I was already able to take more steps than he could. Now, I start to go on longer and longer treks, and he can't. Some mornings, though, I still walk with him down and back the dead-end block.

We gossip about the characters at the Clinic. In the dining room, they call him the Mayor of the Clinic because he knows all the ins and outs, because he's smart, well read, and articulate, and because every community needs a leader. But he's getting cocky. He's telling everyone what to eat. If anybody eats anything off the program, he'll go right up to him or her and say so.

"David, you have to chill out. You haven't been home yet," I say, carefully taking another step forward.

"I'm just trying to help people."

"When you keep the weight off for a couple of years, you can help people."

"I'm going to keep this weight off, no problem."

"I hope so, Davey-baby," I laugh and take another determined step. A part of me wishes that I had his cockiness or confidence.

We talk about the cost of things. Neither of us have much money compared with the others at the Clinic. He's a mortician. He works for a funeral home back home. He doesn't give details. He's very secretive about details, and I don't press him. I know what it's like to have hidden parts of yourself, to keep whole sections of your life from family and friends, to feel scared or ashamed, to wish that you were someone else. If David is practicing being someone else, that's okay with me.

One freezing February morning, Gina and I decide that David needs a coat that fits him properly. We go to the local thrift store and buy him a hound's-tooth coat with black fake fur around the collar, an old gentleman's type of coat. After lunch, we bring it to him, and he hugs it to himself. The coat buttons up over his barrel chest. It fits him perfectly.

The next morning, I parade with him in this very dapper coat. He walks with his hands in his pockets, debonair, his step lighter and more confident.

"It's a wonderful coat, Susan."

"You look amazing in it."

"It's so warm," he says, putting his hands in his pocket. He says quietly, "It makes me feel special."

In April, he has to leave. His visa expires. I miss him. But by now, I'm hiking 3 miles a day on trails, and I've passed him.

In October, he returns. His visa is renewed. A friend has given him a plane ticket back to Durham. Another friend is giving him a place to stay.

"You got fat," is the first thing I say, in a funny, loud booming voice.

"You're still here," he counters. My 1-year anniversary is coming up in November. I'm supposed to leave in November, but my family and friends all want me to stay. They want me to come back the old Susan, which makes me shiver, even though I'm cold all the time anyway. I know what they mean by *the old Susan*.

But nobody has to argue with me because I've already decided: I'm staying. Even though I can't afford it, I can't afford not to stay.

David laughs ruefully. He has changed his glasses to more fashionable wire-rims. But he has also gained back about half of his weight, about 40 pounds. All the fluid and fat are in his chest. He looks worn and gray and top-heavy with spindly legs. A good wind could topple him over.

"Back to eating oatmeal and bran, Davey-baby," I say, kidding him, though I'm concerned and glad that he's back where it's safe. "You're okay, right?"

"Don't worry about me. I'm not going to die today," he says—his old response to my old jibe at him.

We agree to walk together the next day.

But right now, I have to run. I'm working out with Wes, my trainer. I'm training with him three times a week. I'm focused. My leg muscles are stretched, the arches in my feet bend, my toes flex; the memory of being athletic returns. I know that my body is coming back, a renewal after a very long winter.

The next day, and a few times after that, David and I pace the dead-end street. The thrift store jacket buttons tightly around him. He confesses to me that he's on his own plan of eating and fasting. I call it bingeing. He doesn't. David's version of bingeing is devouring an entire jar of peanut butter, or a whole bag of walnuts, or a dozen apples. And then he fasts for a day or so. He's reading books about longevity and drastically-low calorie diets. The books are snuck into the Clinic hidden in paper bags. I urge him to talk with the doctors. But David knows better. He keeps his books close, his bingeing—his secrets—closer. He kids me, "I'm not going to die today." I don't know what to do except to get off that dead-end street and keep walking. I'm afraid for my friend.

One beautiful Sunday morning, I'm in a hurry, running into the Clinic. I had promised David that I would walk with him later that day.

I'm racing out of breakfast and Bea, the social worker, who looks like Betty from *The Flintstones*, except with padding, frantically rushes up to me. "Susan, we've been looking all over for you."

"Hey! What's up?" I say, in a great mood.

"David collapsed this morning on the trail."

"He's okay?" I say, confused and concerned and in a rush.

"He's not." Bea clutches my arm.

My heart drops. "This is unbelievable. I'm planning to go walking with him today."

"He's at the hospital."

"He's not supposed to die today," I say, lurching past Bea.

I hate hospitals. I hate the smell of them. Every hospital smells like Hudson River State Psychiatric, of pee and ammonia and stale cigarettes.

"Where's David B.?" I press a nurse in the emergency room.

"Please wait; I'm going to have someone come talk with you."

"Okay," I say, and wait. I start making a checklist in my head: David's had a heart attack. I'll call Laine. I'll call the doctors.

"Are you the family of David B.?" says a woman to me who's not in a nurse's uniform. She's a social worker.

"He doesn't have any family here. He's from Canada. I'm part of this Clinic, and he is too. We're the closest that he has to family here in Durham."

"Come with me," she says.

"Can't we talk here?"

"We have a room."

"I don't want to go into a room."

She leads me into a little room off the emergency area. It's windowless and airless, light blue, with dusty tan vinyl chairs. It reminds me of the state hospital's visiting room, right down to the crushed cigarettes on the floor. The vinyl chairs are sticky, as if someone had died right there—just slid back in the uncomfortable seat and perished. I crouch at the edge of the seat. The social worker shuts the door behind her.

I say to myself, *This is not good. This is really not good.*

"David didn't make it," says the social worker.

"What happened?"

"We don't have all the details yet."

This is not good, I repeat. *There but for the grace of God*—and stop myself. *I'm okay. I'm okay. I'm not going to have a stroke. I won't let it happen. I know he wasn't listening to the doctors, and I am. He should have listened. I should listen more.*

I'm shaking. "He shouldn't have died today."

The social worker looks at me in that professionally sympathetic way. "I'm sorry."

We all chip in for a bench to remember David by. It's there in front of the Clinic for anyone to rest on after a walk.

Chapter 15

I'm losing weight and aching for a real relationship and compulsively online. My life has to be set up by the time I leave Durham, and that means marriage with someone who wants a kid or two. This is a driving force for me. I'm determined to have a normal life ready to go once I leave Durham.

I meet Bruce online. I think Bruce is the one.

I whisper how hot he is, how sexy, how much I want him, blah, blah, blah. It's phone sex. I'm not as into it as I used to be. There's no Chinese delivery at the end like in Long Beach. But it's something.

He's Jewish. He assumes I'm Jewish. But technically, I'm not. I'm a fraud.

I had once joined a Conservative conversion class, but it was entirely made up of couples getting married, one Jewish and one not, and me. An adult study group in Brooklyn welcomed me. For more than 6 years, I've been studying in one way or another to convert. For me, being Jewish is more than just about dating nice Jewish guys, though that's a plus; it's about filling that hole in my soul.

Bruce wants to meet me, but I'm not ready to meet. Not yet. I make sure our phone conversations are hot and sultry and leave him wanting more. Before I meet him, I decide that it's time I take the plunge. I decide to do something I've never done with a guy, and that is to be honest.

I reveal to Bruce that I'm not Jewish. I expect it to be a big problem because everything in my life has always been a big thing, and I've learned to anticipate everything becoming a big thing. But it's not. In August, Bruce sets me up with an Orthodox rabbi who is willing to officially convert me.

I meet with the rabbi at a kosher pizza place on the Lower East Side of Manhattan, which means no pepperoni on my pizza. My last name, Blech, is fairly well-known in the Orthodox community, and this helps, along with my study history, even though my grandfather was a Zionist socialist nonbeliever chicken farmer from New Jersey.

To officially convert, I have to enter the *mikvah,* a traditional Jewish bath, and be dunked three times. There's a female attendant who speaks no English. She mimes to me to take off even my earrings and contact lenses. Thank God, there are no mirrors. From behind the wall, I hear the rabbis begin the Hebrew prayers. I go under the water one, two, three times. I have to do it one more time because one of the dunks wasn't complete. Fat floats!

Seriously, I feel like I've done something big. I choose Shoshana as my Hebrew name, after my father's mother. I think my father will be really proud of me. Instead, with one long exasperated sigh, he dismisses it, and I feel small.

I'm finally ready to meet Bruce as an honest woman, but he can't meet now. We plan a meeting in late September, and I fly back up to New York. I stay with a friend at her house right on the water in Queens. I'm still over 300 pounds, but I've told Bruce that. I'm honest. It feels good to be honest for once. I'm losing weight. I take time with my hair, making it perfectly curly. I wear a light, tan wool sweater and a long skirt, past my still-thick ankles—long, black silk. I'm so excited. I'm going on a real date!

He's more than 2 hours late. It's after 11 o'clock on a Monday night.

When he finally arrives, I'm so glad. I'm grateful. I thought that he might not show. I buzz the door open. I have to slow myself down the steep flight of stairs to the front door or I'll barrel right into him.

He blows open the door. I step back to take him in.

A dirty white shirt skews half in and half out of his trousers. His collar is open, and both his neck and the collar are streaked with grime. He's short and stocky and swaggering up to me like a man who has done a lot more in life than I know he has. He smirks. I want to step back but I can't. I'm at the bottom of the stairs. I want him to move aside. "Bruce," I say in an upbeat voice.

"Susan," he says, coming closer.

He pushes me onto the carpeted stairs. I don't have a second to react. He pulls my long black skirt down, yanking at my pantyhose, whispering as he had during countless phone calls, "You're so beautiful, you're so beautiful."

"Get off of me, Bruce," I insist, shoving him off.

He sticks his tongue down my throat, telling me that I'm so sexy, I'm so hot, that he wants me *now,* repeating our phone conversations back to me. He sticks his hand down my panties. He puts his face between my legs. I'm pushing his shoulders back. My legs are twisted, caught in my pantyhose and skirt. It's a nightmare because one part of me is thinking: *He likes me, he likes me.*

The other part of me yells, "What the hell are you doing?"

"I thought you were into this stuff!" he says. He has a nervous, buck-tooth chuckle that stammers through his lips.

I'm confused. I don't want him to think that I'm not interested in sex. But I'm not ready for it. And we haven't even had our date yet.

He relinquishes my arm. We decide to go out. I thought we'd see a movie at least. He heads for the boardwalk. "We'll go for a walk," he says, taking my hand, stroking it, holding my fingers tenderly to his face. I wish he had never touched me. But I'm hooked. It's been years since someone has held my hand.

Back in Durham, Bruce calls. I'm lonely; we talk, blah, blah, blah. I push to see him again. After a few weeks of calling and pushing, he says he'll be in Washington, D.C., on business.

"That's only 4 hours from my apartment in Durham, the way I drive! I can meet you there."

On that day, I drive straight through from Durham to D.C. It's pouring rain, a cold, slanted, dismal, autumn rain. I touch base with Bruce the whole way, getting more and more excited as I approach the nation's capital. I had even planned ahead. This is the first time I've set up with the Clinic what I will eat while I'm away. My lunch and dinner from the Clinic kitchen are packed with ice in a large, insulated lunch bag. As I drive, I'm eating pasta (without garlic because I want my breath to be fresh) from a plastic container.

I've brought a change of clothes so that I can change when I arrive in D.C. I find a place to change: a big chain hotel. I park the car in the circular driveway, thinking that I'll just run in and out, but the security guard tells me I have to move my car. The only problem is, my car won't start. The engine doesn't even turn over. The battery is dead. And it's raining.

At least 2 hours for a tow truck! "No! that's not acceptable. I'm meeting someone! I need you here now." I'm more concerned about Bruce than about me. I don't want him to wait for me. It's 1 p.m. I'm supposed to meet him at 4 p.m, after he's done with his business, whatever that is.

"We'll try to get there as soon as possible." Almost exactly 2 hours later, the tow truck arrives. I have to buy a new battery. I haven't told Bruce about all this drama. He expects me at 4 p.m.

I'm back in my car, parked on the side of Embassy Row, flags dripping in rainwater, ready to meet and excited to meet him, on the phone with him, asking him, "Where exactly should I meet you?"

"I'm in front of the Smithsonian," he says from his car.

"Don't move and I'll be right there," thinking there's only one Smithsonian museum in D.C.

"Don't come here; the cops are asking me to move."

"So where do you want me to meet you?"

He lists the streets that he's driving down.

"Just park and I'll find you," I say, drenched and tired and hungry.

"No, you can't. This looks like a really bad area. Don't come here; I'll ask for directions." I hear him ask for directions. But I don't hear a response.

He gets back on the phone with me and says, "Okay, I'll be right there."

So I wait. I figure there's traffic. It's raining. He doesn't know D.C. After a half hour, I call again.

"When will you be here?" I ask.

"Soon. I think I'm around the corner."

I wait. Another 15 minutes. I call. "Where are you?"

"You're not going to believe me—the guy gave me directions and I'm headed toward Baltimore. I can't believe this. This is crazy."

"Okay, so turn around," I say, seething.

"Okay, let me ask directions again."

"Fine." I hang up. I furiously eat through the pasta in my dinner container, hoping it will numb me but knowing that it's not enough food for that.

He calls me back a half hour later.

"You're not to believe this. I'm in Baltimore now. These people are giving me the wrong directions."

"That's impossible, Bruce."

He chuckles. "I know."

Something snapped. I lost it. "Just admit that you were never here."

"I was there," he says, with another chuckle.

"I don't believe you. You were never here. Just say you were never here. Just say you wasted my time!"

The chuckle burns into me. A grating, churning chuckle that swings at me and says, "I've put one over on you."

"Of course I was there."

"You were not here. You're a fuckin' liar. Admit it. Just admit it."

"I was there."

"I deserve the fuckin' truth, Bruce! Repeat after me. 'I was a liar. I was never there. I wasted your time.'"

He repeats it all—and chuckles, rat-tat-a-tat through his big lips.

"Don't ever call me. Don't ever get in contact with me. You're dead to me, Bruce."

He chuckles.

The rain streaks down. The flags on the street are all gone.

"I'm going to eat!" I scream at Lena long-distance. "I'm going and buying a box of Oreos. Two! No! I'm not going to do it. I'm buying four!" I start shouting a list: "Potato chips, and not the no-salt kind! Pepperidge Farm cookies! Ice cream sandwiches! I'm going to start eating and not stop!" I start to cry hysterically. She's such a good listener, though she's only hearing me cry.

"It's not worth it," Lena says, trying to calm me.

"I don't care. How could he do this to me? He was never going to show up, the fuckin' bastard."

"Probably not," admits Lena.

"I'm going to eat. I know I'm going to eat. I have to eat!"

"Sue, calm down. You're scaring me."

"I'm going to call you back." I know she loves me. And I trust her. But I don't trust myself. I can't get home without Oreos. I want to go into the store. I want the Oreos that I know are waiting for me under those fluorescent lights.

"Don't," she says. "Don't get off the phone with me."

And I don't. I want to. I want to fill that hole in me with food. But after a while, after listening to Lena, after hearing her voice in my head repeat, *It's not worth it,* I drive south through the edge of the city. It's the middle of rush hour somewhere in the middle of D.C. Traffic is bumper-to-bumper. I need gas. I can barely see out of the windshield. The rain is worse, sleeting down, slashing against my car. I see something out of the corner of my eye. I'm starving. I park my car. I'm going in—

It's a Bally's. I have a national membership there. I'm going to work out. The treadmills are lined up and empty, and I get on the first one, jack up my legs, swing my arms, jam the speed button higher, pace as fast as I can, numbed, stoic, blocking out the idea of Oreos or chicken wings or Bruce.

Forty-five minutes later, I stop at the first gas station with a food mart that I can find, park right in front, staring at the shelves crowded with food. *He's not worth it!* But I go inside anyway. *He's not worth it,* I mutter and prowl the shelves. The lights are too bright. I need gas. *Just buy gas.* I see what I'm looking for. One small bag of no-salt potato chips, one bag, and 32 ounces of water is all that I buy. *He's not worth it!* I leave the Oreos, along with the candy bars and chips and armfuls of food I could grab. I pump gas in the driving black rain. The air reeks of ozone and exhaust and fuel, a combustible smell. I get back in my car, eat the last of the pasta from the Clinic, eat my bag of no-salt potato chips as slowly as I can, and start the car. I don't stop again until I'm back in Durham.

What I Tell Myself Now When I Want to Binge

- It's not worth it. It doesn't solve anything.

- I'm not going to lie to myself: Those Oreos do taste good. But I'm not going to eat them when I'm in an emotional crisis.

- If I have a fast-food fish sandwich, I won't eat it in my car. In fact, no eating in the car at all.

- I'm never "bad." The food choices I make will always be conscious decisions. I no longer ever have food amnesia.

- I'm not starting a diet tomorrow or on Monday. I'm never dieting again. This is a lifelong journey of healthy eating for me.

And sometimes, all the above doesn't work, and I relapse and binge, but it happens less and less as time goes on.

Chapter 16

By the spring of 2004, I'm down 100 pounds. I celebrate in a leopard-skin bathing suit, size 26/28. People stare at me as I ease into a steamy, lavender-sweet whirlpool at a rustic spa in Asheville, North Carolina. I feel brave and powerful. I stay one night at the spa, by myself. A brief, triumphant moment.

By the fall, I'm down 150 pounds. My weight hovers around 300; I work out intensely and eat at the Clinic for three meals a day. By November, I've committed myself to one more year at the Clinic. I feel strong and determined. And I'm done with Bruce. In early 2005, I meet Aaron online.

Aaron is in his early forties and divorced, with four children. He confesses that an affair with a blonde, thirtysomething woman from Australia broke up his marriage. His business takes him all over the world, and he met her there. She's still there. This is clearly the type my father would call a *shiksa,* and he's an observant Jew from New Jersey, so a *shiksa,* a non-Jewish woman, is a big thing; it's like meat on Fridays for traditional Catholics.

We're on the phone together for hours, and it doesn't involve phone sex but instead big ideas, plans, the future. He's smart and focused.

His four children are all under age 15. But his being from an observant Jewish background appeals to my sense of wanting to find my Jewish soul. The *shiksa* is still in Australia. I figure that I'm a lot closer in Durham.

And I'm in a hurry now.

"Are you still in love with her, Aaron?" I say, referring to his breakup girl.

"I can never be with her."

"That doesn't answer the question."

"Come see me. Meet my children, please."

I go.

I haven't had a lot of experience with second dates in recent years, even though this is more than a date. This is a long weekend with his children, on vacation with him in Virginia.

I want to present my relationship like a gift to everyone: *See, you don't have to worry about me. I don't have to worry. I'm getting married. I'm having normal, fantastic sex (even though we haven't had any yet). I even have a built-in family.*

I drive the 6 hours from Durham in my Altima with over 180,000 miles on it.

Aaron has rented a furnished apartment suite for 4 days. He has one very overweight 8-year-old daughter. He turns on the television and leaves me to the kids, but that's okay. I love kids, even ones who don't want to talk with me. He feeds them TV dinners as snacks. The 8-year-old eats parts of three separate meals. Her brothers make fun of her. Aaron doesn't say anything.

I braid her hair and whisper, "Don't listen to them. You're beautiful." But it's me whom she's not listening to. She won't talk to me.

Yet I like playing wifey and mommy, and I plait her knotty, thick brown hair into pigtails. I want her to be happy. She asks for something more to eat. She reminds me a little of me, a girl without a mother, with a father who always seems to be preoccupied. I offer her an apple from my bag.

"Aaron, what are we going to do this evening?" We had spent a nice day together at Colonial Williamsburg.

"I have to go check e-mails at the clubhouse. I'll be right back," he says, and leaves with a nod of his head to his children and me.

I straighten up the apartment. I run out and buy food for us for dinner. Two and a half hours later, he returns. Dinner is ready. His kids are cleaned up. The table is set. I'm a furious spin of energy. A huge salad, pasta with vegetables, and fruit for dessert waits for him. He scans the room as if he expected nothing less.

Around the table, like a family, we talk about the idea about going back to Colonial times—before e-mail and cell phones and television—*and fast food?* He kids.

I realize at that moment how long it's been since I've even thought of fast food—at least weeks. I take a deep breath and feel a small moment of triumph. I smile to myself and clear the table.

After I give his daughter an extra-special hug and she and the others go to sleep, after I clean up, I wait for him to make a move toward me. "I'm tired," he says, and I follow him to the master bedroom. We lie in bed next to each other. He slides to the edge. His legs are too long for the bed. I want to cuddle, to be held. But he doesn't touch me. I stroke his side. He holds himself as if praying for sleep.

"I'm so exhausted, Susan."

"Oh."

'Do you want to talk?"

"No," he says cautiously.

"Did you have a problem with anything today?" I thought we had a nice day, visiting the restoration, having dinner together.

"No."

"Do you have an issue with my weight? You always said you didn't. Has something changed?"

"I'm just tired."

"I'm not," I say lightly.

He turns his back on me.

We sleep for a while, until 6 a.m. I stroke his back. I kiss his neck.

"Aaron, please tell me if there's something I can do—"

"It's not you. It's me."

I assume it's the weight, The Body. But I'm not going to say it. Instead, I say, "Why aren't you touching me?"

He moves away.

"It's the weight," he says sheepishly half-muffled by his pillow. "Your weight—"

"Don't say another word," I say, and get out of bed.

He stares at the ceiling.

"I'm just not *physically* attracted to you," he says distinctly, as if that makes a difference, as if what I want is a spiritual attraction.

"I'm here, Aaron. I've lost 150 pounds. I may have more to lose, but I'm on my way."

"You don't understand. The other one, the one I left my wife for, she was a model, she was gorgeous, she had a body—" He shudders as if he doesn't have words to describe her.

"I *will* lose this weight!"

He stares at me disbelievingly.

"I will! And when I do, you will contact me somehow. But I will *never* go back out with you."

"Don't say that, Susan."

"I'm saying it."

"Don't go."

I stuff my clothes into my overnight bag. "You're in love with this girl."

He doesn't deny this. "I don't want you to leave—isn't it enough that I'm asking you to stay—"

I cut him off. "I will never be in another relationship where someone is more focused on my weight than on me. Period." I take a deep breath and compose myself. "Aaron, you'll be sorry, because I believed in you."

In the hallway, the 8-year-old in her pajamas runs up to me. "Don't leave, Susan," she says, her pigtails loose from sleep. I wish I had time to fix them. I'm supposed to stay another 2 days, and the kids know it. I'm their vacation with their father.

"You guys are such amazing kids. But I forgot. I have to go to work, okay, honey?"

I tug her pigtails. She doesn't want to hear this. Neither do I. I want to tell her to lay off the TV dinners, to brush her hair, to stand up to her father and brothers, to be happy without eating. But I can't. I have to get out of there.

Aaron follows me down the stairs and to my car. "I know it's me. It's not you."

"I know it's not me, Aaron. You have to change you, not me."

He's crying.

"Those are crocodile tears, Aaron," I yell out on the deserted early morning street.

"If things were different—"

"I don't believe you. What more do I have to do to prove to you that I will lose the weight, you piece of shit?"

I grow quiet. "I want to be with you. I don't to be with anyone else."

He just cries and shrugs, the tears tangled in his beard. The shit doesn't say anything else.

"Look, I have to go," I finally say.

He shrugs.

I drive away, only to realize, a few minutes later, that I have left my cell phone cord in his apartment. I call him. He doesn't answer his cell. I have to park and go back upstairs. I knock and ask for the phone cord. "Why didn't you answer your phone? What were all the tears for?"

He shrugs.

I know it's over.

I go back to Wes. I have appointments with Wes on Monday, Wednesday, and Friday at 9:30 a.m. for 1 hour. He's been my trainer, my savior, my tormentor since the winter. He's a former basketball player, the kind who gets the ball in when the ball has to go in—a quiet, powerful kind of man. He's also a devoted, churchgoing family man, serious and sure and skilled at what he does.

Wes has worked with a lot of obese people. I ask him if I'm the fattest.

"Close to it."

At first, I'm sure he doesn't think I'll show up or do what he says or lose the weight; like I said, he's worked with a lot of obese people. I show up. I do what he says.

In the beginning, I wear my black stretch pants and an oversize T-shirt. As I lose weight, my T-shirts get smaller and tighter. He stays the same: consistent, patient, driving.

"Go warm up," he says, glancing at me as I arrive at the gym.

Five minutes on the treadmill.

"Cardio and core work."

Twelve minutes on the stairclimber. Twelve minutes on the treadmill.

"Let's move it outside."

Four times up and down on one set of the stairs at Wade Stadium, an open-air stadium, home of the Duke University Blue Devils. I hate the stairs. It's like climbing up a mountain three times a week. At the beginning, he'd tease me about doing the entire stadium, but I never believed him. Now, he brings it up seriously. "You're almost ready for the stadium, Susan."

"No, I'm not, Wes," I kid, and focus on one row of steps. My thighs pump up and down; the skin on my legs and stomach and hips flaps up and down.

I have to exercise to music. In the beginning, it's always Mariah Carey. When people start complaining, I switch to J.Lo.

I do core work. The iron bridge—I'm expected to hold up my weight on my elbows.

"Wes, I can't do this."

"Are we whining?" He pushes me, but not beyond what I can do.

"I can't," I say, falling down. I'm making a concerted effort not to curse. Wes doesn't like cursing.

What I say in my head is: *Fuck. Fuck. Fuck.* "Sugar snaps" is what I say aloud. "Sugar snaps."

"Of course, Sue, you can do anything for a minute," he says in a non-judgmental and motivating voice.

"I can't fuckin' sugar snaps *do* it," I laugh, wanting to be heard, wanting to be his center of attention.

"Now, now," he jokes, but with meaning in his eyes. I've never heard him curse. "Enough with cursing. Please, Susan," he says quietly.

"I know, that sounds so disgusting, doesn't it?" I say seriously, wanting his approval.

"You're a smart, intelligent girl. You don't need to talk like that."

I'm totally embarrassed. It's time to really drop the f-bomb from my vocabulary, said or unsaid.

"Okay, just sugar snaps," I say.

Wes smiles. He's my rock. He never lets me quit. He has me do the exercise of the day over and over until I get it. I press myself up. I pull up my stomach, my 300-plus pounds, and form an iron bridge. He's a patient person. He teaches me to be patient. He teaches me self-respect. He believes in me. He believes I can lose the weight, and he helps me believe.

Top Things I Think of When I'm Exercising at 300-Plus Pounds

- One day at a time. It's a cliché, but clichés become clichés because they're true!

- I've got to be patient, got to be patient (and I'm not a patient person) . . .

- I made it here. At least I made it here.

- It's 1 hour out of a 24-hour day. I can do anything for 1 hour. I can do anything for 10 minutes, for 10 crunches, for 10 leg lifts, for 10 steps.

- Good music is a must. Music is a total distraction. The louder, the better. No sad songs allowed.

- Buy a bra that fits well. It saves my back. Also, get professionally measured sneakers.

- Look cute and sexy when working out—no matter what size.

Chapter 17

Nobody else at the Clinic gets olive oil on a regular basis, but I do. The doctor must officially approve my 2 teaspoons of olive oil. He sees that I'm not eating my vegetables because, I tell him, I don't like my vegetables without olive oil and vinegar, so I get olive oil. Everybody is jealous of my extra 2 teaspoons of olive oil, one at lunch and one at dinner.

When I first arrived, the Clinic encouraged me, as they do everyone, to eat their food as plain and as bland as possible because most people, myself included, never really tasted their food. They tasted the salt or the sweet or just ate as fast as they could.

Now, my tongue has been awakened from a long sleep. I munch on broccoli, fresh, crunchy, springy, tasting the way I think the color green should taste. Grapes taste the way purple should taste. I'm in a psychedelic world of food that tastes like colors.

When we have the choice of stewed eggplant, I add it to my pasta and mix in my condiments. Several people point—it looks like I'm eating something different from everybody else. Everyone watches what everyone else eats at the Clinic, as if the rice or pasta or fish you're eating will suddenly turn into a chocolate chip cookie. I'm afraid it would be a *Lord of the Flies* fat mob cannibalizing the one with a cookie.

What I'm eating twice a day—pasta, except for Saturdays when I eat fish—is the same as what everyone else is eating except that I'm creative with my food choices. Some people stop me and ask me what I'm eating. Some days I think I'll go crazy if another person stares at my food, so I sit by myself in the back of the dining hall.

Most days, I eat the same thing for lunch that I ate for dinner. I'm losing weight, most weeks. I'm feeling good: tasting my food, desperately learning portion control, not craving, pausing.

How I Cut the Sodium Habit and Stopped the Cravings

- Fresh fruits and vegetables. No fast food. No processed foods.

- I redefined my snacks—a cold can of Diet Rite Orange Soda (one of the few sodas that has no sodium—check labels!) in a pretty glass. Sometimes, I need two cans.

- I put down my fork at least once during each meal—more often is better. Take time for my meals. It should take me 20 minutes to eat a meal. I have to realize what I'm eating so that I don't crave more. I time myself.

- Throw out the table salt, the soy sauce, the ketchup, and, yes, the Tabasco sauce. Double-check spices for salt. My sister had a seasonings pepper for grilling. I checked the ingredient list. The first ingredient? Salt. Ingredients are listed in order of their quantity. Anything that has salt as the first ingredient should be suspect.

- Experiment with spices. My favorite "new" spices are cumin and ginger, both fresh and in a jar—whatever's easier.

- I fancy up my water, whether it's with lemon or with lime. Or I'll make my own lemonade with water, ice, fresh lemons, and two sugar substitute packets.

- Dark chocolate has zero sodium. One piece. Enough said.

- I remind myself: *I'm worth all of the above. I'm worth taking care of myself, taking the time to eat and to eat right.*

- I've learned to forgive myself. Why this? I'm not perfect. I'm going to fail at some point. I'm going to eat a big, juicy, crunchy, sweet, salty _____ (fill it in, I've probably eaten it!). I try to learn something, about my food choices, my emotional state of mind—learn one thing—from each setback, each binge, then I forgive myself and go on, with knowledge that will help the next time.

It's spring of 2005, and I'm feeling good. But I'm going broke.

I work the phones trying to drum up the computer products business. I arrange with the Clinic to meet people at the airport and drive them to the Clinic. For a month, I'm a bookkeeper for a camp that specializes in overweight kids.

My father gives me an idea: to substitute teach. This is how he made ends meet when we were growing up. I've never taught anything before in my life. I was never a camp counselor. But I go to the high school down the street. I think I'll walk in and they'll hire me. I have a 4-year degree from the department of education at Florida State. It doesn't occur to me that they might not hire me—even though I have absolutely no teaching experience, and my experience with children has been limited to my 4-year-old nephew.

I stride into the high school and am directed to the vice principal. She's very polite in that North Carolina way that's really all about appraising me. "Are you approved by the city?"

"No."

"Well, honey, if you want to do this, you have to go downtown to the Board of Education. You can do that?"

"That's it?"

"Once you're approved, you get on the list."

"The list?"

"The list."

I get on the list.

I substitute at the elementary, middle, and high schools. After one day in elementary school, I say, *Never again.* High school was too scary. How could I teach kids who knew more than I did? I actually like middle school, though: The kids are young enough to draw you a picture and old enough to take direction.

I make a deal at the middle school: I'll substitute teach every Tuesday and Thursday. My first day as a regular substitute is in a sixth grade social studies class. The classroom smells of feet and bologna sandwiches, and I'm excited. I'm supposed to show them a movie. As the movie is being shown, I'm writing down quiz questions. The class outline didn't say to give them a quiz, but I'm thinking that this is a great movie—I'll ask them a few questions at the end.

In the middle of the movie, I notice one kid slumped over the sports section of the newspaper. *At least he's reading,* I think, though he should be watching the video.

"Can you put the newspaper away?"

"I'm reading it," he confirms.

"If you don't put that newspaper away, I'm giving you an *F* on the quiz that I'm giving you."

"What quiz? You didn't tell us we were having a quiz," he says, but he rolls the newspaper up under his arm and watches.

The movie ends.

I give a quiz of 10 questions.

"You're not from here," he says in the middle of the quiz (obviously, this is not someone who completes what he starts). "You're from New York?"

"I'm from the Bronx," I say, quickly thinking that it will give me street cred. I was born in the Bronx. I did live there for the first 1½ years.

He hands me back the quiz. I glance down at it. He's aced it. "Bronx, huh?" he says.

"*The* Bronx," I correct him.

The next day he shouts down the hall, "Hey, there goes *the* Bronx," and I wave back.

One day, I spend an hour focusing on one eighth grader in a special education class. He's big enough to be a grown man. He can't add or subtract. We work on one problem over and over. We work on adding fives, starting with five plus five. We count on our fingers. I show him how to use a calculator. I don't know if what I'm doing is "right." But I'm excited. He's getting it. He wants to be a mechanic. I tell him that mechanics need to add and subtract. He looks at me confused.

"How are you going to be able to give a bill? Or see whether your pay stub is correct?" I say.

He concentrates. He seems to get it. I want so badly for him to learn.

"You're doing great."

"I can't do this," he says, scattering the worksheet on the floor.

"You are. You can get this—"

His fingers are too big for the keypads on the calculator.

"You can do anything for a half hour—"

He stares at the numbers, making them out. Slowly, he seems to be understanding what it means to add and to take away. He gives me a half-smile. "Five plus five equals 10," he says with confidence.

It's that fragility of life that breaks my heart.

I decide to go back to graduate school and study for a master's in education with a focus on special education. I take classes as a nonmatriculated student at North Carolina Central University. It's the closest university to me, a relatively inexpensive state school, and a famous, historically black university.

But I'm scared to death to go back to school. I haven't been a student for more than 25 years. I tried taking a class in the spring of 2004. I was so excited about it: It was a writing workshop. I had never taken a writing class before. My sister was always the writer in the family, not me. But I wanted to put my memories down on paper for the first time in my life.

The class was held in a regular classroom with a wonderful published writer and novelist who, in the oddest turn of coincidence, had taught my sister in a summer writing workshop in Iowa. But that's the way with Caroline and me—our lives intersect in strange ways. I assumed that there would be regular seats in the classroom, i.e., seats that were not attached to desks, seats that I could fit into. I couldn't get into any of the seats.

The only thing I could think to do was ask for a special table and chair. I arrived at the class a half hour early. The school set up an old wooden table, an eyesore, in the front of the class for me. I couldn't concentrate on anything that this instructor was saying. I thought that everyone in the class was looking at me. After three classes, I hadn't written a word. I quit.

So my biggest concern at North Carolina Central University isn't *Can I handle the work to become a special education teacher?* My degree at Florida State was from the department of education, in leisure studies. What the hell I was going to do with that I didn't know, but my father made it very clear that every one of his children was going to graduate from college.

Now, at age 39½, my question is, *Can I fit in the seats?*

I arrive at my new class 45 minutes early. The seats are plastic and bolted to the desks. There's no leeway in them, no stretch. I search for an open classroom, but all the classrooms are locked. I pace. I decide on a chair that I'll try. The professor shows up, and I ease into the seat.

Before this . . .

I couldn't sit in movie theater seats.

I couldn't sit in plane seats.

I couldn't sit in restaurant seats.

I couldn't fit in friends' cars, certainly not in bucket seats.

I couldn't fit on my toilet seat. I tried never ever to have to use public restrooms and squeeze into a stall.

I focus on the blackboard. The class is Psychology of Education. All I can think of at that moment is: *I can fit in the seat!*

I'm 268 pounds and losing. I buy two sets of expensive earrings, one for each of the 100 pounds I've lost. It's a beautiful spring in Durham. The pines are tall and majestic and infuse the air with their cool scent. I walk 3 to 5 miles a day. I listen to the birds while I stride out into the world. The birds remind me of my father, who loves birds, who'd always take time to show us a cardinal or blue jay in our backyard in New Rochelle. I had foraged in a local bookstore and learned that in North Carolina, there are more than 460 different types of birds—it's one of the richest areas for birds in North America. I see cardinals, mockingbirds, hawks, and hummingbirds. I hear, in the woods among the tall, towering trees, the different birds in full-throated song or in whispers and catches, and I feel less alone.

Chapter 18

I turn 40 in May, and I have plans to party.

The year before, on my 39th birthday, when I was still over 300 pounds, I visited my brothers in Atlanta. I flew from Durham to Atlanta—my first plane trip in years. The seat belt just fit.

In Atlanta, Mark made a perfect, salt-free, healthy food barbecue party: grilled vegetables and absolutely the most creative fish tacos, made from tilapia, a flaky white fish, with lime and cilantro. I love parties where you get to participate in making the meal as part of the party.

My father came up from Florida, and I made him sit by me, and we ate together, holding the fresh, overflowing fish tacos with both hands. My father eats fast too, with gusto. I had to say aloud to myself: "Slow down."

"Who's slowing down?" said my father. "Not me!" He called out to Mark appreciatively, "Who ever thought to make tacos with fish?"

My younger brother, David, and his new girlfriend, Cindy, prepared a sugar-free Jell-O cake, which reflected the light in its rainbow of colors.

My father asked for seconds and thirds. I got them for him. We hadn't eaten together in years. "And how about you, toots? You look good."

"I feel good, Daddy." *I take it back. I don't want to use my mother's words.* "I feel like I have a lot of possibilities," I say carefully. I'm waiting for him to say he's proud of me, but he doesn't. He munches happily on his fish taco.

Mark's friends bring me gifts, including a delicate white and purple orchid. Somewhere Mark had found a piñata, no small feat right after Cinco de Mayo. Everyone gets a turn to break it, and when all the toys come flying out, we laugh and gather them up like kids.

That was the first time in years that I had been with both my brothers.

When I flew back to Durham from Atlanta, snapping the airline belt across my waist, I was overwhelmed. Everything was happening too quickly: I felt so loved. I almost couldn't accept it.

Here's my brother Mark's recipe for fish wraps:

MY BROTHER MARK'S TILAPIA WRAPS

4 fillets of tilapia, very fresh
1 tablespoon olive oil
Juice of 1 lemon
Ground black pepper to taste
Salsa (see recipe on page 228)
8 soft, low-sodium wraps (sold at specialty food stores such as Trader Joe's and Whole Foods)
1 medium jalapeño pepper, diced very fine
Chopped fresh cilantro to taste (plus extra for garnish)

1 In a heavy sauté pan over medium heat, place the fish in the oil. Add the lemon juice and a small amount of water—just enough of each that the fish doesn't stick to the pan. Add black pepper to taste.

2 Turn the fish at least once and cover while cooking. Cook the fish until flaky, less than 5 minutes per side. Do not overcook. While you are waiting, prepare the salsa, adding the jalapeño pepper and cilantro.

3 Drain the liquid from the fish.

4 Garnish the fish the with extra cilantro and set the fish and salsa aside.

5 To prepare the wraps, take a clean dish towel and wet it until just damp; squeeze out any excess water. Place the wraps in the dish towel and put into the microwave oven. Heat about 45 seconds, until warm and slightly soft. Serve the wraps alongside the fish and the salsa.

6 Let the guests build their own fish tacos—it's part of the fun.

Makes 4 servings (2 wraps each)

Now, for my 40th birthday, I want to celebrate with everyone. My friends Marcy, Lena, and Elle come down to Durham. This is their third trip down to visit: Marcy, so thin and crisp and sophisticated; Lena with her dark Italian looks; and Elle, 6 feet tall and naturally blonde—they're my Charlie's Angels. We eat all our meals at the Clinic together, except for one. My friends love eating there—they think it's too much food. Elle knew enough to bring salt, tiny packets that she sneaks in her jeans like cocaine.

I set up a private gyrokinesis class with my Pilates instructor, Rue. We relax and stretch our backs, arms, and legs. We use Rue's circular, flowing patterns to move the energy in our bodies. My friends have never done a class like this, and they are totally surprised that I can stretch and bend and swing so freely.

I learned to walk again in this studio. When I started Pilates, my feet were wretched and swollen; it was like hobbling on sponges. My thighs pushed and pulled together. I couldn't line up my feet and take one normal step in front of the other. I would topple over. I waddled, side to side, swaying, taking up enough room for two or three people in any corridor, pushing the fat forward.

But as I lost weight, Rue had me practice stepping with one foot directly in front of the other across the studio in a straight line. I had to stand straight. I had to align my legs and feet, press down on the heels and balls. I had to hold my head up and shoulders back. I had to take one step, slowly, directly in front of another. I cried. Everything hurt.

And I was so embarrassed. I didn't want to learn how to walk again. I didn't want to practice walking. I wanted to run. But I had to learn to walk first.

n Saturday night, Charlie's Angels and I make sushi together. It would have been fish night at the Clinic, so I'm staying perfectly within the program. I even learned how to make it at the Clinic: with cooked fish, scallions, alfalfa sprouts, carrots, and sheets of nori (seaweed) and sushi rice. My friends drink two or three bottles of wine. I sip water. We make too much sushi.

"What about plastic surgery, Sue? What's with that? When are you doing it? Have you seen a doctor? What are you doing first?" asks Elle in her rapid-fire New York way. I have to catch her speech. I've become too used to North Carolina cadences.

"It's all about my stomach."

"What about your stomach? How much work? What do you need to have done?"

I'm wearing workout pants. I pull up my T-shirt. They see my stomach, with all its sagging flesh and loose skin, for the first time ever. We stare at *It:* the sinking, shriveled, sagging folds of skin that make up my stomach. Elle backs away. I grab my skin and pull it toward her.

"Get that thing out of here!" shrieks Elle.

"Touch me, feel me," I kid, making my stomach "talk."

"Stop that!"

"*It* has a name. Rebecca!"

"You've named your stomach?" shouts Marcy.

"It's part of me!"

"Susan!" Elle cries, laughing, backing away. "Seriously, don't touch me!"

"Love me, love my stomach!" I say, running after her with my stomach, holding it out in my two hands like The Thing, The Blob, a 4-o'clock movie monster. Marcy and Lena cheer. Tears are running down my face, I'm laughing so hard. But the truth is that I don't want to hide my body anymore. I don't want to live in shame.

That night, my friends give me a birthday gift: a circle diamond necklace in white gold. I call it my "circle of friends" necklace. We decide after that to buy Marcy the same necklace for her birthday. By the end of year, we all have the exact same necklace.

SUSAN'S SUSHI

¼ pound salmon
Wasabi powder
1 cup cooked sushi rice (cooked according to package directions)
½ cup rice vinegar (Make sure this vinegar has zero sodium!)
2 sheets nori seaweed (I like the toasted seaweed sheets best)
Sesame seeds (optional)
¼ cup carrots
¼ cup alfalfa sprouts
2 scallions
Balsamic vinegar
You will also need a bamboo sushi roller, plastic wrap,
a bowl of water, and a sharp knife.

1 Poach the salmon with water for 11 minutes in a pan or aluminum foil. When cooked, let it stand in the oven or on the counter for a few minutes.

2 Stir a small amount of water into the wasabi powder to make a paste. Place in the refrigerator.

3 Cook the sushi rice in a rice cooker or pot as per the package directions. Put the cooked rice in a bowl, add ½ cup rice vinegar, and stir. Add more rice vinegar to taste, if desired. Place in the refrigerator to cool.

4 Prepare the bamboo sushi roller by wrapping the plastic wrap around it in order to roll the sushi.

5 Place a sheet of nori on the plastic-wrapped sushi roller. Take a handful of the sushi rice and spread it evenly onto the nori sheet. Keep enough of the rice for your next sheet!

6 When your hands get too sticky, dip them in the bowl of water and wipe them clean.

7 Lightly shake some sesame seeds around the rice-covered nori sheet.

8 Turn the sheet over so that the rice is not showing. Place half of the fish and any of the vegetables that you would like onto the nori sheet, on the side closest to you. This will prepare you for rolling. Go easy on the toppings, or the roll will not hold properly.

9 Take the sushi roller and start to roll. Make sure your first roll holds; adjust the roller if necessary and roll again. Keep doing this until the entire roll is finished.

10 Wet a knife and cut at least 6 pieces from the sushi roll. Enjoy!

Makes at least 1 dozen pieces

Making sushi seems like a lot of work at first, but once you get the hang of it, it will take you no more than 20 minutes to prepare an incredible meal!

I love seeing my friends, yet what I really want for my birthday is for my family to be together and for them to see how my life in Durham has changed me. I want us all to *eat* together.

Growing up, we ate dinner together almost every night. We each sat in our designated spots at the dining room table. My father sat at the head of the table, I sat to his left, and Mark was on the other side. David sat across from my father, and Caroline sat next to David. The seat at the opposite end of the table went empty. That's where my mother would have sat.

Caroline splits up the spaghetti and meatballs into five equal servings. The meatballs are counted out equally: She has made the exact number to divide by five. We do the same with chicken or steak or meat loaf. For a while, we have chicken cacciatore every other day.

We're noisy, vying for attention, eating so fast to get to the next thing in life and not wanting to leave the table—alternately ignored by my father, who's reading the newspaper, and quizzed by him on what happened that day. Our idea of portion control is five equal servings of anything we have for dinner.

I could be 10 or 12 or 14, and we'd eat dinner the same way. Yet, by the time I'm 15, my sister has fled to college, and our dinner meals, along with many other things in our family, fall apart.

Before my father arrives, I'm focused on what I need to have in the house for him and what I need to have for my 40th birthday picnic celebration with my family. My father plans to stay with me for 5 days. Mark and I fight, and he says he won't come. I feel horrible, but that's what Mark and I have done—fight, make up, and fight some more—all our lives. I clean. I cook. I shop.

I make a pasta dish with my own tomato sauce, a potato dish with peppers, and my own fresh salsa. I had cooked the whole day before my father arrived. Grapes, cantaloupe, strawberries, and peaches burst on shelves more accustomed to holding water and diet orange soda. My refrigerator in Durham has never been so full.

My father arrives on my birthday: Wednesday, May 11. I pick him up at the airport around lunchtime. I haven't seen him since Thanksgiving, when we celebrated together in his one-bedroom Florida condominium. Turkey legs, cranberry sauce, broccoli, and a huge salad was our Thanksgiving meal, and I was thankful.

What really marked Thanksgiving in Florida wasn't the turkey legs. I wore a bathing suit. The last bathing suit in Florida had been black and white with an old lady's skirt. I had to wear biker shorts under the bathing suit in order not to chafe and get diaper rash. In Florida, I wore a size 26/28, black one-piece bathing suit. Everyone else was a good 70-plus, with aches and pains and bent knees and thinning hair, so I felt good. Being able to shop at Lane Bryant was an accomplishment, even though I dreamed of a white thong from Victoria's Secret. I swam in that condominium pool in my 26/28 bathing suit like I was training for the Olympics.

Today, when my father steps off the plane, his left hand shakes. He looks confused for a second. His broad shoulders are stooped forward, and his feet, in brown collegiate boat shoes, are shuffling more than walking. I stand up straight. I want him to be proud of me. I'm here! I'm on time! And not because I drove like a mad person, but because I planned this day to be special for the two of us.

"I didn't even recognize you," he says, and lets me hug him.

He wants to get going. It's 3 p.m. and he hasn't eaten lunch.

At my apartment I prepare a tasting plate of all the treats I have in my refrigerator for my 40th birthday celebration. I tell him to sit, and I serve him.

"So, Mark's not coming?" he asks.

"No," I say, wanting to explain, but he cuts me off.

"You can't make up with him?"

It's always my fault.

"How do you like the pasta?" I ask. I don't want to focus on what we won't have. No, we won't have four of us here. But Caroline and David are coming, and I'm here, and I've changed so much; doesn't he see that?

I eat nothing, since I had already eaten lunch at the Clinic.

He finishes off the last forkful of pasta on his plate and makes a face.

"Don't you like it?"

"Feh," he says dismissively. "It has no taste."

I'm shocked.

He doesn't say anything else. He's finished everything. His trembling fingers push my plate away. He looks at me with the sad, hooded, tired eyes of a man who has seen too much. "What else have you got?"

I don't want him to push my plate away. I feel my old rage in my throat. *I don't want my life to be like this. I don't want to need so much from this man.*

"Let me get you something you like, Daddy. I'll be right back."

I grab my pocketbook.

I drive straight to the closest Burger King. I swing into the drive-thru and order a fish sandwich. *Why can't he be proud of me? When is enough enough for him? What else can I do to make him change?* I order without really thinking. I eat without thinking. *I have to eat. I need this fish sandwich. I'm a failure. I'm a fuckup. I don't care. I want to eat, now.* I shove the sandwich into my mouth.

I race to the supermarket and buy cheeses, all kinds (my father loves cheese); also tuna, mayonnaise, onions (I'll make a big thick tuna salad; we'll spread it on long Italian bread); and several loaves of bread. I throw in some bagels and cream cheese. Boxes of Stella D'Oro cookies and bags of Doritos join them in my shopping cart. I'm racing through the store, thinking, *What else should I get for him?*

I'm off. I start fantasizing. *I'm going to make stuff that I know my father will like and screw it. Screw it. I'm going to eat it too.*

I'm gone for an hour. When I return, heavy with grocery bags, and lug them into my spotless white kitchen and spread them across my countertops, my father is sleeping, curled on the futon in the second bedroom, snoring. He doesn't wake. I start eating, first the chips. I make a tuna sandwich, smearing on the mayonnaise, spreading it thick on the Italian bread, using half a loaf of bread. I don't care. I'm not going to the Clinic for dinner tonight. I just want to finish the sandwich before my father wakes up.

My sister drives up around 7 p.m., and she is huge.

She is 6 months pregnant. Her feet are double their normal size. She wears flip-flops and stretch pants and waddles, holding her hard, round, high stomach.

"How was the drive? How do you feel?" I ask, hovering around her.

"I can't sit, walk, or stand. Other than that, being in a car for a couple of hours was a lot of fun," she says, stepping aside as my nephew races toward me.

At age 42, she's carrying my niece, my girl-baby. She wanted this baby, trying for years to get pregnant again. I want to stroke her stomach, though she hates that.

"You look beautiful, sister." We often call each other "sister" and "brother." It has no religious overtones. It was started years ago by Mark, for no other reason than that it set him apart to call us that instead of by our names, and it stuck.

"I look fat," she says, leaning against the wall.

"You'd fit right into the Clinic," I joke, and see how distressed this makes her. I can't say anything right today. "Why don't you sit down? You just look pregnant, wonderfully pregnant."

"It's you who looks wonderful," she says softly. "You really do. Look at you! I haven't even said happy birthday! I can't believe you're 40."

"I don't feel 40. I don't think I look 40. Do I?"

"You don't. You look incredible. You're really staying focused down here, aren't you?"

"I am," I say, pushing away the thought of the BK, the chips, the tuna sandwich. *That binge doesn't exist. It's the first major binge since I've been down in Durham, but I can will it not to have happened.*

I can't admit to her, or to anyone in my family, about how I've been eating in the last few hours. I can't let them know that I screwed up again. I'm too ashamed.

I change the subject back to her. "Are you taking it easy? Your feet look a little swollen."

"You don't know what it feels like! I can barely walk."

"I do," I say quietly. "I really do."

Caroline, her husband, and her son are staying in a corporate apartment I arranged for them. It's graduation week in Durham for Duke and the University of North Carolina. Every hotel has been booked for months. The first thing she wants to do is go food shopping so that they have a few things like milk and cereal at the apartment. For the third time in 2 days, I go to the supermarket. But this time I don't race inside. I can't look at more food. I can't be tempted. My father insists on going inside. He says I didn't buy salami. He wants salami. I haven't eaten salami in 2 years.

I stay in the car with Mikey, and that lasts for about 30 seconds. Mikey doesn't want to be in the car. He's just traveled for hours. He wants out. So do I, but for other reasons. I unlock his car seat and free him. I have an idea.

I put him in an empty shopping cart and start pushing him in circles around the near-empty parking lot. I'm the engine. He can rev me up. He can steer me anywhere. We crash into another shopping cart like bumper cars. He screams in laughter. He says, "Do it again!" and I do. I howl at the moon. I roar and make him roar, too. I may be 40, but in my heart, I'm 16. I'm free. I can do anything that I want. I have my whole life ahead of me.

My sister, however, isn't happy with us. "He could have gotten hurt. What where you thinking?"

"She doesn't think," says my father, holding another bag of groceries to bring into my house.

"I'm fine, Mommy," says Mikey in my defense. "I want to come back and do this again with Aunt Susan. Can we?"

I head back to my apartment. It's 9 o'clock. We watch television together, the History Channel, and after a half hour, my father says he's going to bed.

It's my birthday. I'm 40 years old. No one ever says that I look 40, whatever that means. I've even passed a test—I've safely passed the age at which my mother had her stroke. I made it over that imaginary line. My life has been on hold for the past 10 years, I could be any age between 25 and 40. I want my life to start already.

Soon my father goes to sleep. He snores. I can't sit still. The apartment is too small with my father in it. The walls rattle with his snores.

I jam my finger on the remote and race through the television channels. There's nothing on television except the Food TV Network, these days my absolutely favorite channel. I throw the remote across the room. I want to wake my father up. *He has to talk with me.* But of course I don't wake him. I'm frantic, and I'm angry at myself for being frantic.

I can't stay in the apartment. I decide I need a different salsa for my birthday dinner the next day, one that my father, in particular, will like. I remember the Mexican restaurant that I went to with Caroline the night I arrived in Durham, and how good that salsa tasted. *That's what I need.*

And it still tastes good. It's smooth, chock-full of tomatoes, and salty—extremely salty. I order 2 pints of salsa and a huge bag of their chips, to go, even though I've made my own salsa at home. I sit down at the bar, alone, and watch everyone eating, and I begin obsessing. *How long does it take to pack up salsa and chips?* When the waitress comes over and asks if I want anything else, I say, "No," fast and hard.

What if anyone from the Clinic sees me eating here? I've lost 213 pounds. I'm one of the most successful people ever at the Clinic. The *New York Times* has even interviewed me for an article in a series called "Obesity Inc." about the prevalence of diet programs in Durham, which is supposed to appear in the business section sometime in the near future.

But this birthday night, I heave myself into my car, break open the salsa, and tear open the chips. The salt burns my mouth. My tongue leaps out and licks the corners sore. I wolf down an entire pint of salsa, and I'm left wondering whether I should go in and order more. My ankles swell as I push the chips into my mouth. I don't think of my family and how they all believe that I've been focused on the program. I don't think of the program. I don't think of the 213 pounds I've lost and the 100 I still have to go.

I'm focused on the salsa and nothing else.

I don't care.

Since I've already eaten the salsa, I think, *Why not? It's my fuckin' birthday. I can eat what I want.* Jimmy Johns Subs is right down the street. I order the #15: the tuna sub without cheese, but *extra* olive oil, vinegar, and hot peppers.

I don't care.

A greasy-haired townie with a pimply face and the slow-moving insolence of a 20-year-old makes the sandwich. I can't look him in the eye. I want him to hurry. *I need it.* I pay for it with the last dollars in my pocketbook and eat it in my car, on the side of the road, in the shadows. I eat it all.

I don't care.

I go home. I go straight to bed. I will myself to forget what I just ate. The feeling is like before I went to Durham: forced amnesia. My birthday is over.

The next day, my father is up early, ready to go to the Clinic for breakfast. All I'm thinking of is how to go to breakfast and avoid getting weighed in. I can't have my father see that I've gained weight—not that my father even knows that I get weighed in every morning—or he'd be all over me. At the Clinic, I go in the front door instead of the side door, which I regularly go through in the morning, directly to the Inspiration Room and the weigh-in.

I'm excited to introduce my father to the doctors. I skip the weigh-in.

I show my father that I'm on the board that lists weight loss. I'm in the 200-pound-plus section. I'm up there in black and white, but my father is preoccupied, distant, grayer this morning. I introduce him to Ray, who takes my father's shaky hand in his beefy one and pumps away. I bring my father over to the coffee-klatsch of over-50 women, which includes Betty from Connecticut. She's 60 pounds overweight or so, plump with rolls of soft fat that have accumulated on her upper arms and hips over the years. She obviously thinks he's adorable, and she perks right up with her decaf growing cold in front of her. Later, she'll ask whether my father is single. He's both: single and adorable. He has an impish grin and flashes it now. His dimples light up his face. Later, he'll ask whether she's single. But there's no time for me to make a match.

I make sure that he orders what I usually eat: Irish oatmeal, with measured-out cinnamon and maple syrup and fruit. He likes it.

"Pass the salt," he grins at Betty. He knows there's no salt at the clinic.

"What about milk? I need milk for my coffee," he laughs.

There's no milk at the Clinic. "We all drink our coffee black," giggles Betty.

"I don't even know why you're here," he says to Betty. He admires her figure. I think she's going to twirl around or kneel at his feet.

"Morris, you have such a wonderful daughter. I can see where she gets her sense of humor and fun," says Betty, her arms jiggling.

"I want to introduce you to the doctors, Daddy," I say. I've had enough of this *Cocoon* replay.

I bring my father into the Inspiration Room. The weigh-in is over now, and the room is empty. I introduce him to the country doctor. "Doesn't your daughter look great?" says my supporter, my champion. I'm a huge success at the Clinic, 200 pounds in just under 18 months.

"She looks good," my father agrees, looking around the room. I want him to look at me, to really see me. He shuffles his feet. The doctor beams at me.

I introduce him to the senior doctor. I lead him to the other people at the clinic, to the kitchen staff. I'm the Queen of the Clinic with my father. I want him to be proud of me.

Back at our table, we sit drinking a second cup of coffee. My father pulls out a newspaper and starts reading. I'm suddenly back at home with my father at the head of the table, and me vying for his attention.

That night again, my father goes right to bed—it's past 10 o'clock. And that night, again, I race to the Subway–Dunkin' Donuts–Baskin-Robbins combo drive-thru—my dream fast-food palace—and order a 12-inch tuna sub and a brownie sundae with an extra scoop and extra *extra* chocolate sauce. Forty cents extra for the extra *extra* chocolate sauce!

This fast-food palace is opposite Rue's workout place. I'm supposed to be there tomorrow. I eat the ice cream first, not wanting it to melt. I lick the container, wanting all of my extra *extra* chocolate sauce, and avoid looking across the street. I love the ice cream. I want more, and I hate it.

I hate myself. I'm angry with myself for the anger—and the stupidity and failure. I bite into the sub, hardly breathing, wolfing it down, wondering what else might be open. Now that I've started eating, I want to eat as much as I can. I stare blankly ahead. I finish my tuna sub with my eyes closed and feel the full numbness envelop me.

But as soon as I'm done, I feel greasy. Bloated. Gross. My thighs spread. My hips inflate. My stomach pours down to my knees. My face breaks out along my chin. I have two chins, at least. I want to eat more and feel less. But I haven't scoped out 24-hour delis in Durham. I'm trapped.

How am I going to get weighed in tomorrow? How can I face the scale?

I can't. The next morning, I gulp down an extra-large coffee with milk. I don't go to the Clinic. I cancel my Friday workout with Wes. I agree to go to the zoo with my sister.

We all pile into my sister's minivan and drive to the North Carolina Zoo. She's at the wheel even though she's pregnant. She'd get carsick in the back. But she can't sit in the front row passenger seat because my father would get carsick if *he* sat in the back. So my father is navigating up front, even though he has no idea where we are going and refuses to look at the map. I sit behind my sister and also give her directions. Her husband braves the bumps on the third row and keeps out of all the arguments about which way to go.

My father comments on the buffet prices posted at the various family-style restaurants.

"Look at that, $6.99 for all-you-can-eat steak dinner."

I eat all the Life Savers in her side seat pocket until my sister yells at me, "What are you doing? I need those in case my stomach gets upset."

"I'm sorry," I say, "but I finished them."

"Two packs?"

"I'll buy you more," I promise.

"It doesn't matter."

But it matters to me. She caught me eating. *I have fruit in my bag but I ate all her Life Savers. I'm drowning.*

"Look at that," points out my father, "$2.99 for an all-you-can-eat breakfast buffet. Do you think they serve all day?"

After about 2 hours, we finally get to the zoo. We're all aggravated, hungry, and hot. "The North Carolina Zoo is the nation's largest walk-through natural habitat zoo," I read from the print out. "This will be great exercise."

"It's not the Bronx Zoo," says my father, skeptically looking at the acres of zoo. "Remember how we always used to go to there every year? That zoo is right off the highway. Or you can take the subway there."

"Well, the Bronx Zoo is in the Bronx," says my sister.

"And we're as far away from the Bronx as you can get," adds her husband, groaning, climbing out from the third row of the minivan. Alan looks like he felt every bump on the road. "It must be a hundred degrees out," he says, not exaggerating by much. "How are we going to do this?"

There's nothing but zoo anywhere you look: zoo and mountains. We soon learn that the zoo is built on the Uwharrie Mountains, though locals call them hills. Five miles of trails wind through the park, including 37 acres of African plains and 11 acres of North America prairie. The highest "hill" in the zoo is Purgatory Mountain, and it rises 937 feet above sea level. *No, Dorothy, you are no longer in the Bronx.*

We decide to take the day slow and easy, no pushing my father or sister, though my father grumbles that he's fine and my sister insists even more loudly that she's not. She's pregnant, in case anybody forgot in the last 5 minutes. And Mikey wants to see everything. He's hungry/thirsty/hot/tired/bored/wondering where all the animals are, and will he see kitty cats, because he suddenly remembers that he misses his cat, and when is he going home? We haven't left the parking lot yet.

Five hours later, we're all hot, sweaty, and exhausted. We drag ourselves off Purgatory Mountain and out of the North Carolina Zoo and back to the oasis of the minivan. I convince my sister to head to Chapel Hill for dinner.

"This is my birthday dinner, and the only time I'm going to go off the program this week," I say, blocking out the last 2 days, the fish sandwich, the tuna subs, the brownie sundae.

"Are you sure?" Caroline says skeptically. "You really want to go off the program?"

"I'm sure. This will be the only time," I lie.

At the restaurant, it's like we're dining in a garden in Rome. Not that I've ever been to Rome, but there are murals and plants and it's cozy and there's Italian music playing. We gobble all the bread and more is brought again and again. It's fresh, warm, and crusty. I sink into it. I'm truly hungry, not just psychologically hungry but, after all the walking, physically hungry. It's an unfamiliar sensation.

When we finally stand up and leave this Roman garden of an Italian restaurant in Chapel Hill, I'm bloated, swollen, stuffed on bread and pasta and a chocolate seven-layer cake. I can't cross the street to look at the pocketbook my sister is pointing out. I can't lift my nephew, even though he wants me to. I don't want to move. I've screwed everything up. I make a pact with myself. I'm going back on Phase 1 as soon as my family leaves. I'm eating nothing but grains and fruit. But I know that I'm a failure and a fraud. I'm ashamed.

On Saturday, I don't want to walk anywhere. I don't want to undress or shower or look in the rearview mirror because I may see myself. Of course, I don't go to get weighed. But I'm throwing a lunch party for my family. All the food I prepared, everything that's within my food program, is going to be served, along with everything else I bought for my father. I want to throw it all out.

My brother David and his fiancée, Cindy, arrive from Atlanta first.

We spread out on my back porch.

"There's enough food to feed an army, Susan," announces my father. I'm expecting six people, and he's right: There's enough for two dozen.

I open up a Corona. I haven't had a beer in at least 5 years. I don't even like beer. But I can have one if I want it.

"I'll take the Doritos and bread away," says my brother-in-law.

"I say this with love," I say, without much love. "But if I want to eat 10 bags of Doritos and 14 tuna sandwiches, that's what I'll do."

"Okay," he says, dropping the bag, giving my sister one of those *What did I do wrong?* looks.

"Everything looks delicious, Sue!" shouts David, playing with an airplane with my nephew, running around the backyard like the biggest 5-year-old kid in the world.

"Try my salsa. If you don't like it, I have other salsa from this Mexican place."

He scoops up a chip of my salsa. "This is the greatest, Sue!"

I think he means it. He grins. Even at age 38, he has a baby face, all cheeks, all big broad chest and 6 feet of him. His eyes are puffy these days. He's put on weight. He's also going back to school to become a nurse anesthesiologist. I'm so proud of him. I wish Mark were here, too.

"You really like it, David?" I say.

"What's not to like? Tomatoes? Peppers? Onions?" he laughs, big and friendly, and eats more.

"Since when do you like tomatoes or salad?" interrupts my father, his salami sandwich at his side.

"I like tomatoes," David says lightly. He's not being baited. "Why'd you go and buy more salsa, Sue, when the stuff you made is terrific?"

I want to hug my little brother. But instead, David grabs the plane from Mikey and wings it around his head, into the air. The plane zooms over the trees. All three of us chase after it. I can feel my body move, scrambling after my nephew, tagging my brother.

Everyone cheers when Mikey dives to the plane first. I wrestle him to the ground, tickling him and shouting, "Aunt Susan loves you!"

"Look what I can do, Mommy," he calls out to Caroline. "I can almost hug Aunt Susan all the way around. I just need longer arms."

SUSAN'S SALSA

5 to 10 Roma tomatoes (depending on size), diced
1 cup finely chopped fresh cilantro
Juice of 5 limes (more if needed for taste)
½ large red onion
1 cup frozen roasted corn, if available (you may substitute 1 cup frozen corn)
1 cup canned low-sodium black beans (optional)
Freshly ground black pepper to taste

1 Mix all the ingredients together.

2 Place in the refrigerator overnight.

3 Serve with no-salt tortilla chips or large chunks of green pepper as "scoopers"!

Makes 4 to 6 servings

I also served a simple but delicious dessert. The key here is to serve it in funky sundae glasses. I bought mine at the local store that sells everything for 99 cents or less.

SUSAN'S DELICIOUSLY FAST DESSERT

1 cup diced strawberries
1 cup blueberries
1 cup Cool Whip
*1 bag (8 ounces) semisweet chocolate chips (Use the whole bag in the
dessert—no in-between tastes . . . well, okay, just one or two!)*

1 Chill six to eight 8-ounce glasses a half hour before you're ready to start.

2 Layer the fruit, Cool Whip, chocolate chips, and more Cool Whip.

3 Sprinkle the top with a few pieces of fruit and chocolate chips. Serve very
cold.

Makes 6 to 8 servings (8 ounces each)

Chapter 19

My birthday party is going on without me. I'm in the kitchen cleaning up, but what I'm really doing is finishing off the chips and salsa. I shove them into my mouth. Chips crumble into the sink. The faucet on high washes them away. Salsa dribbles down my arm, redder than blood. More follows, into my mouth, into the stainless steel, out of the bag, into my mouth: more wet salsa, my salsa, the restaurant salsa, more dry chips, more. I eat bread and cookies too. I'm not anybody's sister or daughter. I'm nothing.

If I could shoot salsa and chips directly into my veins, I would. I'd rather feel nothing than this overwhelming, undernourished anxiety.

"What are you doing, Sue?" David says, striding into the kitchen.

"Nothing," I say, wiping my mouth, dropping the chips in my hand back into the bag.

"Well, come into the living room with us."

"No, I'm okay. I want to do the dishes."

"Don't eat the chips and salsa by yourself," he says, stepping toward me. "You can eat with us. Don't eat alone."

I'm so busted. So exposed. Like my brother caught me naked.

I bring the chips and salsa into the living room. I'm so tired. I want them all to go home. I eat some more chips and salsa. I can show him that I'm not ashamed of eating out in the open, with everyone around, even though I am.

Monday is the day. I'm going back on Phase 1, I bargain with myself. One more day, and I'll be back in control. After the celebration at my apartment is finally over, I drive David and Cindy to their hotel. On the way back, I think, *The day is ruined—all those chips. I can have one more treat.* Before I can change my mind, I zoom into the Cookout and order the cheese fries, onion rings, and an Oreo cookie–Reese's peanut butter cup–Heath bar toffee vanilla shake. I desperately want a burger, but I haven't eaten red meat in a year, and I shut my mouth.

Sunday, my brother and Cindy return home to Atlanta. The rest of us go to the farmer's market. One more day, and I'll get back to the program. Trays of strawberries are offered at every stall along with homemade pickles, jellies, pastries, pies, brownies. Even the cheeses are fresh, like soft, new goat cheese. There are samples everywhere, too. The array of sharp smells—new onions, organically grown garlic—rises up. Even the smell of the earth is mouthwatering, as if the dirt has just been shaken from roots and leaves, fresh and clean. This is the abundance of food that makes this country great.

I, however, want to eat everything. I head for the strawberries. I can eat those in front of anybody. I taste one succulent strawberry. Picked that day, the farmer with no teeth assures me. I don't buy anything.

Strolling through the market, we stop at the pecan pies, expansive pies, falling-out-of-the-pie-shell pies, the smell of sugar and nuts rolling out.

"I love pecan pies," says my brother-in-law, born and bred in Long Island, New York—not exactly the home of pecan pie makers. "I also love biscuits and gravy. How about some biscuits and gravy?"

"How about some hush puppies—onion, oily, cornmeal pieces of joy!" I counter.

"How about grits. Smothered in butter?" he says.

"Fried chicken or chicken-fried steak, Alan?" I say, getting into this.

"Chicken-fried steak, of course."

"That stuff could kill you, Alan," laughs Caroline, obsessing over jars of homemade pickles.

"I'd die happy," says Alan, holding half a dozen shopping bags.

"Give me an everything bagel with lox and cream cheese any day," I laugh. "I guess I'll always be a northerner."

"I'll take my biscuits and gravy any day. And I'm getting hungry. When are we going to eat?" he says.

I hadn't planned on eating here.

"How about we go to that restaurant?" he says. He points to the restaurant on the hill: the Farmers Market Restaurant.

This will be the last time I go off program this week.

We traipse in and are greeted by a line of pies: peach, cherry, apple, and pecan. The homemade smell fills the restaurant. "Goodness Grows in North Carolina" circles the top of the restaurant along with scenes of cows and barns. I can think of other things, such as my hips, that are growing just by standing in the restaurant. The restaurant is bright, airy, and packed. I scan the room, hoping there is no one I know, and there isn't.

Plates whip by us, cradled on the waitresses' hefty arms. Pancakes, eggs, grits, ham steak, and biscuits—huge, made-from-scratch biscuits—brim over each serving. Each slice of pie commands an entire plate—just the slice—with its fruit flowing onto the dish and over the edges and on to the table. This is my last meal before I go back to the program, so I can eat.

The first thing we do is order hush puppies to share. The waitress is the nicest. She keeps bringing out the food until my brother-in-law announces that he's had his biscuit and gravy quota for the next year. Two deliciously gorged hours later, we're debating whether we should buy a pie for later.

"Let me buy you a pie," I offer.

"We don't need a pie," says my sister.

"You should have one. For Mikey."

"This kid didn't eat anything again," chimes in my father.

"He doesn't like pie," insists my sister.

"How can you think of eating anything else?" says my brother-in-law, rubbing his flat stomach.

"One pie. An apple pie."

"Stop pushing the pie, Susan. We don't want the pie. If you want pie, buy it for yourself."

"I don't want pie! I'm absolutely going back on the program this minute," I say, finishing my cup of coffee and staring disbelievingly at my empty plate. My sister avoids my eyes. "I know what I can eat and what I can't eat!"

"I didn't say anything," says Caroline, whose two eggs over easy and a ham steak, along with her share of hush puppies, are gone. Pregnant or not, she's packed it away, too.

We slowly leave the North Carolina Farmers Market Restaurant, where goodness grows without pie.

It's over. The week is over for me. And I just need everyone to go home now.

Caroline, Alan, and Mikey head back north. I take my father to the airport. "Did you have a good week?" I ask anxiously, holding on to his arm.

"It was great to see you," he says tiredly. "You look great, Susan," he says without really looking at me, because if he did he'd see my hush puppy eyes, my Cookout feet, my brownie sundae pants tight around the waist.

He steps away from me.

"Now let me go, Susan, I don't want to have to run to my plane."

I don't want him to go. I want him to say—well, it doesn't matter, because he's not going to say it. He's on his way through security.

That night, I lie in bed in disbelief. I haven't been weighed since Tuesday. It's the biggest relapse I have had since I came to Durham. I feel like an addict, like I can't stay straight. I was sick. I want to eat even now, with my stomach sagging to the side like the biggest bowl of Jell-O ever. I force myself to stay in bed. *If I move one foot off my bed, I'm driving to the nearest fast-food drive-thru.* I try not to breathe. I don't blink.

I'm a fat shit.

Chapter 20

Finally, it's Monday morning.

I haven't slept at all. I wear my old clothes, my black stretchy pants, and a baggy green plaid 4X T-shirt that I've been sleeping in. The Body should be hidden. I feel dirty.

Slinking out the door, I skip breakfast at the Clinic. I stall until mid-morning, doing nothing before I arrive at the Clinic, hoping I'm using up some calories just living. I wait until the Inspiration Room is empty and weigh myself, thinking I may have gained 10 pounds, give or take. I'm sure everybody knows that I've binged.

The week before, I had weighed 250. *I could deal with 260,* I bargain with myself. *Even 265.* I step on the scale.

I look down.

290.

I step off and on again: 290 pounds. *I gained 40 pounds! How did I gain 40 pounds in less than a week? What did I do?*

I know what I did.

I stumble out of the Inspiration Room.

I run into Gina. She's back. Like a lot of people, she's gained back some of her weight, and she's returned to refocus. She tugs at my shirt with her long red nails. "What are you wearing?" she says loudly.

"Leave me alone, G."

I push past her. I stare at the board that lists all the food choices. I'm going back onto Phase 1, just grains and fruit. I know I'm punishing myself.

Tuesday morning, in the doctor's office, I confess all: the bingeing, the shame, and the lies. It's what I imagine confession to be—a bare space, me barely able to face a man I respect and admire. I would get on my knees if the doctor thought that would help.

"Why do you think you did it?" the doctor asks quietly.

"I think it initially started because I wanted my father to be proud of me. I wanted him to see how I'd changed, and when he didn't react the way I thought he would, I was so angry. I was filled with this rage. I had to eat. I just had to, Doctor. I'm sorry—"

I gulp air.

"I wanted my birthday to be perfect. I wanted my father to be proud of me—"

"Why can't you be proud of yourself?" he says.

"I think I'm proud of myself, but maybe I'm not."

"That might be something you want to think about—being proud of yourself."

I slump in his office in my oversize clothes, and cry even more. He offers me tissues. I need the whole box. My head hangs down. I want to punch myself in the stomach. My whole body caves in on itself.

"Susan, we're here for you. Let's get back on the horse, let's get back on Phase 1, and you'll be okay," he says warmly and firmly. I cover my face with tissues. I fear I'll suffocate on my own tears.

"Be proud of yourself," he says again, as if these words will not stay with me for the rest of my life.

And something clicks. That proverbial light goes off. I know what he is saying.

Grow the hell up—that's what the doctor is saying to me in his kind way. *Grow the hell up.* Daddy didn't make me eat at Burger King. I ate at Burger King. *Grow the hell up, Susan.*

Being truthful to myself is so raw to me. Sharing the truth is like fire, searing.

The doctor pauses and looks at me. "We're behind you. You don't have to worry about anything. We're behind you 100 percent."

It's another turning point in my life. Suddenly, I realize that I have to take responsibility for myself. I don't like that person who binged and lied and binged some more and was ashamed of herself and her actions. I don't want to be that person. I want to have pride in myself. I want to love myself.

Grow the hell up.

I wear the same clothes for a week. I drop all my workout appointments. I cancel substitute teaching.

Grow the hell up.

I don't shower. I don't want to see The Body at all.

Grow the hell up.

I'm starting over. Back to grains and fruit. I'm exhausted, dragging myself to the Clinic and back to bed. I ignore Gina and her constant questioning about my clothes. My family calls and tells me what a great time they had in Durham. I tell them that I did, too. I'm ready to admit my lies to myself and to the doctors at the Clinic, but not to my family, not yet.

The following Monday, I see Wes, my trainer, for the first time in a week. I come clean. "What happened this week?"

"I've gained 40 pounds."

"Let's walk the treadmill."

"I can't." My feet and legs are so swollen, I feel as if I'm hobbling again on sponges, lurching forward, thighs thick, the skin rubbing together and splitting open. I almost break down.

He looks surprised. His placid face is careful not to show more emotion. He runs both hands over his head as if freeing himself.

I wait for him to say that he had reservations about the Clinic, but he doesn't. Some people think it's a very drastic way to lose weight. Some people think that it's not a diet suited for real life.

All he says, with studied calmness, is, "Let's take it slow today."

Wes teaches me patience. With patience, perseverance, and discipline, a person can do anything. At least according to Wes.

I don't feel as if I'm "in" my body. I don't emotionally sense my legs or arms or toes move or step or stretch or even take a simple step. It's as if I have lost the sense of movement or of purposeful sweat tearing down my sides or the reward of wind on my face. I look at myself from the outside in for the next 3 weeks.

"How do you feel?" asks Wes.

"Nervous. Angry with myself," I say, sweating, on the treadmill.

"Why? You're doing great."

"Really? I don't feel it."

"Keep going," he says calmly. And I do. The huge, back-and-forth swings are harder than just being fat. I want the bingeing to stop. I want to be back in my body. And peace—that's all I wish for: peace.

My skin breaks out. My chin is slashed with pimples. I feel porous. I'm sweating or peeing all day. I'm ice-cold. I sleep as much as I can. It's as if my body is in detox mode. It's as if my body is returning to life.

By the end of week, I lose 24 pounds (now I've learned that it's mostly water weight). By the end of May, I'm back to 250 pounds.

What I Learned from My Trainer and from My Worst Binge in a Year and a Half:

- Patience and perseverance.

- An all-or-nothing attitude never works because . . .

- At some point, I'm going to have a setback. I just am. And if I have an all-or-nothing attitude, which means either I'm perfect or I'm shit *(I mean, in my new commitment to eliminating potty mouth, "less than perfect," but it never feels that way—it feels like shit—so I have to say it)*, it's going to be devastating.

- I grow and change by making mistakes and recovering from them.

- I have to put myself first. I have to make sure that I am taking care of myself before I take care of anybody else.

- Go back to the first point. Have patience. Persevere.

Chapter 21

At 6 a.m. on May 19, the phone rings, and I panic: *Is my mother okay?* Early morning calls are almost always from the nursing home.

"We want you on the show," a pleasant female voice asks with some urgency. I miss what she says in the beginning because I'm thinking of my mother.

"Who?" I mumble, thinking it's a joke or a wrong number. I'm half asleep.

But she insists that she wants me "on."

"On what?" I say, now more awake than asleep.

"On *Good Morning America*."

"Oh my God!" I shout, fully awake.

The producer has seen the article in the *New York Times*. I haven't even seen it yet. The article, on the front page of the business section, apparently features me in the first four paragraphs.

As soon as I hang up with the producer, I find the article online. "Penny-Wise, Not Pound-Foolish: City Cashes In as Mecca for the Hefty (With Wallets to Match)," announces the broad headline. The reporter, Stephanie Saul, even includes how I'm going to have surgery to remove "dangling skin" and fill out "sagging breasts" (see the third paragraph). But the best part is—because I'm truly thrilled to be part of this article, besides *GMA* calling me!—my before and after pictures. I look like I've cut myself in half.

Good Morning America flies me up on Friday. A car meets me. I've always seen those drivers at JFK or LaGuardia, holding out placards with names written out on them, waiting for someone important. No one has ever held up one with my name on it, except for today. I'm so excited that I ask the middle-aged driver if I can keep the card with my name written on it.

Good Morning America has arranged for a hotel for me, the Millennium, and I'm thrilled to find out that I'm in the VIP section. I've never stayed in a hotel's VIP section. I'm sure I'm going to see stars. But what I find out is that VIP really means GFF—*get free food*. Platters of fruit and cookies and pots of coffee and tea seem to appear by elevator, on some unknown but regular schedule. I'm not focused on food. I should be preparing for my Monday morning appearance on *Good Morning America,* but I'm really just as excited about Saturday night and my date with Hugh, another guy I've met online.

We agreed to meet at Columbus Circle. He's from Scarsdale: tall, handsome, and slim, divorced with kids, and almost too good-looking. He's couture, full retail, and I'm the Lord & Taylor Clearance Center.

For 5 or 6 hours, we amble through Central Park circling through the zoo, up to Strawberry Fields, down past Tavern on the Green with its sparkling lights against the trees, and back east until way past any sensible hour to be in the park.

We don't kiss good night. We hail separate cabs. I head south and he travels east, but before his cab makes the turn, just like in the movies, we both turn around and look at each other, holding one another's stare for a long, desirous moment that's better than any kiss.

The next day, I see Caroline. I borrow a suit from her. My ankles are like heavy logs. I tell her it's from the plane flight. But if mine are logs, hers are tree trunks. Her doctors are worried. I'm worried. She's pushed herself to the limit to have this baby—first with all the fertility drugs, and now with the pregnancy that has seemed to sap all her energy. She kids that she has an alien inside her, not a baby, and today it looks like that.

"Have you cut the salt from your diet?" I ask.

"I can't eat anything without getting nauseous."

"You have to cut the sodium. Cut out bread. If you have to eat bread, buy no-sodium bread at Trader Joe's. I'll buy you some."

"I'll try."

"And you have to drink a lot of water. Not tea. Not juice. Definitely not soda. Water."

She gives me a small smile. Neither of us are used to me telling her what to do.

"Have you tried asparagus? It's a natural diuretic. It will help the swelling in your feet."

"I just keep on buying new sandals. I'm up to a men's size 11 triple wide," she says. She looks me up and down. We both know that I look good in her blue suit with my silk top and circle-of-friends diamond necklace. "But I feel terrible saying this, Susan—"

"What?" I'm thinking it's about how I look in the suit.

"I don't think I can come with you to *Good Morning America.* I think it's too much for me."

I'm relieved. I thought she was going to ask me about my weight.

"Are you going to be okay, sister?" she asks.

"I'll be fine. I love being on camera. I'm an old pro at it because of the German television show, you know."

"This is live, Susan."

"I'm very alive!"

We laugh together. Caroline clutches her stomach.

"You have to take care of yourself!" I say, not telling her my true worries: that this pregnancy could be the one that pushes her to a stroke, like our mother, who had her stroke weeks after my younger brother was born. I can't lose my sister.

"Don't worry about me. My blood pressure is fine. I'm not going to have a stroke," she says as if reading my mind. "I'm at the doctor twice a week." She breathes hard and sits down at the edge of her bed with great effort. Her stomach is twice the size of what it was with my nephew—or maybe my perception has changed. Maybe I didn't think she was so big then because I was so much bigger.

"You don't have to take care of everybody all the time," I say, knowing that she has just taken care of me, with her suit and advice.

"Go to bed early, get a lot of rest tonight," she says with a small smile. "Alan will go with you, okay? You'll be great. You look so thin."

"Really?" I say.

"Yes."

"What time do you have to be at the studio?"

"At 5:30 a.m."

The night before my live taping on *Good Morning America,* Hugh comes over to the hotel. We're planning to go out, but we never get any-where. We snack on no-salt, gluten-free rice crackers. Hugh's allergic to gluten. We talk. That's all. I watch his lips as he eats. I'm stretched out long and lean on the bed. He sits opposite me and snacks carefully, one cracker at a time. He's clearly in control. He doesn't even get crumbs on the bed. He doesn't leave until 1 a.m.

When he finally kisses me—and I had been hoping all night that he would kiss me, push me back on the bed, and make out like hot high school kids—he lands a soft kiss, safely and chastely, on my lips and leaves.

I'm too excited to sleep.

The phone rings. It's Hugh. "I just want you to know I kiss much better than that."

We talk for another hour while he drives back to Scarsdale.

T wo weeks later, it feels like our phone call still hasn't ended. I'm back in Durham. Hugh's 38th birthday is coming up. I put together a package of gluten-free goodies including brownies, birthday candles, matches, and (from the 99-cent store) streamers, a pin-the-tail-on-the-donkey game, prizes, a *Happy Birthday* hat, and a birthday horn. I don't hear from him for days. I think, *He's in the middle of his son's visit—maybe that's why he hasn't called.*

So I call him. Late in the evening, a day and a half later, he returns my call.

"Did you get my package?"

"It took me a few days to open it."

"Okay, so what do you think? Wasn't it fun?"

"Don't you think it was a little much? I mean, for someone you don't really know that well?"

"I don't think so," I say with an edge. "If I thought it was a little much, I wouldn't have sent it."

"So, what are your plans now?" he's switching subjects. "When are you coming back up?"

What do you mean? I think. *Are you an asshole? I want to hear that you like the package.* Now, I want to punch him, but at the same time, he's asking when he's going to see me again. He wants to see me again; that's all that matters.

"When would you like me to come up?" I say, calming down. *I can play it cool, too. I can do this Susan goes to Scarsdale, upper-crust thing. I'm a classy chick.* "Or maybe you'd like to come down to Durham?" I say coolly.

"Let's discuss it on Sunday."

"That's wonderful. Okay. Sunday."

We have a plan. Every relationship has its issues, but this is going to work out.

I go exercise. I run, pump, jump, flex, and stretch. I'm seeing Hugh again.

On Sunday morning, his name pops on my phone screen. "My new boyfriend is calling!" I say to the table and run off in the middle of a spoonful of shredded wheat and mandarin oranges.

"Hi!" I say, pacing in the Inspiration Room. "What a surprise to hear from you so early!"

"You know, I've really been thinking a lot about us, and I don't think it's going to work."

"What do you mean?"

"It doesn't seem like we have enough in common on the day-to-day stuff."

"What does that mean—'day-to-day stuff'?" my voice cracks.

"Look, Susan," he says. "I just don't think it's going to work."

I stop pacing. "You're breaking up with me, and you're not giving me a reason?"

"We don't have enough in common on the day-to-day things."

"You don't want to give me any specific reasons? You want me to just accept what you're saying?" I'm crying. He says nothing. I'm saying to myself: *This is just another test for myself. This guy is manipulative and controlling. This guy isn't right for me.*

I hear him take a deep breath and slowly let it out in one long, careful swoosh. He's controlling even his breathing.

"I wish you the best," I say and hang up. I delete his phone number from my phone. I'm definitely through with guys online. It is, in itself, an addiction.

But *Good Morning America*! My first time ever on American television! June 6, 2005. I arrive at 5:30 a.m. I'm so scared that I'll oversleep that I barely sleep after I say good night to Hugh at 2 a.m. I don't eat anything. I skip breakfast. I'm out of my routine again.

"Let's go into hair and makeup first," says the producer, who meets me at the entrance to the *GMA* studio in Times Square.

"I did my hair and makeup."

"We'll do it for you, honey," she says, crinkling her nose, guiding me back to the hair stylist.

In the makeup room, I see someone I know or at least recognize. He arrives with a mini-entourage, looking sleek and fit. Good thing I don't say, "Can I get a grill?" I almost think he's George Foreman. But then I realize he's Evander Holyfield, and he's gorgeous.

"Are you in a fight?" I ask.

"No," he says, and gives a smile. "I'm dancing."

"You're dancing? I don't think anyone is going to be looking at your fancy footwork with that incredible body." His posse lets out a major laugh, and I flash him my biggest and brightest Susan smile.

Before I know it, I'm up next. A stagehand adjusts my shirt and skirt. "Just look into the camera," she says with a warm smile. "And talk into the camera like you're talking to a friend."

Robin Roberts strides onto the set. She touches my back and says. "Come on, Susan, let's inspire people." I want to be her friend forever.

After the segment, I'm thanked, brought to the elevator, and shown out. It's over. I'm on the street. I go back to the hotel, planning to take a nap and wondering what I'm going to do about lunch and dinner. I down a decaf coffee and an orange juice, munch through an apple, and go to my room.

My phone rings continuously: my sister, my brother, one friend after another calling to say that they've seen me on TV. I hear from everyone but my father, so I call him.

"What channel was it on?" he says from his condo in Florida, sounding very far away.

"Didn't you see me?"

"I think I was watching the wrong station."

"So you didn't see me?"

"Nope."

"I'll send you a tape," I say, trying not to get too upset. *How could he miss me?*

"Okay, send me a tape. I'll watch that," he says with regret. Everyone else saw the segment; everyone is so excited for me.

I fly out that night.

A car arranged by *Good Morning America* picks me up at my hotel. I'm running late. I haven't eaten dinner. I ask the driver to stop at a grocery store to pick up a bag of no-salt tortilla chips. I say to myself, *I should be eating fruit, but I want something more comforting.*

Inside the store, all the checkout lines are long, and I'm so late. Every single person pushes a full shopping cart. I head for the shortest line, which snakes toward the back of the store.

I announce, "Would anybody mind if I just bought this one item?" I hurry to the front of the line. "I'm really late getting to the airport. Is that okay? Thanks. Thanks," I say nudging my way to the cashier.

Nobody minds except a fortysomething woman clutching a full plastic basket full of low-fat yogurt at the front of the line. She's one of those girls who you know works out just to meet a guy. "You know something? I mind," she exclaims.

"I'm really sorry. I'm late for a plane. I just have this one thing—" I say, undeterred.

"Doesn't look like you need those chips," she pronounces, one hand on her bony hip.

I turn to her, my anger flaring. I'm ready to give it to her. But somehow I recall what the senior doctor said once: *People who say hurtful things to others are hurting within themselves.*

And I hurt. I had just battled off 40 pounds and appeared on *Good Morning America*—even if my father had missed it—and what the world still saw was the chunky chick buying no-salt tortilla chips.

I glare at the woman, but what I say is, "My hope and prayer for you is that you find happiness sometime in your life."

I hand the checkout person my $3, take my change, and leave without looking back.

The driver and I split the tortilla chips in the bumper-to-bumper traffic to the airport. He's on high blood pressure medicine, I soon learn, so I use the drive to share with him what I've learned about low-sodium foods.

"These chips aren't so bad," he admits, and we arrive at the airport 45 minutes before my flight.

My flight is canceled due to a lightning storm. The airport is eerily empty, hot and airless. Most of the flights are canceled. I panic. I don't know what to do. I call my sister. She says she'll come pick me up, but to call the *Good Morning America* producer first and see whether she can help. The producer is wonderful, arranging for a car and another night at the Millennium as if it's the easiest thing in the world.

At the hotel, I check back in, and they put me back into the VIP section, in a beautiful room overlooking Times Square. Lightning flashes over the city. Rain threatens but doesn't fall. I hurry down to the street, on the prowl. It's late. The crowds from the Broadway shows are gone. Straggling couples dash across Times Square. Billboards flash, advertising coffee, soup, television, and Broadway shows. I don't know where to look. Asian street hawkers sketching one last portrait or selling one last souvenir photograph of the city close up for the night. High school kids lope down the streets in packs.

I want to eat, and it's not worth it. I want a bagel and butter. I want to eat, and it's not worth it. Can I find a no-salt bagel with no-salt butter? Does it even exist? I enter a 24-hour deli with cramped aisles and the smell of old coffee. Music from the Far East twangs on a scratchy radio. I start reading packages. *Is there a cookie with no salt, no calories?*

"It's not worth it," I say aloud. It's not.

Back in the hotel room, I have a normal-size bag of M&M's out of the minibar, but that's all, and go to bed.

I get on an 11 a.m. flight the next morning. It takes off without a problem. I'm relieved because I'm going back home—to the Clinic. I step on the scale the next day. I'm down a pound. I'll take that pound. I didn't gain anything being away for 5 days.

Chapter 22

I do what I think is impossible.

I wake up very early and eat breakfast early and alone and in studied silence. I make sure that no one speaks to me. It's my game day.

I arrive early at the Duke University football stadium, home of the Blue Devils, early on a perfect, cloudless day. Banners commemorate past glories, the Rose, Cotton, and Orange Bowl appearances; Rose Bowl was in 1942.

"Are you ready to do it?" asks Wes.

"I'm ready to do it," I say, tentatively. My legs quiver. I'm cold even though it's warm.

I never wanted to do it. It's such an overwhelming task to think of, like losing 300 pounds. I don't want to take the first step, and this time, it's a literal first step.

"Take it easy," Wes says, in his crisp white polo shirt and blue shorts.

I'm going to run the entire stadium, every single step.

start on aisle A at the pit of the stadium. I run. I don't stop. I don't stumble. I keep focused on Wes or the sky or the Carolina pines whispering, *Keep going, Susan.* To run is so good. I'm grateful I can run at all. And I'm on the way to fitting into that white thong bikini.

Wes stands at the top with a glass of water. Every time I get to the top of the stairs, he says, "Okay, focus, focus. When you get up to the top of the stairs, don't walk; *jog* to the next staircase. Get your breath back when you're going down the stairs. Don't walk down the stairs. Jog. Keep your legs moving. Thirty-two minutes and 30 seconds. You're doing it, Susan. You're done. 33 minutes. You did it."

I gave 100 percent, but Wes gave 150 percent to get me there. I know he's proud of me. He tells me.

Wes high-fives me. I want to cry, but I can't because I'm too happy. I'm absolutely elated. I almost feel invincible. I can do anything.

I'll do the entire stadium again a few weeks later. My best time is 27 minutes and 50 seconds, but nothing beats the sense of accomplishment the first time.

But today, I still have 30 minutes left of my workout with Wes. We pace around the entire stadium to cool down. Back in the training center, I work on weights. I'm on a high, and it has nothing to do with chicken wings.

I lie down on my back on the therapy table, just as I do at the end of every workout. Wes takes one of my legs and pushes it as far back as it will go, then pushes it to the side. He cuffs my leg in his arm and stretches my quadriceps. He flexes my leg. My body hurts, but today, it's a good hurt, it's an I-did-my-job-today hurt. More important, I can feel, really feel, my leg and my muscles stretch, reach, flex. I can *feel* inside; I can *feel* my body.

Exercise as My Job

- Exercise is my other job. This means that the responsibility and dedication I have for exercise is the same as I have for a job. I wish someone would pay me to exercise—I'd be rich! This is how I've come to the realization that I have to take exercise seriously.

- I need to have a trainer—if exercise is my job, I need a boss.

- When I say to myself, *I can't afford a trainer,* I remind myself, *Susan, you never had a problem dropping $300 to $400 a week in fast food. What are your priorities?*

  What else do I do when I say I can't afford a trainer? I won't buy that pair of shoes or pants. Or I'll get my hair cut for less. Or I'll find a trainer that works three or four people and costs less. Or I'll get friends together and form a group with one trainer. Or if I really can't find the money, I will find a workout partner. In Durham, I exercised with a trainer three times a week. I now exercise once a week with a trainer.

- I visualize my body where I want it to be. I envision Jennifer Lopez. I love her curvy, sexy-mama body. White thong bikini, here I come!

- I have learned to readjust my goals as I go along on this journey. As I lose weight, it becomes harder, not easier, to reach my goal. The weight comes off more slowly, not more quickly, for me, and the last 40 pounds is the hardest. Let's be real: Those last 40 pounds are an absolute bitch! But more about that later.

- Be realistic. Not every hour in the gym, walk, or bike ride needs to be "perfect." Even now, there are days when I don't want to move or walk or ride my bike. I don't want to go to the gym. But I don't do what I used to do; I don't sit in my parked car outside the gym and count that as "going" to the gym. I bike for a mile. I go to the gym for half an hour. I move.

- *I have to be in my body.* This is the most important aspect of exercising for me. When I was almost 500 pounds, why did I feel like I wasn't "that heavy"? Certainly, I didn't think I was obese. Why? I made the least effort possible. I didn't feel fat because I didn't move the fat. I didn't feel *in* my body.

It's not an option not to go to work for me. I wasn't born rich. I always kid my father that he "forgot" to give my siblings or me a trust fund. I had the good fortune to be born into a family that valued education and hard work. I was born healthy and strong. It's my "job" to keep that pact with myself and with my Creator to work at getting myself healthy again—and at keeping myself that way.

At the end of the day, I remind myself: *I have one life to live. How do I choose to live it?*

I'm caught in the vortex of news about obesity in America. After the *New York Times* article and *Good Morning America,* I did interviews with a Danish newspaper, an Italian magazine, and a South Korean television show. I was on German television twice. The doctor asks me to be part of a two-person debate on diets—specifically, the high-protein/low-carb regimen of Atkins versus the high-healthy-carb/low-fat regimen of the Clinic—before about 80 first-year medical students at Duke University. I've never spoken before a professional crowd. I'm nervous, but I go because the doctor asks me to go.

Among the many questions I'm asked is one about my choice of a restricted-calorie diet as opposed to surgery. Here, I veer off into one of my monologue subjects: doctors. How little time and focus doctors have for a patient. My Long Island internist said he was making an appointment for me to have a gastric bypass while running out the door to see another patient—without asking me whether I was in therapy, whether I had tried diets, or what the hell else was going on in my life. He didn't ask me much of anything in the 5 minutes I spent with him.

The moderator intercedes. "Let's not turn off these students from medicine before the end of their first year."

High-healthy-carb/low-fat/low-sodium comes out on top of this debate. But more exciting than that is the students' curiosity afterward. An entire group of students approaches me with more questions.

How was it that I was able to gain 300 pounds? What made me want to lose it? Why come down to Durham? Why couldn't I do it on my own? What made me want to make those changes? What do I think should change in the American diet?

"I only know what worked for me," I say. I laugh at all the attention. I wish I had all the answers. I'm not an expert on the American diet or on obesity. I know what I've learned about healthy eating. I know what I've learned about overeating—and most of my eating has little to do with food and more with how I feel about myself.

"What would you have liked your doctor to ask you?" asks one fresh-faced student, who looks about 12.

"I would have wanted him to sit down with me, look me in the eye, and ask me what was going on. Talk to me. Ask me how I felt physically and emotionally. I deserve to be treated like I'm a person, even though I'm fat."

An hour later, we're still chatting. If these students are at all representative of the next generation of doctors, I have some hope.

Twice, Wes asks me to speak before his adult continuing education classes at Duke University. I'm "on" all the time, and I like it. It helps me to talk after years of lies and shame.

I'm also in the middle of my course on the psychology of education when I'm given an assignment to write a motivational paper based on a poem or song or story.

Here's part of it:

> *1968 was an interesting year for most. President Lyndon Johnson delivered the State of the Union Address. Martin Luther King, Jr., led a march in Memphis, which turned violent. The 10,000th United States airplane was lost over Vietnam. Andy Warhol was shot in New York City, by Valerie Solanis, a struggling actress, and Louise Blech had a debilitating aneurysm that left her brain-damaged and paralyzed for the next 37 years and counting. She left behind a husband and four children, all one year apart—the youngest a few weeks old, the oldest four. I was her third.*
>
> *I remember being 12 years old and the excitement I used to have when my father would say to us on a bright, sunny Sunday, "We're going to see your mother today." I used to spend the morning making lunch for us and for her. Always Italian food, always homemade, and always yummy. Today, we're going to be a family, I thought. We all piled into the yellow station wagon, which*

smelled from orange rinds left by my father 2 days before. We were off. I didn't know which highway we took or how long it took to get there, but I knew it was Exit 13. I used to count from Exit 6, "Only seven more exits to go!" My heart would be racing.

In my mind, my mother never "lived" anywhere. She didn't have a house or an apartment or even a street I could refer to. It was always "my mother's hospital." As we walked up the outside staircase at the Hudson River State Psychiatric Hospital—Ross Pavilion—I started to breathe only through my mouth because the smell of the urine mixed with Clorox was so offensive that the stench penetrated the glass doors in the open air. We could smell the odor 3 feet before the entrance.

There she was in her chair, a chair that was a bed on wheels so my mother's limp body could collapse onto the sticky vinyl. We all ran over and hugged and kissed her. She was disheveled and smelled like urine. She had most of her teeth but not all. Her hair was matted as if it hadn't been brushed in weeks or months. She didn't have roundness to her limbs. Instead, her unmoving left arm and legs looked flat from the atrophy of her muscles. Her skin was pasty white and very dry and scaly. She looked at us with cloudy, unfocused, hazy eyes, and smiled and said hello. She didn't really know who we were. The doctors made sure to dispense as much Haldol, lithium, and a cocktail of other psychotic drugs, which are usually dispensed for severe mental illness, so that she would be easy to handle.

We usually spent a few hours there. We ate, and one of us would try to feed my mother the food we had brought. I always wondered if she could taste how good it was. Always on the drive home, I would ask my father, "Daddy, what happened to Mommy? Why can't she come home?"

Always the same answer, "Your mother is sick. She can't come home."

I knew not to ask any more questions.

My mother was once beautiful. She was tall, 5 foot 9, curvy, with striking high cheekbones, full lips, and beautiful, clear, milky white skin. My mother should never have been in a state psychiatric hospital. But there wasn't any money or resources to have her anywhere else. My father had four kids, so this is where she stayed for a long time.

In the late '80s, thanks to New York State, the pavilion where my mother was housed was closed, and she was sent to a private nursing home in Connecticut. The doctors there were appalled at the shopping list of narcotics my mother was taking. When I saw her for the first time at this nursing home, she was sitting up, in a standard-size wheelchair, with makeup, a dime store necklace and earrings, her hair combed and cut, and smiling, eyes amazingly clear and focused. She recognized me.

I fainted on the floor right in front of her. Seven years later, my sister and I moved her to a nursing home in Long Beach, 5 minutes from my apartment.

I saw my mother sleep for the first time on September 14, 1995. I had never been able to visit at her bedtime. I held her hand at her bed. But before she closed her eyes, she told me she loved me. She slept, and I watched her, and cried. I was 30 years old, I wanted my mother to come home, and I knew she never would.

Over the next 8 years, I began to deal with the "loss" of my mother. I spent 4 years in psychotherapy, twice a week, rarely missing a session. The emotional pain was horrific. I cried enough tears for a lifetime. And I ate through the pain.

By November 23, 2003, I was 468.1 pounds. I had been athletic throughout school. I was involved in the sport of body-building from age 19 to age 30. But the scales didn't lie. I was 468.1 pounds. I was scared out of my mind.

It took every ounce of energy, courage, and bravery that I had to shove aside my fears, panic, and terror and move from New York to Durham, North Carolina—alone—with my life savings in my pocket and the sheer determination to change my life. I left my family and friends, left my mother, to whom I was the primary caregiver by now, packed my car, and left. I had no idea if what I was doing was going to work.

Each day that I was at the Clinic, I would look at a poem my friend had given me, which gave me hope and strength at times when I didn't think I had any left. This poem gives me the power to trust in myself and hold on tight. I keep this poem on my night table and look at it daily to reaffirm that I will be okay, as long as I believe in me. The poem I choose was given to me by Laurie. It reads:

> *The jump*
> *is*
> *so*
> *frightening between*
> *where I am*
> *and*
> *where I want to be. . . .*
> *because of all I may become*
> *I will close my eyes and*
> *leap.*
>
> *—Anonymous*

My hopes and dreams are bright now. I have surpassed what I thought was capable. I've lost over 220 pounds in 21 months. I'm going strong.

I recently took a 45-minute train ride from New York City to Long Beach to see my mother. My sister was meeting me there with her family. It was my job to bring my mother downstairs to the backyard of the nursing home, where my sister had set up a nice lunch. Italian food, of course. My heart raced the same way it always did when I knew seeing my mother was seconds away. The elevator doors opened and my mother was sitting in her wheelchair watching some TV show. I ran over to her, just like I always did, and gave her a big kiss and hug.

"Going outside?" she said.

"Of course, we're going outside," I said with a big, toothy smile.

As I pushed her down the hall and into the elevator, I said to her, "Guess who's downstairs waiting for you?"

She turned her face up to me and said hopefully, "Susan?"

I just stared into space for a moment and tears automatically streamed down my face. "Yes. Susan. She can't wait to see you."

Everyone had to read his or her essay aloud. I didn't know what to expect. I haven't shared my story with many people. And the story about my childhood, my weight, my mother, and how it's all wrapped together— or, more precisely, tangled like a ball of twine—was particularly difficult to share with strangers. I felt so exposed. I never wanted people to know the real me. The real me was a kid without a real mother. The real me was someone who ate because that kid was still inside, angry and alone and hurting.

By the end of the essay, most of the class was crying.

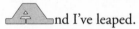nd I've leaped.

I also aced the class.

Chapter 23

My little brother is getting married, and I need to buy a dress. I haven't bought a dress in years.

Besides the bridesmaid dress for Marcy's wedding (remember? I had to buy two size-16 dresses and have them sewn together), the very last dress I bought was for a business associate's wedding. That dress was custom made even though I wasn't a bridesmaid. I was just huge—a size 34. I hid myself in that long tan dress, with its high neck and long sleeves and equally long matching jacket with dull sequins. Every part of my skin was covered. I could have been one of those Afghan women in a full veil and looked more appealing. I couldn't fit into pantyhose. I had to wear biker shorts underneath that dress so my thighs wouldn't rub raw together, so I could walk. I sat off to the side, where I hoped no one could see me.

My brother's wedding is set for July 23 in Atlanta. A luau theme.

But I have no money for a new, tropical-themed outfit. My car is

268

sputtering with more than 190,000 miles on it. I'm going to have to fly, and buy a present. And I'm going to have to wear pantyhose. Not only have I not bought or worn a skirt or dress in years, I also haven't worn pantyhose.

On the clearance rack, I find a dress: sleeveless and V-necked and form-fitting. Light pink, cream, and white flowers streak across the silk, and it's the right length—below my knees—to hide the fat I can't seem to lose around my knees. Plus, it's only $10! It makes me look like I've stepped from the set of an exotic James Bond movie. Size 20 is a little too big, but I think it's better to tailor, and at $10, I can afford to have it really be perfect.

But the tailor screws up—he ruins the material—and it's the day before the wedding. I hurry back to the store. On the rack, there's only one size left, an 18. I pull it over my head. I don't care who's looking at me get dressed. I'm moving as fast as I can. It fits! Perfectly. I'm 40 years old, single, going to my little brother's second wedding, and, like a miracle, a size 18 fits.

The wedding is held at the clubhouse in David and Cindy's apartment complex. My brother's co-worker leads the ceremony. This young, energetic, black Christian preacher sways in front of old Jews from Florida, my family; Cindy's family from Ohio; and the bride and groom's raucous friends. Everyone is thrilled to see David and Cindy married.

"That was a nice ceremony," my father announces. "Short." He stands up, ready to go to the buffet. He's in the middle between Mark and me.

Mark and I are barely talking.

"Good, Pop, because that's the last wedding you're going to go to," says Mark. His comment is directed at me. My brother may be 41 years old, more than 6 feet tall, built like a linebacker, and an incredible artist, but he can be a mean 10-year-old in a moment. This was a continuation of the fight we had had that kept him from coming to my birthday celebration. It was a test.

I say nothing. He knows I heard it. He meant for me to hear and to be hurt. He doesn't think I'm ever going to get married.

But nobody is going to beat me back. In the past, a remark like this would have sent me reeling to the buffet. All I think is: *This is just another little test. You, Susan, are going to win.*

I've brought a cooler with my own food to the wedding: pasta, fruit, and broccoli, and extra just in case I'm tempted. I drink only water. Everyone else eats plates of barbecued chicken and ribs. I skim past the hors d'oeuvres. Although they look good, though I could sneak one grilled chicken kebab, though no one would say anything if I ate one, I don't.

I came here in a size 18 dress, and I'm going home in a size 18 dress.

I dance with everyone: with my father, who comes from the generation that knows how to dance. He tells me not to look at my feet, to look at him and follow him, and I do. I'm dancing the way I always imagined my mother dancing with him. But I don't say this, because I don't want a sad thought coming between us. His fingers know how to swing me out and back. His feet keep the beat. I'm full of grace.

I don't want the song to end. But when he's done, he's had enough. If Caroline was there, she'd have him dance with her, too, but she's not. She's 9 months pregnant. My father sits. I see him watching me carefully, and I think, *Does he see my mother in me tonight?*

We do the Electric Slide, with nobody going in the right direction. I slow dance with David and give him back to his beautiful new wife. I dance with David's best friend from college. He's really cute in that shaggy dog, never-quite-grew-up way. We dance together until my updo becomes a down-do. It's July in Atlanta and hot and humid, and the air conditioner in the clubhouse sputters warm air. A few of the men try to fix it, but the sun's going down, and isn't it getting a bit cooler? The sweat slides down my bare arms. I feel my body move.

Chapter 24

We ate. On Sundays—not every Sunday, but often—my father would announce that he had a certain yen for something. He'd say it just like that—"I have a yen for—" and we'd be off.

Sometimes, it meant an adventure: a trip to Chinatown and a search down the narrowest of streets until we'd find the most packed slip of a Chinese restaurant. All five of us would tumble in. He'd order the dishes and we'd share—whatever sounded strange or exotic, prawns or dumplings, with urgings of "let's try something new." Everything, including tip, under $20 or so for all of us.

But more often, my father would announce that he was cooking. He'd have a "yen" for a roast, or a stew, or for his famous noodle pudding. My father loved his own noodle pudding. He always used the same long, clear glass pan—I always think of it as the noodle pudding pan. My father sold pots and pans, but ours were all old—originals from the first few years of his marriage to my mother, battered, blackened, and scraped. We were the shoemaker's children without shoes, the gourmet cookware purveyor's family without any nice pots and pans.

He'd take charge of the kitchen. "The raisins have to be soaked first!" "How much should we make?" "Heat the oven!" "Do we have enough honey?" Sticky, stuck jars of honey were pulled out. We always had half a dozen half-empty jars of honey in our house. He'd pull out the butter, applesauce, and honey, gripping the stainless steel bowl in the crook of his strong freckled arms. "Boil the water!" "Add the noodles!" "What time is it?" he'd demand, as if we were suddenly in a hurry, even if it was Sunday and it wasn't even noon yet. *He* was in a hurry. We had noodle pudding to make and eat.

He'd spoon the mixture into the glass pan and center it on the oven rack. The smell of cinnamon and honey would encircle the house from the kitchen, sweet, enveloping, into the dining room and living room and back around into the kitchen. The windows would fog. Gray and cloudy days or rainy or snowy days—those were the days when he'd cook noodle pudding.

We'd watch old black-and-white movies. Our house was still fighting World War II. I'd snuggle on my father's lap, my brothers at his feet and my sister on the side of his chair, and watch the Americans win. During the commercials, we'd all jump on him. He'd tickle us. He'd put all four of us on his back and ride us around the house. He couldn't sit for long either.

Finally, after about 45 or 50 minutes, the noodle pudding would be ready, maybe a noodle or two burnt on the outside. "Caroline! Mark! Susan! David! Who's hungry?" We didn't let it cool. "Be careful. Don't burn yourself." "Smell that! Just smell that!" He'd cut it straight away into perfect squares for us that held together until we tore into it. "Get plates. This is the best noodle pudding we ever made!" He was right. Nothing has ever tasted as good.

Here's how my father makes his famous noodle pudding, though I've modified it to eliminate the salt. First, you've got to have a pan. If you still have an old Pyrex pan somewhere, use that.

MORRIS BLECH'S FAMILY NOODLE PUDDING

Traditionally, Jewish people eat this as a side dish and call it kugel. Is this the most low-fat dish in the world? Of course it isn't. It can easily be made sodium-free, so that's a plus. And it's a dish with memories.

1 pound broad egg noodles
1 cup raisins
½ cup butter (unsalted is okay, although my father would never use it)
1 jar (8 ounces) applesauce with no sugar or salt (double-check the ingredients)
½ cup honey
4 eggs
1 teaspoon pure vanilla extract

1 Cook the noodles according to package directions. Do not add salt to the water. While the noodles are cooking, soak the raisins in water to soften.

2 Preheat oven to 350°F. In a large bowl, mix the cooked noodles and the butter, applesauce, honey, eggs, drained raisins, and vanilla extract.

3 Pour mixture into a greased 9" × 13" glass baking dish.

4 Bake for about 50 minutes, or until the top is slightly brown.

5 Serve hot or cold with salad or vegetables.

Chapter 25

Shelton flies me to New York.

First, I dawdle with Shelton on the phone for 2 weeks after "meeting" him online. He lives in Brooklyn. He wants to fly me up. No one has ever offered to pay for an airline ticket for me anywhere. I hesitate. But after David's wedding, I'm even more broke, if that's possible, though I'm now a shrinking size 18.

If he had asked me to come up any other weekend, I would have said no. But Caroline is having her scheduled C-section on August 12. Shelton doesn't know this, of course. He thinks I'm coming to see him. A part of me is flattered by the invitation. We seem to have so much in common, but I can't tell you what. We talk for hours on the phone beforehand, but I don't remember any of it. He's Jewish. I feel safe saying yes to the airline ticket; it's almost like an expensive dinner, and he won't be bringing me out to eat, so it all works out in my head.

He says he'll pick me up at the airport on an early Friday afternoon. I can't find him in the airport. No one looks like him.

"Susan!" a scratchy nasal voice calls to me—a voice that I recognize but is attached to someone who looks nothing like his online picture. His nose is too sharp and takes over his face. He's wearing designer pants from the '80s and a Members Only jacket, with his hair parted in the middle. He's too young to have had these clothes in the '80s, so that means he either has an older brother and he's wearing his clothes, or he thinks this is a cool look.

Worse, he's thinner than his picture. His wrists are bony. His Adam's apple wobbles. He's worse than thin. He's skinny, and I don't do skinny. He has the same eyes as his photo: big, blue, long-lashed, bedroom eyes. He stares at me intently. He doesn't kiss me hello. He takes a step back and says my name again as if hoping he has the wrong person. I'm not what he expected either.

He shares an apartment on a busy street with a roommate. He didn't tell me about the roommate. I'm 40 years old and he's 30 going on 18 with a roommate.

The apartment is claustrophobically decorated with oversize oil paintings in ornate gold frames, two or three to a wall throughout the living room and dining room. Most are portraits of stern people, unforgiving in their stares. The blinds are all drawn.

"Who are these people?"

"All dead. And worth a lot of money."

His business is growing, and he's going to be rich someday, and why is he telling me this? I'm not what he expects. I'm in the dark with an '80s freak and the painted and the dead.

I want to leave.

But I'm supposed to stay the weekend at his place, in his extra bedroom. Caroline doesn't know I've flown up. I didn't tell any of my friends I was coming up. I want everyone to think I'm focused on losing weight, not on guys.

And I want to surprise my sister. She had my niece this morning: 9 pounds, 10 ounces. *Isn't that a big baby?* But I push the thought out of my head. She's healthy. My sister is healthy. *But isn't that a big baby?*

"That's a really big baby," says Shelton, after I voice my concerns in order to change the conversation from him and his investments. "Is it something that runs in your family?"

"No."

"How much did you weigh when you were born?" he asks.

"I don't know."

"What do you mean, you don't know?"

"I don't have anyone to ask. My father says he doesn't remember, and I've told you about my mother—"

"That's right," he says. Now it's his turn to change the subject. "I just want to make sure it's not genetic—"

"No, Shelton. Her son, my nephew, was only 7¼ pounds when he was born. I may not know how much I weighed when I was born, but I wasn't born fat, okay? Can we talk about something else, please?"

"Sure, but first I have to just check my e-mail."

I don't believe this is happening.

He disappears into another dark room. I fall asleep in his bed—alone. I'm so weary of all my stupid mistakes with guys, and Shelton is definitely a mistake. At 2 a.m., I'm searching the house for him. I want to leave. But I'm trapped. I don't have enough money for a cab. I don't even know what cab company to call and where it could take me.

I call Marcy and desperately explain that I'm in Brooklyn, and I need her help. I need to her save me. "You've got to pick me up."

"Now?" she says.

"Okay, first thing in the morning."

"Sue—"

"Just come." I give her the address.

I open up the refrigerator, which is packed with food, grimy, perspiring, groaning, and crackling. Packages of precooked meals, frozen bagels, hot dogs, and half-eaten store-bought chickens drizzled in salt crowd the shelves. I don't want any of his food. I need to store my pasta, which I packed for the weekend, but there's no room in his refrigerator.

I'm chilled from the freezer air. The pasta containers shove into the produce drawer. A cold sore puffs out on my lips. I want out of here, but now it's the middle of the night. I'm ashamed that I'm in the kitchen, mesmerized by all the food. I slam the refrigerator door shut.

Shelton is in the bedroom adjacent to the one where I had been sleeping. I kneel beside the bed, covering my cold sore with my palm. He opens his eyes.

"This kind of sucks," I say.

"Yeah, whatever," he says sleepily.

"I'm really kind of nervous here, Shelton."

"Why are you nervous?" he says, looking at me sideways.

"I'm in a strange person's house. You're not making me comfortable."

"Yeah?" His eyes don't blink. He stares at me intensely as if full of meaning, but I know what he's full of, and it isn't big thoughts.

"Do you want to sleep with me—in the other room?" I know this is a come-on, but it's the middle of the night, I'm in this guy's house, and I don't want to be alone.

"Yeah."

Between the bedrooms, the portraits glare at us. Outside it sounds like drag racing. *I could stop a car,* I think. *I could call a cab, even at this time*

of night. I could go to Laurie's or to my sister's, even though she's in the hospital. I could leave now, but I don't.

He has a humongous bed, red velvet cover, silk sheets and matching heavy gold and red velvet curtains, a total mojo sex bedroom.

Cars screech outside. I slide around the silk sheets and realize that they are polyester. The room is pitch black, but not dark enough for me. I won't take off my clothes. I don't trust him. He doesn't make an effort to even try to convince me.

He rubs his hands through my hair. His knuckles grind on my skull. He doesn't kiss me. He gives me a meaningful wide-eyed stare. He thinks he knows me, but he doesn't and never will.

I give him a hand job just because.

I feel like a prostitute.

In the morning, I tell Shelton that my friend, my oldest friend—tall, smart, a fun, fabulous girl—is coming to pick me up.

I want him to know that I have a great-looking girlfriend coming, because I want him to know that I'm the type of girl who hangs out with other cool girls. I don't want him to think I'm the fat girl with fat friends.

He nods his head, leans back on the bed, and goes back to sleep.

Marcy arrives by 10 a.m. She drives all the way from Westchester. I'm so relieved to see her that I run out onto the front steps with my bag. "Thank God you're here. Come in, meet Shelton, and then let's leave. I really want to surprise Caroline this morning."

She steps into the house. She's wearing tight workout pants and a cut-off top. Her black hair swings down around her shoulders. She smiles at Shelton, who has just showered.

"I want to go," I whisper, pulling her arm.

"We're going," she says, not going.

"Let me make coffee first," he says, smiling back at her.

So we sit on his cheap fake leather couches under the portraits of scowling dead people.

We drink bad coffee. His roommate joins us. He's GQ slick, a hair-gelled-back-before-noon kind of guy. The lies people tell—that's what we talk about—along with online dating, older women and younger men. Perfect brunch conversation, except there's no food but boxes of sugared cereal and acidic coffee.

"I know. In general, in my opinion, a 30-year-old guy would never want a long-term relationship with a 40-year-old woman. They both do it for one thing," says Shelton. "What do you think, Marcy?"

"You knew that I was 40," I say. I won't be invisible.

"Did I?"

"You were the one who spent the $400 flying me up. I didn't take out my credit card. What was that about?" I laugh, trying to keep it light.

"I thought we had a lot in common," he laughs back, adjusting his knobby, hairy knees protruding from an extra-tight pair of gym shorts, and giving Marcy a conspiratorial smile that Marcy, to my great surprise, returns.

"Obviously, both of us were disappointed in person with each other, Shelton."

"You look exactly like your picture," his roommate says, also looking at Marcy. The two guys duel for her attention. "But in person you look very strong."

"What's wrong with that?" I love looking strong.

"You're not a small girl; you're *strong*," he says, snidely looking at his friend. *He's calling me fat without calling me fat; I know it.*

He repeats it, "Really strong."

"What does that mean?" I say.

"Strong. I'll leave it at that," he says to Marcy as if they are sharing a secret, and Shelton joins in, and they all three laugh. I could kill Marcy.

"You look nothing like your picture, Shelton."

"What does that mean?" he says, indignant.

"You were bulked up in your picture."

"I had football padding on."

"What does that mean?"

"Football, the sport. I play touch football. I was wearing a football jersey. Didn't you notice?"

"Everybody lies online, Sue," says Marcy.

"I never lie," Shelton says, laughing and lying. He gives Marcy one of his trademark big-blue-eyed looks, deep into her eyes. He's lying on the pleather.

"Marcy, when are we leaving?"

"Sue, wait, wait, wait. I just want to finish this conversation." Marcy stares back at Shelton, wide-eyed, like she likes him. But I know her too well. She's just playing him, and me.

"Marcy, either we're going to leave now, or I'm going to take a cab to the hospital," I say and get up.

"Okay, in a minute, Sue."

I try to be cool. I really do appreciate Marcy coming out to pick me up. I give her the "let's go" look. I give her the "these guys are losers" look. She ignores me. When that doesn't work, I nudge her side and hit her leg and send her mental telepathy signals that it's time to leave as she and Shelton compare notes on the New York dating scene. Neither of them can meet anyone, and they can't figure out exactly why.

Four hours go by.

Finally, I stand up. "I want to leave, Marcy. I want to go see my sister."

Shelton stretches. "You don't really have to go, Marcy?"

"We have to, Shelton," says Marcy.

I wave good riddance to the dead people on the wall.

When we reach the hospital, I leave Marcy in the car and totally surprise Caroline.

"I can't believe you're here, sister!" Caroline says, half sitting up in the high hospital bed, cradling the baby.

"How could I miss seeing my baby niece?" I say, avoiding how I flew up to New York.

Caroline is in her hospital bed, holding this tiny, red-faced, wailing baby with all this brown hair matted on her round head—her baby girl, my niece, a joy and a wonder. She hurts from the C-section. I push away the thought that my sister looks like my mother in the hospital bed because she doesn't look like my mother—she looks like her, and so happy with the baby in her arms.

"Let me hold her."

Reluctantly, she hands me the baby wrapped tight in her striped newborn blanket. I don't want to give her back. I open up her hands; they wave free, 10 fingers. She's beautiful. She looks straight at me and squints as if recognizing me.

"She's a big baby, isn't she?" I say, and want to take the words back immediately.

"She's perfect."

"That's what the doctors think about her weight?" I say carefully. I don't want to upset my sister. I don't even know why I'm mentioning this.

"Don't go there, Susan. I'm not thinking about my daughter's weight when she's 1 day old."

"You're right," I say. *What am I doing? Stop it!* Though I also think, *Aunt Susan will make sure she's into sports early.* I can't help it. "She's perfect," I whisper, cradling her close, seeing how strong she is as she takes my finger.

"Give her back to me."

"Let me hold her."

Caroline has to pry the baby from me.

Chapter 26

I've come out. I'm telling everyone that I know: I want to find the guy who will be forever, and I want to have him by the end of the year. I will be at my goal weight by then. I'm a girl with a plan. I want a normal life when I leave Durham.

At the end of August, I'm off to a singles weekend at a hotel in Fort Lauderdale. It's not South Beach chic; it's more Bridget Jones meets the Catskills. My father is pressuring me to move to Florida after I'm ready to leave Durham, so I've been following up with guys from Florida I've found online.

I bargain with myself: *If I meet someone in Florida, someone I could marry, maybe I will move to Florida.* I get there on Thursday night, and I know I'm going to meet Adam, whom I've been e-mailing and talking with, and whom I'm hooking up with because we have *so much in common.* Actually, I know I don't have much in common with him, except that he's single and Jewish. He's 35, not completely bald yet, and he has straight perfect white teeth.

I wear a tight pink top with black Capri pants and a pair of little black high heels. He opens the door to his rented convertible for me. I'm stepping into a movie—cute guy, great car, and the babe—and in a moment of it-can't-be-me realization, I'm the babe.

"I've made reservations at the *best* steak house. Let's go. Let's go," he says, swerving the car out into the street and grinning at me.

"I don't eat meat and I don't eat salt. Everything else I eat," I say. In an instant, I know I'm being much too serious.

"Why?"

"I just lost a lot of weight."

"How much is a lot?"

"Is 250 pounds a lot?" I say.

"Wow," he looks at me sideways. He drives fast. I smile. My hair flies out, tangles. I swipe strands from my eyes. I'm laughing. How do they keep their hair looking so great in the movies?

"I'm going to take care of it." He calls the restaurant, acting like the big man, all in charge, a *macha,* if you know that word, making sure that I can eat a low-sodium vegetarian meal, and I kind of like it.

I eat a baked potato and sautéed vegetables. He has two drinks, stuffed mushrooms as an appetizer, and a steak for his main course. We share a fruit and sorbet platter for dessert.

After dinner, we stroll around the hotel grounds.

"You're so beautiful," he says.

I look at him. The moon reflects off his bald spot. *Did he just say I was beautiful?*

"I'd love for you to come upstairs," he says.

I lean against his car and he leans into me.

"Come upstairs with me," he repeats.

I demur, thinking hard-to-get is the better way with him. "I don't think so," I say, easing away. "It's getting late." I'm sure we're going to spend the weekend getting to know each other.

Adam ignores me for the rest of the weekend.

I had brought my own food, but the singles weekend has enough food to feed a small refugee camp. There's breakfast, snack, lunch, and tea, and, in between, there's hooking up, sex, and seminars on being single and Jewish, as if anyone needed a seminar on that.

Here's a recipe for one of the dishes I often bring with me on overnight trips. I pack the pasta in plastic containers that each hold approximately $1\frac{1}{2}$ cups. I stuff everything in a freezer lunch bag with those blue ice freezer blocks stacked around it. The pasta keeps nicely for 2 to 3 days.

SUSAN'S ORIENTAL VEGETABLE SPAGHETTI FOR ONE

2 ounces angel-hair pasta or regular spaghetti
1 teaspoon toasted sesame oil
¼ cup chopped Spanish onion
1 teaspoon grated fresh ginger
1½ cups frozen oriental mixed vegetables
1 teaspoon rice vinegar (Make sure it's zero sodium!)
Powdered ginger to taste
Ground black pepper to taste

1 Make the pasta according to package directions. Do not add salt to the water.

2 In a frying pan over medium heat, heat the oil with the onion and ginger. Sauté until brown.

3 Add the frozen vegetables and stir-fry until tender, about 5 to 10 minutes.

4 Drain the pasta and add to the vegetables.

5 Add the rice vinegar, ginger, and pepper to taste.

met Leo online before deciding to come to the event this weekend. *We have so much in common.* He meets me at the hotel, though he's not attending the singles weekend. He follows me through the hotel lobby, a 5-foot 6-inch puppy. He has that Mr. Brady, Jew-fro hair. He's wearing a polyester maroon shirt, and he's critical of everyone else at the singles weekend.

I agree to go, but I ask the third guy of the weekend—Dylan—to give me a "save" call and pretend to be a girlfriend in distress. When he does it, I stretch up on my tiptoes and kiss Mr. Brady good-bye on the cheek. I check out of singles weekend and meet up with Dylan. He's very goofy. A cutie. He lives near my father. He owns his own house. *We have so much in common.*

I wear the same pink shirt and black Capri pants to meet him. I've added a pink denim jacket. I think maybe this third guy will be The One.

What's big about him is his giant projector screen; it's the centerpiece of his house. He has an immaculate house and no roommate. A DVD of Elton John songs plays. We're singing and laughing. I close my eyes. I sway my hips. I'm loose and tight at the same time. I don't want to see him looking at me, but he takes my arm and dances along.

He's chosen a movie from Blockbuster: *Ladder 49.* His mother calls.

He asks if I'll say hello to his mother. I do. I love that. I whisper, "Should I tell her we're making out?"

"We aren't—yet," Dylan laughs, and I'm charming with his mother.

He folds his arms around me. His kiss is fun and light, and soon we're making out like teenagers. He leads me into the bedroom. He's goofy and long-limbed and grabbing at me.

I go happily, thinking that we'll kiss and cuddle and that's it. But I'm so into him and the night.

No one has seen me naked in 6 years. He unsnaps my bra. My boobs are down to my knees. He pulls my pants off. My skin flaps down off my thighs.

The lights are off, but it's summer so it's still light enough. He has a double king bed, a huge bed. He's cuddling and hugging, lean, slightly taller than me, smiling, stroking my hair. I don't want to touch him because I don't want to encourage him. Yet all I want to do is to feel him.

My stomach. Oh my God. My pants are coming off. My stomach is hanging down to my knees. Is he going to think that my stomach is gross? It is gross. I'm wearing French-cut black nylon underwear. I try to cover my stomach. Every stretch mark on my body is part of my drama and trauma.

I'm glad I'm lying flat on my back. I try twisting my legs to the side to hide my thighs. I feel so naked. I don't want him to touch me. I don't lie sideways. All the skin from my stomach flops to the left or the right if I turn that way. I cover my stomach with my hands. I'm glad my nails look good.

Dylan takes off his clothes confidently and smoothly and flings them to the end of the bed. He has a broad chest, muscled legs, and curly chest hair I could play with all night. He leans back, grinning, all ready, and I am too. I'm going to do it. I'm going to have sex for the first time in 6 years—and what do I finally touch?

The world's absolutely smallest penis, a smidgeon of a penis, a speck. I wait for more. But that's all.

I can't believe it.

Dylan holds his arms out to me. He tells me I'm wonderful. He wants me to come to him.

But I'm not ready to have sex with him. I can't. I can't even see what I'm supposed to have sex with. It's like chocolate. If I'm going to eat chocolate, I want really good, really satisfying dark, rich (no sodium!) chocolate. I don't want a candy bar from the drugstore. That won't do it for me.

"Why don't you go on top?" he urges.

There's no way I can go on top. Not with The Stomach.

He reaches toward me, and I playfully sidle away. I don't want him to touch my stomach. I'm sure he's looking at my stomach because he looks so quickly away. I move closer to him, I distract him by playing with his chest hair. He can touch my back. I don't have back fat anymore. I have a normal back with shoulders and bones and the line of a spine. If I curve toward him, press against his side, I can hide the hanging heaps of skin almost completely. I give him the world's quickest hand job.

Chapter 27

"Why don't you focus on losing weight right now, Susan, instead of trying to find Mr. Right?" asks my exasperated sister. "Why don't you focus on you?"

I'm in the car. I don't tell her anything about my disastrous Florida weekend except that I had a few dates. I'm never moving to Florida. I'm back in Durham and driving past Murderer's Row. I'm going to keep driving. I grip the steering wheel. I should have taken another route.

"I want to be married."

"You know you could marry the wrong guy. That would be worse." She's been married for 20 years. She still holds her husband's hand. She doesn't know anything about dating. The smell of meat grilling dizzies me. *The Cookout.* Shakes. Onion rings. Fries with cheese. Grilled meat smells pumped into the air. *Keep driving,* I say to myself. The North Carolina pines bow ever so slightly in the breeze, but the winds only carries the Cookout aromas to me, personally to me.

"I know," I say. I wish she weren't so negative. The baby cries in the background. Caroline seems distracted. I'm distracted, too.

"I'm going to get off-line." I know I won't, I haven't yet, but this sounds like a good thing to say.

"Good."

I close my window, but it's as if the smells are trapped in the car; the smell of pines never get caught this way.

"You don't get what it's like to date. Everybody lies, all these guys."

"So stop going online. Stop having these long, intense conversations. What could you talk about? Go out and meet someone. Isn't there anyone to meet in Durham?"

"I don't want to stay in Durham. I want to live near you—"

"Susan, you have to do what's best for yourself."

"I miss the sea."

"Okay," she says carefully.

"I want a normal life."

Silence drops between us.

"Don't you have anyone to fix me up with?" I say lightly. I've seen some of the very cute soccer dads out on the field with my nephew. "Any desirable divorced dads out there?"

She won't play along. "Everyone I know is married. Or they have problems."

"I'm okay with problems. Everyone has issues. Look at me—"

"I don't know anybody," she says quickly. "I tried."

"Twenty years ago." My sister's one big fix-up was a good one, not that I thought it at the time.

"I have to go, sister," says Caroline, exasperated. The baby wails.

I'm driving her crazy. I'm driving myself crazy.

"So do I."

I slump in my car. *I'm fat. I'm never getting married. I'm never going to have a baby.* I drown in self-pity. I want to eat.

But I do what I've learned. I want to change. I know I really don't want to eat.

I think, *HALT!* It's commonly used in various 12-step programs, according to my friends who have been through them, and it's one of the tools from the Clinic. So, *HALT.* I ask myself, *Am I . . .*

Hungry?

Angry?

Lonely?

Tired?

Usually, it's a combination. I'm usually more angry, lonely, and tired than hungry. But I literally stop in my head. I stop my thoughts. *What is going on with me? Am I hungry? Angry? Lonely? Tired? I'm lonely. So what can I do about it? Am I being honest? Am I being honest with myself?*

I stay with my emotions. I think about them. I breathe.

I stop. *I'm okay. I'm lonely, but okay.*

I'm not going to eat.

"I'm not going to eat!" I demand of myself.

I'm here. I'm in my body. HALT. I swing my car into the parking lot.

My hip-hop dance class starts now. Usher, Missy Elliot, and OutKast blast. I'm dancing.

Chapter 28

It's Saturday morning at the Clinic. "What do we want to do tonight?" I ask.

"What do you feel like doing?" the question circles around the table.

"Dancing? Line dancing, anyone?" I call out. Nobody listens. Across the table, there's the professionally brilliant woman, who's been coming here for more than 40 years and eats so fast she makes me nervous. There's Bradley from the Midwest, who's hanging out with the psycho chick, Jenny. There's Annie, who's been thin for months now and can't seem to leave. And Black Stallion, in his sixties, battling obesity all his life. His hair is a jet-black mane, and his stomach plunges down to his knees.

"You're looking good, little Bradley," calls out Black Stallion. "Seen your *johnson* lately?"

"How about a movie tonight?" I push. I don't want another conversation to devolve into sex—fat sex. Our last conversation was about sex with pillows. Sex with pillows to support sore backs, pillows to balance on with weak knees, and sex with pillows so you don't hear your stomach flapping. When you're having sex doggie-style, you put the pillow under your stomach and you don't hear it flapping. I don't want to talk about sex at breakfast again.

"I haven't had sex in 10 years," whispers Joy to me with a wistful sigh. She's short and chunky and perky, but from the way she talks about herself, you'd think she was huge and ugly. In real life, Joy's a fiftysomething swim instructor.

"You haven't had sex in 10 years?" I turn to her and forget about the movie.

"I haven't met anybody."

"You haven't met the right person in 10 years. You've got to be kidding me."

"Okay, I heard you the first time."

"Ten years?" I scream. I haven't had sex in 6 years, but I was almost 500 pounds. "You know the best kind of sex?" I say.

"What?" says Joy, wide-eyed.

"Any sex after you've lost weight."

"We want to hear about the real thing," calls out Black Stallion.

"That's all you're hearing from me," I jostle back. "So are we going to the movies tonight?"

"What do you want to do?" The question circles around the table again.

I'm caught in that old movie, *Marty,* with Ernest Borgnine, about a butcher in Brooklyn who can't get a date. His mother pushes him to put on a suit and go to a dance at the Stardust Ballroom on Saturday night. He doesn't want to go. He screams at her. "Blue suit, gray suit, I'm just a fat, little man. A fat, ugly man." I won't give away the end, but it's happy.

We decide to go the movies. But which movie theater? One has all the cookie and ice cream shops outside the movie theater. The other's seats are too small. There's a third, but it smells like wet musty feet. We have this conversation every time we go to a movie.

We have nothing to do but talk, and we talk and talk until at least 10:30 a.m. before dispersing. We agree to a movie. Some go for a walk, like me. We'll meet up at lunch and at dinner at 5:30. Since it's Saturday night, it's fish night. Once a week we have fish, salmon, tilapia, sea bass cakes, swordfish, or flounder with a vegetable stuffing. My favorite is salmon with honey-mustard dill sauce.

The bare tables have tablecloths on them for Saturday night fish nights. There's a sense of accomplishment in the air every Saturday night. We've all made it another week. Someone says, "Did you know that *diet* means 'way of life' in Greek?" I didn't. But I remember it, for later.

After dinner, we have to figure out which cars we're driving. I used to say, "Thank God, I'm the heaviest, because I always get the front seat." But tonight, the front seat is up for grabs. I'm no longer the heaviest.

I want everyone to get going. But nobody rushes. They are too old or too fat or too distracted. They want to travel together. Everyone waits for everyone else. I want to go.

"Oh my God, the popcorn smells so good—"

"Look at those M&Ms—"

"I used to eat two of those—"

"I used to eat three—"

I don't participate aloud in this one-upsmanship of who ate more; it's a kind of mutual masturbation for the emotionally overweight. *I was so fat that I couldn't go to the movies* is what I could say, but I don't. I want to focus on getting thin and on the future. Everyone from the Clinic trudges close together, as if by moving en masse, they won't be seen. I walk ahead.

"It's not what you really want," I shout. "Get moving." Yet I'm seeing the concession stand and seeing the heroin. *It's not what you really want,* I repeat to myself. *Get moving.*

When I first came down to Durham, I didn't go to the movies because I couldn't take the smell of popcorn. But I'm here. I finger my snack, a container of grapes. I'm so frustrated with everyone. I just want to sink down in the dark.

Others buy extra-large cups of diet soda as if the sodium won't affect them or set them off. It would me. I've said it before and I'll say it again: Sodium is a trigger for me. The ones who cheat later in the evening won't be at breakfast on Sunday. Or maybe they'll slink in on Sunday, use the side door, eat breakfast. But they won't weigh in. I've been there. Everybody knows you cheated, there are those knowing looks, the jealous greedy questions: *Where have you been?* Which really means, *What did you eat?* I'm moving past that concession stand. The movie can't start soon enough. When did 15 or 20 minutes of previews and ads become standard?

The dark engulfs me.

The microcosm of the Clinic forms my life. Not many people are down here as long me. Most people come down for a week, 2 weeks, a summer at most. The Clinic has been my Band-Aid. It's getting old, dirty, stuck to my skin, and I'm not taking it off. My second anniversary of moving to Durham is coming up.

After the movie, some go for coffee, and I go home. I don't eat or drink after 8 p.m. I don't want to be tempted.

At home alone, I turn on my favorite network, the Food TV Network. My absolute favorite show of all times is *The Secret Life of . . . .* I want to know the secret life of Twinkies, milkshakes, gum, garlic, cafeterias, succulent seafood, and even salt. Did you know that salt was the world's first food additive? That salt was once traded instead of money? That it was more valuable than money?

My favorite episode of my favorite show is "The Secret Life of Sandwiches." When I see this show, it reminds me of my favorite sandwich—one prepared at this deli on Arthur Avenue, a famous Italian block in the Bronx, with mortadella, salami, provolone cheese, extra mayonnaise, and oil and vinegar on fresh-baked slabs of crusty Italian bread, hard on the outside and soft on the inside, absorbing all the oils and fat inside. Or my other favorite is the tuna sandwich made by José in Long Beach. He makes it from chunky flakes of oily Italian tuna on braided Italian bread with sesame seeds, and he always used to give me a little extra—a little more tuna, a longer piece of bread, olives or pickles. If someone offered me sex with Matt Damon or one of those two sandwiches, I would go with the sandwich. I don't know what I would do if I could eat both and not gain a pound. But I'm keeping to my 8 p.m. rule. I can fantasize about food; I just can't eat it.

So, I dream about it.

What I always dream of is chicken wings. How it tastes to crunch into them. How they would be boiling hot. I'd have to dip them into the jar—straight into the jar—of Marie's blue cheese dressing. How I would cook them exactly 20 minutes, and then 2 minutes under the broiler just so they would burn a little. I'd eat the bits of burned Tabasco and ketchup, which would taste sweet and burnt at the same time, I imagine. Or, I dream of club sandwiches with extra *extra* Russian dressing and how the cheese melts on the club sandwich. Or the Chinese scallion pancakes and how greasy and good they taste.

I stare at the ceiling and imagine the food. I fall asleep on my back with the taste of my dreams in my mouth.

In September, I talk with the doctors about leaving. I'm done. I can't be here. Everything's going on my credit cards, and I'm paying minimums and shifting balances and wanting this all to be over. I'm someone with little patience. I've learned patience down here, but clearly not enough. One morning, I push the senior doctor.

"I want to leave."

"Not yet," he says. He's a down-to-earth, brilliant doctor in Birkenstocks. He teaches meditation classes. He teaches about patience and inner peace and believes in it.

"Isn't the whole point to leave Durham?" I say, hesitating. I didn't mean I wanted to leave today. I know I'm not ready right now. I just want an end date.

I want a normal life, and I want it now.

"I really want to go," I say.

"Not yet. The end of the year."

"Okay, the end of the year," I agree; it's only 4 months off.

The other doctor asks me how I feel about this decision, about my plans. What am I going to do when I get home? How's it going work?

"How are you going to duplicate the structure?" He's not challenging me, but he's asking me. He's analyzing the situation. He wants it to work for me; so many gain the weight back.

"How are you going to handle going into the grocery store and shopping? How are you going to do this? Are you going to move back into an apartment? Do you have it set up? Are you going to get a job? How are you going to do this?"

"I'm not sure," I say. I don't have a place to live in New York. I don't know how I'm going to pay for the move back. I haven't been grocery shopping for myself in more than 2 years.

September in Durham is one of the most beautiful months: The tall trees turn all the golden colors of autumn, and the clouds are high, the skies blue, and the town bustling with college kids. I'm fluctuating between 210 and 215, the lowest weight I've been in 10 years. I've lost 250 pounds; wasn't that enough?

I write up to-do lists connected with leaving Durham and starting my new life, and I throw them away. I call my sister and Lena and relate to them my to-do list instead of doing anything on the list. I paste up a new list by my computer, scrawled out in my oversize script. The lists tumble from the computer screen to the floor. I make a favorite dish, thinking that I'll soon be cooking for myself every day. I want to be ready for my life on the outside.

SUSAN'S PASTA AND SAUTÉED ZUCCHINI FOR ONE

2 ounces pasta (about 1½ cups cooked)
2 teaspoons olive oil
½ cup diced Spanish onion
2 cloves fresh garlic, finely chopped
1 yellow zucchini, diced
1 green zucchini, diced
2 Roma tomatoes, diced
5 fresh basil leaves, chopped
Ground black pepper to taste
Garlic powder to taste

1 Cook the pasta according to package directions (no salt) and set aside.

2 Heat the olive oil over medium heat in a medium-size saucepan.

3 Sauté the onion and garlic until brown.

4 Add the zucchini; cook until tender and a little brown, about 10 minutes.

5 Add the diced tomatoes; cook until tender, about 5 minutes.

6 Add the basil, pepper, and garlic powder.

7 Pour over pasta and serve!

Why Does Pasta Work—But Bread Doesn't—for Me?

- First, I don't keep bread in the house. I could breathe 10 times, 100 times to de-stress. Yet, when I open the refrigerator and see bread, I eat it right away. Even if I put the bread in the freezer, it's 30 seconds in the microwave and I have bread. My solution: Don't keep bread in the house.

- Pasta takes effort—at least, enough time and effort to focus and calm down. Cooking pasta (or anything) tells me that I'm putting myself first. I'm preparing a meal. I'm not just shoving a piece of bread in my mouth or slapping a sandwich together. I'm slowing down. I'm waiting for the water to boil.

- Note: I make enough pasta for only one meal at a time.

Dear reader, remember this is just my take on food. I'm not a doctor or a nutritionist. I'm the anti-expert. I lost my weight eating pasta twice a day. Bread is a food that I've found leads to my binges. Know what sets you off and be honest with yourself. If one slice is going to set you off, slice it out of your life!

ere's another pasta recipe that I love. Again, it's for one, but this is easy to make for a family by increasing the ingredients proportionally.

MACARONI AND CHEESE FOR ONE

2 ounces elbow macaroni (about ½ cup cooked)
2 teaspoons no-salt butter
½ cup chopped Spanish onion
1 clove fresh garlic, finely chopped
1 ounce low-sodium Jarlsberg cheese, cut into small pieces
1 fresh basil leaf, finely chopped
½ cup no-salt bread crumbs
2 teaspoons olive oil

1 Cook the pasta according to package directions (no salt!) and set aside.

2 Preheat oven to 350°F.

3 Place the butter in a medium frying pan over medium heat.

4 Add the onion and garlic; cook until brown and tender, about 3 to 5 minutes.

5 Pour the pasta into the pan and stir; turn off the heat.

6 Pour the pasta mixture into an 8" × 8" baking dish.

7 Add the cheese and mix.

8 Add the basil and mix again.

9 Evenly sprinkle the bread crumbs onto the mixture.

10 Evenly sprinkle the olive oil onto the bread crumbs.

11 Place in the oven and bake for 15 minutes, or until the bread crumbs are browned.

Chapter 29

Snapshot. At almost 500 pounds, I was the head in any group picture. I hid myself behind the couch, or in the last row. Or I refused to be photographed at all. Now, after losing more than 200 pounds, *Woman's World* asked if I would be willing to be photographed for the cover of their magazine. I would be seen by millions of people in the supermarkets across America paying for their bread and milk. The article was essentially a profile of the Clinic and their diet. I was grateful to the doctors, to the second chance I had been given. I couldn't believe anyone was asking me to be on the cover of anything. I wanted to cheer. In fact, I did.

In January 2006, with cold rain striking down, *Woman's World* flies me to New York City for the photo shoot. After landing at the airport, I'm in a cab, stuck in traffic, and late.

I race into the photographer's studio and find a team of people waiting for me; the photographer and her assistants, the makeup artist and her young daughter, the calm stylist, and funky downtown hairstylist all turn to look at me. I'm panting, ragged, and drenched.

The stylist has a full wardrobe of sizes 16 and 18 for me to try on for the shoot. I've brought a white pantsuit a friend had given me. This suit still has tags on it. All I know is that I don't want to wear black. I have spent the last 10 years wearing black.

They love the suit!

After hair and makeup, which takes about 2 hours, I'm falling asleep in the chair. The rain is pounding on the windows. After I change into the white pantsuit and step in front of the camera, rock music pumps on, and I'm on. I'm as ready as I can be.

"You look beautiful. Gorgeous. Space between the teeth. Space," shouts out the photographer. She opens up her mouth and wiggles her index finger between the top and bottom of her teeth to show me how to smile. I grin.

"You're right on. Beautiful. Move left. Now, the other way. Leg back. Hips out. Twist. Twist."

"Twist where?" The photographer is making me laugh, and I'm giving her the space between the teeth naturally.

"Give me more, Sue."

I feel like Tyra, like Christy, like Cindy, like Gisele.

"This is really hard work," I sing out. It's ridiculous. Unreal. I swing my hip out. Pop up my thumb.

Music blares.

All of the pain, all of my inability to walk, all the time I hid myself, all the shame, flashes before me—and is gone. In that moment, I can cheer the weight loss and the change in me. I can reveal who I want to be to these wonderful strangers: happy.

I appear on the cover of *Woman's World* on March 21, 2006, touting an obesity cure next to a St. Patrick's Day article on chocolate Irish cream cheesecake and crumb crusted corned beef. I frame the magazine cover for inspiration.

Chapter 30

So, it's the end of March and one in the morning when the phone rings next to my bed. I'm still in Durham.

I've received these calls before: "Your mom bruised her elbow and we brought her to the hospital," or "Your mom is running a fever."

I always answer the same. I don't say hello. I say, "Is my mom okay?"

"No, she isn't," begins the nurse. "She has a very bad infection. We're not sure she's going to survive. You really need to come up."

"What else can you tell me?"

"I can't tell you anything else. You're going to have to talk with the doctor."

"Let me talk to her doctor."

"He'll be in first thing in the morning."

I'm shaking. I don't know what to do. I know I have to call Caroline. But I don't want to wake her up.

I call Caroline. She doesn't answer the phone. Her phone is in the kitchen. She sleeps like she's dead. I call 11 times. I try Mark. I try David. I don't call my father. He also has the phone right by his bed. He'll wake up. I don't want to upset him. I call Caroline again and let the phone ring over and over. On the 12th attempt, Alan answers. He wakes Caroline up.

All I keep thinking is that I didn't go through these past 2 months to lose my mother.

I'm on a 6 a.m. flight out of the Raleigh-Durham airport and at the hospital by 9 a.m. My mother is in intensive care, on a respirator, unconscious. She's having problems breathing even with a respirator. The nurses didn't have a lot to say. We have to wait 24 to 48 hours to see if she'll survive. I smooth down her hair and pull up the sheets, covering up her wide shoulders.

I call Caroline when I get there. She's at the hospital within the hour. She wets a paper towel and dabs my mother's head. She whispers to her, telling her that it's okay, that we're here, and that if she wants to go, she can.

"Don't tell her that."

"Susan, hasn't she been through enough?"

"I want her to get better, don't you?"

"What if she doesn't get better? She could live like this. Is this how you want her to live?"

"Do we have to talk about this now?"

We've been through this once before with pneumonia, 5 or 6 years before, and we should know what to do. But we've forgotten. There's nothing to do but wait.

I rant at her doctor, who's patient and explains that he's doing everything he can, including bringing in specialists. He tells me how these things happen in the elderly. He listens. He lets me go on until I can't think of anything else to say. My mother is 78 years old. I don't think of her as old, though. She never had a chance to be young.

For all of my life, until I went to Durham, I never went to sleep without thinking about my mother. *What if her medicines weren't appropriate? What if she wasn't being washed? What if no one cut her hair or nails or took her outside? What if she were being abused or left in bed for too many days?* I didn't want to forget her. In Durham, I realized that the "what ifs" were killing me.

Now, my worst "what if" is coming true. What if my mother dies or, worse yet—worse than death—is unconscious and on a respirator and in ICU where the lights never go out and the nurses stare at computer screens because there's nothing left to say, and you're not dying, but there's no life left. No watching television, or eating pasta or visits in the back on the porch by the bay with your daughters and grandchildren. It's a life without life.

I stay at Caroline's house. Nothing changes with my mother for 3 days. We visit. She's in the dark except for the lights from the monitors. We find the dark comforting. But the nurse is too helpful and turns the lights on. I ask for the 10th time if there's been any change, any improvement, even though I can see that there's none.

In the late night, Caroline and I sit in her kitchen and talk about her funeral, about how there's a grave for her next to her mother, our grandmother, somewhere in Westchester. Caroline hugs the mug of tea to her cheek. The babies sleep, my niece, 8 months old, my nephew, 6 years old. How I wish I could hold one.

"I don't want to think of that, sister!"

"I don't want to think of it either." Caroline pauses and drinks her third cup of tea for the day. "But what if she doesn't get better?"

"We can't just pull the plug. She's alive."

"We should have signed the DNR forms."

"Can we talk about something else, Caroline? Please, anything else?" My sister and I have talked about this before. We don't trust the hospitals. We think a DNR form will give them permission to do nothing. Now, I don't know. *What if she doesn't regain consciousness? What if she has to live on the respirator? What if* . . . I can't think of it.

It's what we don't talk about that weighs between us. I drink water. I've had nothing salty since coming to New York, but I can't stop drinking water. My sister has these large, 24-ounce plastic glasses. I keep filling up my glass. I want to drown.

"When are you moving back to New York?" Caroline asks.

"Not April 1. Not now. That would be next week. I'm not ready. I'm not even packed. I planned to finish packing this week. I didn't expect this! I can't move back April 1!"

"When?" she says calmly, folding into herself, her cup of tea.

"May 1. Unless something else happens, May 1."

"What else could happen?"

"May 1."

"Are you sure?"

"No."

"I'll come down and help you move back?" she says this in her way of telling me by asking a question.

"You will?"

"I moved you down there, I'll move you back. I want to make sure you come home, if you're ready."

I nod my head and get up and fill my glass, chug it down all in one gulp, and gasp for air at the end.

On Saturday, after almost a week in ICU, my mother regains consciousness. I visit her. She recognizes me, or at least she knows I'm one of her daughters. On Sunday, I fly back to Durham. May 1 is my new move date.

My mother is in the ICU and then the hospital for another 2 weeks.

Caroline is there every day. I'm on the phone with the doctors every day. We're both exhausted. As my mother recovers, she's perky and funny and very alert. And an odd thing happens. My mother asks what day it is. This is a startling question from my mother. For 39 years, she has lived without a sense of time passing. It's Sunday or it's Wednesday; it's the day my mother is asking us what day it is. Maybe all the oxygen charged up her neurons for a brief moment. But it makes me think again how fragile and dear life is. Soon, she is moved back to the nursing home and fades back to being my old mother, and every day is the same.

One bright spot in my last few months in Durham is Dudley. He works out with Wes, after me. He's a minor league baseball player, a total North Carolina homegrown boy.

I'm in a *Bull Durham* daydream with him. I'm Susan Sarandon and he's Tim Robbins. Dudley always comes early and hangs out with Wes and me. I'm usually finishing up my workout, on my back or side, my leg, quadriceps, glutes, hamstrings, calves all stretched out for him to see. One fine spring day, he ambles into the gym.

"You look good today," he calls out. The scent of his spearmint gum wafts over me.

Dudley is not here to lose weight. He's here to gain. He's in the 190s and wants to reach 208 by building muscle. He's all hardtack muscle as far as I can see.

"My Dudley's here!" I shout back at him.

He pulls up a chair, stretching out his long legs.

"How was your weekend?" I ask.

"Couldn't gain weight," he says, chomping on his gum.

"Want me to make you some of my famous chicken wings?"

"I ate two steaks last night."

"Oh, poor Dudley. Did you have some ice cream after that?"

He can't gain weight, and I can't lose weight. I'm about 215 pounds. There's a nursery rhyme about this situation.

Dudley and I even have this bet. He'd gain weight and I'd lose. If he wins, I will do these abs exercises for 10 minutes that Wes makes the baseball players do. Dudley can't even do them easily. If I win, he'll have to run the stadium stairs in under 30 minutes.

This fine spring morning, by the time my session is over, I have four gorgeous twentysomething minor league baseball players hanging out with me. I only wish I knew something about baseball.

"What team do you like?" asks Dudley.

"I like the team with the cutest guys on it," and I give a sidelong glance at

Dudley and back at Wes. "And if Dudley was playing, I'd root for his team."

"Okay, now we're going to do the iron bridge," says Wes evenly.

The iron bridge is when you lie on your stomach and lift yourself up on your forearms and toes, keeping your stomach taut. You have to be level as a plank. Your butt needs to be down. The most I've lasted on the "iron bridge" is 45 seconds.

"I'm only going to do the iron bridge if Dudley does it with me."

He gets down beside me on the mat.

Forty-five seconds is like 45 minutes. For Dudley, it's no problem; he winks at me in the middle. I'm pouring sweat. My hair is a tangled mess. My arms quiver.

"You know I'm going get into my white thong bikini, Dudley."

"There you go," says Dudley with a happy inhale and long, hearty exhale. Life is good for that guy, and yes, on many days for me, too.

ltimately, neither of us win the bet.

When I'm finally ready to leave Durham, I say to Wes, "Watch— I'm going to get to 208 and you're going to have to give me Dudley's phone number."

In April, I buy a size 16—not a 16W—pair of white crepe slacks. That's my moment. I stare at them. I stare at me in them. They fit. I wear them around the house. I'm almost too afraid to wear them out, as if another person, another Susan, will have to go with them.

As I'm getting ready to leave Durham at the end of April, I write this letter and send it to my family and friends.

> *To the people I love the most—my family and friends:*
>
> *I am in my last week of my 2-year-and-5-month emotional and physical transformation at the Rice Diet Program. As I return to the mainstream, I will need continued support from my friends and family. I hope that you all will be able to assist me in maintaining the changes that I have made toward a lifelong pattern of healthy eating and regular exercise. Sometimes, people, even though they mean well, do things that are not helpful or supportive. Here are some things you can do that will help me:*
>
> *1. Avoid offering unsolicited "advice" or "constructive criticism" about diet or weight loss. Keeping focused is a fragile thing that can be damaged by unsolicited advice. I know what I need to do to succeed.*
>
> *2. Do not try to enforce my "good" behavior. I am not*

"good" or "bad" as it relates to my lifelong pattern of healthy eating and exercise. This is a journey. No beginning and no end. Most people rebel against being controlled and this will only make adherence to my eating and exercise guidelines more difficult.

3. Remember, the word diet *comes from a Greek word meaning "way of life." Do not think of what I will be doing as deprivation. My program is aimed at helping me to better health and longer life, and that is what I have chosen.*

4. You will already be able to see significant changes in my lifestyle, including increased physical activity. Eating and exercising properly are the keys to success. Please be careful not to sabotage that success by raising doubts about my chances for long-term success. Even subtle hints about failure can erode the confidence and self-discipline I will need.

5. The road to sustained weight loss is long and sometimes treacherous. Please understand that I may not want to give you reports about my progress and status. Questions about my weight may seem supportive, but let me do the sharing of this when and if I think it is appropriate. In the meantime, know that I rely on the kindness and goodwill of all of my friends and family.

I want to take this opportunity to tell everyone who is reading this letter that they are receiving this letter because you have each helped me through this incredibly difficult time in your special way. I would never have been able to be as successful without all of your love and support. You are so special to me. I feel so lucky to have had this second chance at life. Thank you for giving me that second chance to rebuild and nurture relationships. Thank you all for believing that I could do it. Thank you all for being incredible human beings.

I would be happy to talk to any of you more about the Clinic itself, and about the ways that you can help me reach the goals I have set for myself. Communication is the cornerstone of this process. I want to be able to count on you as an ally.

With my love, gratitude, and loyalty always,
Susan

Chapter 31

The last week in April, right before I leave Durham, I chance my first Clinic hookup. He's younger, so much younger that I could be his mother—or at least Caroline, who's 2 years older than me, could be his mother. It's like the last weeks of college or summer camp I want to cram the most out of what's left. I had the feeling that I would be here forever, that I would never lose the weight, and now, in a rush, it's all over. I want to hold on to something. He's young, but I hold on to him. This isn't going to last. All is bittersweet.

Caroline flies down. All three of us go to a Bo Bice concert at a local redneck dance bar that smells of beer and manure. We park in a field next to tricked-out pickup trucks. They check our IDs at the door. I'm sure they're really checking my new guy, who's so sweet-faced. All three of us circle around the crowd. Twentysomethings in last year's lingerie blouses swing their beers and shout, "Bo!" The music blasts out from extra-large rock speakers. I realize how much I like quiet now.

The next morning, Friday, I say good-bye to Wes by working out with him one last time. We throw a ball on the field. The sky is a perfect blue. The high pines summon a cool breeze. I sprint back and forth. At the end, I climb into the Bod Pod. It looks like a space module. It weighs me, and more importantly, it reads my percentage of fat versus muscle.

I weigh 221 pounds. I'm leaving on Sunday.

"You going to miss it?" says Raj, one of the cooks, after dinner when I'm hanging around, one of the last to leave. He's a big, handsome black man dressed in a white cook's coat.

"I'm scared."

"It'll be like college," he says, sorting through silver pots and pans. "You'll miss it. But you can't never come back. It'll never be the same, like college is never the same when you visit again, and you're old and everyone is so young."

"I'm going to come back. At least to visit." I can't quite let go of the safest place in the world for me.

"It'll be different. You'll be different. You'll see."

At the end, in a fancy hotel bar, my sister and close friends from the Clinic pour champagne for me.

Advice is given; it's been flowing solicited and unsolicited from people at the Clinic for the last few weeks . . .

Not many people keep it off.

You'll be back.

Everyone gains it back.

You're going to date right away?! How are you going to go on dates and not go out to dinner? (I can't go for a walk instead of going out to dinner?)

Everyone gains at least 30—at least 40!—at least 50 pounds!—the first time out.

You can always come back.

Remember what you learned. Remember the struggle.

Get a system going. Keep walking and moving. Call us. Call us anytime. We're here for you.

Sue, can you handle it! (Guess what? I'm not perfect. I'm afraid. I'm not finished myself. I'm struggling like everyone else is.)

I celebrate with water. I thank them all. And I say to myself—and to everyone—that I'm going to give myself a 20-pound leeway. I won't beat myself up if I gain a "freshman" 20 going back to the "real" world. I thank them again, and it's time to leave.

On Sunday morning, the car, the same Altima, now with more than 200,000 miles on it and grinding with the weight of everything I didn't send up by truck a week earlier, is ready to go. My sister squeezes in next to me. Unlike on the trip down here, I'm unreservedly glad that she's with me.

I weigh in one last time. I'm 218 pounds. I've lost 250 pounds in 2½ years.

I drive off with 40 pounds or so plus surgery to go. It's over. I did it. Even though I haven't made it to my ultimate goal yet, it doesn't matter. I had nothing at 500 pounds or at 400 or even at 300. Now, I have my life back.

What I take with me—and go to—is a support system.

I've developed a support system. Here's how I define a support system: one or more people whom you trust, and who love you unconditionally, and they trust you. But talk is cheap. I talked for 10 years about losing weight. I lied. I cried on the phone with friends about how I couldn't lose weight, and then went on binges. I ate up their emotional support and gave little in return. A support system is a two-way street. When I stopped talking and made that commitment to do—and to change—everything I could to lose weight and become emotionally healthy, I reached out to family and friends and gained their support and trust.

Here's How I Built My Support System:

* *I started with me.* I mended myself. I trusted myself. I can't look to someone else to save me. This takes time. And I learned that I could start at any age.

* *I include only a very select group of people in my support system.* Yours may only be one person. Or, in my case, it's five or six people, depending on the week.

  There will be people you love who can't be included. You don't want to know that the people you love have faults that make them untrustworthy or undependable or unreliable or any number of "uns," but there are, so be kind to them, forgive them; just don't depend on them.

  Sometimes your support system is made up of those you least expect. It may not be your husband or wife or your best friend. People in my support systems have different roles.

  For example, my father's role is to just to be there for me to call up and cry, to listen, to hear me. I don't want him to do anything, to take an action, to spend money. This is very hard for a man of action like my father. But he's realized over the past 2 years that that's not what I need—because I've told him what I need. I need him to pick up the phone when I call; that's all. And as he gets older, I'm there in the same way for him. At 76, living alone in Florida, he wants to know he's not alone in the world. He's not, and I'm not.

- *I include people who are good listeners and I try to be a good listener.* Support systems are there to listen, to empathize, and not to judge or analyze me. I try not to use the phrases "you should do this" or "why aren't you doing that?" with others. If I need mental health advice, I should find a therapist. I don't use my support system as a substitute for therapy.

- *I am my own support system.* I trust myself. I trust what my body needs and doesn't need. I'm *in* my body. I am aware and mindful, and it's hard and it hurts some days, but this is my journey, my life.

If I sound like I have all the answers, I don't. In New York, freedom from the structure of the Clinic is almost too much for me. I find a new gym and a trainer and get on a workout schedule. But I don't find a therapist or support group soon enough. I have two slices of pizza and two chocolate cookies, and that's good for 7 or 8 pounds.

I'm anxious about work. I rent a studio apartment in a stately Tudor building in Long Island, a world away from Long Beach. I'm only half-way to a teaching degree. I need to complete it. My credit cards are maxed out. I don't want to, but I borrow more money from my father. I search for a job in Manhattan.

A shawarma sandwich—it's grilled turkey and lamb and onion, hummus, tahini, and spices rolled in a thick pitalike wrap that's as long as my forearm—"solves" the issues temporarily.

I want to enjoy food without using it as a way of numbing myself, of shaming myself. I want to enjoy food as food, not as heroin. I want to taste meat, the way the juices drip down my arm. I want to enjoy the people I'm with, even if they are strangers eating pastrami sandwiches next to me. I want to take what I've learned over the past 2 years into my real life, every day, not just on "good" days.

My 41st birthday arrives. My father flies up. He questions the sushi I prepare for the celebration with him and my sister. I refer to the letter I sent to him. I pull it out and read him parts aloud. He gets it. His broad shoulders are stooped, frail, and all of a sudden, he seems much older. I realize how much stronger I am.

There are two different types of relapses. With one, I have a slice of pizza, and I'm back on track the next day. The second is the binge that lasts a week or more. With the latter, I remember to be especially kind to myself. There are things I have to say to myself: *This hour, I'm not going to binge. This meal, I'm going to do well. This minute, I'll drink water.* And I'll forgive myself.

I will take a little bit of a walk. I'm going to walk to the mailbox instead of a car. I'm going to move. I'm going to be *in* my body again.

I will get on the scale. I will acknowledge what my weight is. I will take responsibility.

I will e-mail a friend every day with my weight. I join Weight Watchers, for the meetings and the weigh-ins. I go every Sunday morning—for a while.

I will take care of myself: take my vitamins every day, shower, wash my hair, put makeup on, get my nails done, acknowledge that I'm worth taking care of.

I will remember: This is my journey.

I gain weight. Not the 20 pounds everyone at the Clinic said I would gain. I'm proud of that. Nineteen pounds. In 10 weeks, I gain 19, and then I stop with the help of my support system, by using tools like HALT, and by using everything else I've learned that says to me—well, really screams to me: *It isn't about the food*. It's midsummer, a hot, glorious sun-dappled summer in Long Island, and I regroup. My goals:

1 Get under 200 pounds. On top of the last 40 pounds or so I need to lose, I have approximately 20 pounds of excess skin from my overall weight loss. What I decide to do about plastic surgery is my next big challenge.

2 Look great in clothes. Buy a few great-looking outfits.

3 Remember the struggle.

4 Eat consciously.

5 Weigh myself every day.

6 Move every day.

Over the last 2½ years, I've accomplished much of what I set out to do—because it's not just about the weight. I changed my entire life: the way I think about food, the way I relate to people, the way I deal with rage and anger, the way I forgive myself and others. Most importantly, I've changed the way I think about myself. I don't live in shame. I'm finally proud of myself.

I've stopped the lies. I've stopped making excuses, and I know every excuse in the book.

Every Excuse in the Book (That I Can Think of Right Now) for Not Losing Weight:

333

- *I'm happy.* Immediately followed by: *I can't be happy. I don't deserve it.* This thinking set me off on my last minor binge of the summer. Everything is going well. I have a plan beyond the office products business. I have the possibility of a real date or two. I'm spending time with my sister and her family doing fun things. I'm working out. I'm losing weight. I'm writing this book. I've found a new Pilates instructor I love.

    I panic. I'm a wreck. Everything is going to fall apart. I know it will.

I'm scared. I'm alone. Maybe a new career won't work out. Maybe I'll never meet anybody. Maybe I'll never have a kid. I fall back on what I know. I eat a foot-long hero as if it will save me from myself.

I call my younger brother. "David, what is wrong with me?"

"You're afraid to be happy, Sue. For some reason you want the drama and the chaos in your life, and the only way right now you can have it is by eating like this."

"I don't want the chaos. I want to be normal."

"Then be happy and be normal. Don't sabotage yourself. Don't find excuses to overeat."

I don't know why, but this felt so simple and so smart. I *can* be happy. I have a right to be happy.

If I take the time to focus on why I'm eating—the emotional reasons why I'm eating—and use my tools, I will eat less. I will make better food choices. I don't eat because I'm *Hungry*. I eat because I'm *Angry, Lonely,* or *Tired* or a combination of the three, or in this case because I was scared of the unknown. Understanding the emotional underpinning of that hero sandwich binge was a breakthrough for me. It's not the binge; it's what you learn from the binge that counts. My little brother helped me repair the hole in my soul by being honest and nonjudgmental. In the same way at different times, Lena, Laurie, and others did as well.

- *Something's wrong with my thyroid.* Like, less than 1 percent really have a problem, according my own unscientific and nonresearched analysis, and less than 1 percent of those people actually go get it diagnosed.

- *I just can't get the water down.* I never had a problem chugging diet sodas. Now, I drink at least eight glasses of water. I aim for a gallon of water a day. Everything becomes a habit. I've made drinking water my habit.

- *Healthy food costs a lot of money.* Recently, a week's worth of grapes costs me $9. That's a lot for grapes. I just had to remember how much a fast-food binge used to cost me (try $100!).

- *I really don't eat a lot.* Lena said this to me recently: "You're the only one in history who doesn't eat a lot and gains weight. The reality is that you're not eating a lot in front of people. The issue is what you're eating when you're not in front of anyone."

- *I can't help it, but I crave fattening foods.* So uncrave them. I felt absolutely addicted to fast foods. I felt it in my throat, that lump. I had to have a fish sandwich to calm down. What I've learned is that salt makes me crave, and fast food is loaded with salt. I was addicted. It's the old Doritos commercial—you can't eat just one. I certainly can't. I had to change my behavior. I had to eliminate all fast foods and processed foods loaded with salt. I had to become an expert at reading nutritional labels.

- *I can't deal with changing my life or relationships.* It's too hard. A friend recently said to me, "If I lose weight, I'll be attractive [she's already attractive, but 50 to 60 pounds overweight] and guys other than my husband will notice me, and I'll cheat. I know I will because I can't stand my husband. And I'm afraid to leave him." Does this make any sense? She's afraid; that's the key part. She's made up her mind to just stay fat—because it's easier, because leaving what she knows for the unknown is too scary. She hasn't dealt with the emotional underpinnings of her eating issues. I spent almost 10 years living and working in a place where I progressively isolated myself, thinking that I couldn't change, and reaching 468.1 pounds.

- *I don't have time to exercise* . . . but you have time to sit in front of the television because you had a hard day. It's all about choices. I could very easily sit on the couch and watch *Good Will Hunting*, my favorite movie, for the 50th time. I keep my bike near the front door. I ride into town to buy a magazine. I walk down to the mailbox and back. Even if I'm not having the perfect workout, I'm moving. Remember: Exercise is my job.

- *I don't have time to weigh my food.* Recently, Lena outed me again. She said, "Sue, that's at least 4 cups of pasta you're eating."

  "No, it's not."

  "Measure it."

  She was right. I was eating three times the pasta that I should have been eating because I had convinced myself that I knew better. I thought I knew what a cup and a half looked like, or at least what I wanted it to look like! Now, I measure everything out. I can eat more, but I know exactly how much more. At least I'm not kidding myself about how much I eat anymore.

- *The basic formula—calories in versus calories out—which was told to me on my first day at the Clinic, somehow doesn't apply to me anymore.* I'm smarter than that. And sure, Susan, the world is flat. I'm *not* smarter than that.

- *I'm on a diet.* This is my favorite excuse. Why is this is an excuse? If I'm on a diet, I can go off the diet. There's always an excuse to go off your diet. I have finally realized that I'm not on a diet; I can make choices. I can eat a bit more, but I'm doing it consciously. And if I eat a bit more, then I'm at the gym or walking or biking or moving a bit more.

Most importantly, whatever I eat, I'm not eating to obliterate thoughts or feelings. I'm not hiding. I'm not lying. I'm not ashamed. I'm a grown-up making choices.

t the end of June, I'm in midtown Manhattan during lunchtime. It's the summer of halter tops and flip-flops, and Capri pants or miniskirts swishing by on bare legs stripped of any fat. Every girl is a size zero. Nothing sticks to them in the muggy streets. The only things oversized are their sunglasses. I'm off to a job interview in a new silk blue pantsuit, a size 16, and feel like the chunky chick on the block. Yet, I march on.

One airless August evening in my new studio apartment, I'm on the phone with my father. Unprompted, he ends our phone conversation with, "I'm proud of you, toots. You know that, don't you?"

My heart drops. He has finally said it and meant it.

Even more importantly, I realize as I reach for another glass of ice-cold water: *I'm proud of me.*

Chapter 32

You may have figured this out already: I'm not someone who over intellectualizes her situation. I like to believe that what people say is the truth or close enough to it. I'm not someone who reads tons of books (unlike my sister), though I devour anything that Jennifer Weiner writes. I love my family. I'm hung up about my mother and my father. I can't quite get over my childhood; maybe nobody ever does. My favorite sounds are the Who, Mariah Carey, the start of a hip-hop dance class, and being called Aunt Susan. I don't dream of food anymore. I have the same good friends I've had since high school. I'm fiercely loyal and expect others to be so, but I've learned that people don't always live up to my expectations, and that's okay. And yes, I've made mistakes with men, but hopefully I'm learning from them.

I look back and think, *How did I do it?* I thought the first 100 pounds would be impossible. And when I lost it, I thought I would never lose the next 100. I took it a pound at a time. Pound by pound. I don't want to forget the struggle. It makes me walk up the stairs instead of taking the elevator.

But I confess, the last 40 or so are the hardest, and that's where I am now as I end the book, working on the last 40 or so.

But I've learned that it's not about the food.

On most days, food doesn't dominate my head. I used to think all the time of what I would eat next. I don't anymore. That's a big thing; that's an accomplishment.

I wish I could have ended this book with everything resolved. I would be under 200 pounds. I would have had plastic surgery; it would have gone great. I would be a perfect size 12. I'd be dating seriously or planning my wedding. But I'll say it again: I'm not perfect.

I've started celebrating Shabbat, the Jewish Sabbath, on Friday nights, because it gives me a chance to pause and be thankful.

I like myself a whole lot more, and not only because I found the courage to lose weight but also because I've stopped the lies and the shame.

One Sunday, I race my nephew Mikey down the Long Beach boardwalk. With his 6-year-old hand tight in mine, we dodge bicyclists racing down the center of the boardwalk. We stop to watch a heated volleyball game between the girls in bikinis and the boys in hip-slung bathing trunks. At the ocean's edge, a group in white enters the sea and is baptized to the beat of drums. The breeze sweeps in off the ocean, fresh and cool. I pour water on my nephew's new crew cut, and he squeals and tumbles into my arms.

He hugs me, his thin, sunburned arms pressed against my back, all the way around. He asks me: What am I? A grown-up or a kid? I confess. I tell him I'm a happy, grown-up kid.

We run, laughing and shouting to one another, the sea at our side.

Feeling my body breathe and go forward on its journey, wondering what the next step will be, is its own blessing.

Photo by Rick Newby

Epilogue

Sunday night, March 25, and I'm in a karaoke club in Manhattan. He's singing "Will You Marry Me?" by Alabama—to me. To me!!

❦

I found him, my fiancé, after dancing on the streets of the Upper West Side of Manhattan during a block party. "Are you going to the party on 86th Street?" a guy on the corner asked me.

"Sure." Beat. "What party?"

It was there that I met my future husband.

Over the next few months, his arms encircle, embrace, enchant me. Elegantly, we're in love.

❦

The job. A Fortune 500 in midtown Manhattan snatches me up as a paralegal. I work with a trainer twice a week at 6 a.m. before boarding the Long Island Railroad to commute to work. I am out in the world. Every part of me acknowledges the realization that I have changed. But no one in my new life knows the old Susan. The morbidly obese Susan. The Susan who is always with me, inside me—500 pounds of fear.

❧

February. I ask for help. I search for and find a new therapist. Absorb her words. Have a revelation with her: I don't have to be perfect. I don't have to be "in control" or "out of control." I don't have to be "good" or "bad." I change the tape in my head, heart, and soul. Snap! This is a moment of quiet triumph, and I want to scream it aloud. I don't have to be on or off a diet! I don't have to be perfect!

❧

June. I ask for a personal leave from the job. Drive down to Durham. My fiancé understands, maybe better than I do, that losing this last 40 or so pounds is less about the weight and more about the fear. I know, in another moment of quiet triumph, I will get under 200 pounds. It will be my gift to myself. I don't have to shout this.

❧

This summer I start keeping a diary for the first time in my life. *June 18th* . . . Woke up and walked the trail. Had half a grapefruit for breakfast and a banana for my snack at 11 a.m. Work out with Wes for an hour. Went to walk the Eno Trail—the HARD one to boot! I seriously barely made it back. I have never been that tired from so many workouts!!! However, these were amazing workouts! You try hiking up a mountain. Yes, you heard me correctly! A mountain after working out for 2 hours prior! But I survived! Regardless of what the scale says tomorrow—I'm proud of myself!

👑

July. One hundred and seventy-five wedding invitations drift through the U.S. mail.

👑

This is more confession than memoir, mutters my sister. We are kneading these words. My life rises as we are writing.

👑

The epilogue is the end after the end. But this is a journey. There is no end.

👑

Latest diary entry: Life is good! Peace out and much love to the universe!!

Acknowledgments

Daddy, sometimes you have to talk . . . and sometimes you just have to talk to your dad. Thank you for your love through the toughest times when I didn't think I'd make it. You'll forever be the best dad ever. I love you! Mommy, you're my ray of sunshine. Caroline, you've been mother, sister, and friend. Thank you for always believing in me when I know it wasn't easy! Mark, I'll always look up to you! David, you're my inspiration! Richard, Cindy, Hal, Fran, to the best extended family ever! Michael and Sara, please stay little! E.T., your never-ending love and support helped make my journey possible. My love and loyalty forever! M.F.B., P.K., L.G., E.G., M.B., A.D.—my beautiful girlfriends who listened to it all—I love you! Dr. Rosati, Dr. Neelon, J.C., and everyone at the Rice House, and to my amazing trainers M. and R., thank you for helping me save my life! To my new extended family, thank you for being such wonderful people! To my husband, thank you for your love, laughter, and wisdom. I love you for forever. Thank you for making me feel safe. I can now exhale. —*Susan*

To my husband, children, and family, with you all good things happen, and to my sister, for her courage. —*Caroline*

From both of us, to Art Harris, agent extraordinaire, whose passion and drive helped us keep the faith and keep on going, and to Michael Broussard and Carol Martin, with us from the start, thank you! And to Nancy Hancock, our editor, whose dedication, skill, and belief in our story sustains us. The world is bigger—and better—because of all of you!